PROTESTANT
PASTORAL
COUNSELING

BOOKS BY WAYNE E. OATES
Published by The Westminster Press

Protestant Pastoral Counseling
The Revelation of God in Human Suffering
Where to Go for Help
Anxiety in Christian Experience
The Bible in Pastoral Care
The Christian Pastor

PROTESTANT PASTORAL COUNSELING

by
Wayne E. Oates

THE WESTMINSTER PRESS
Philadelphia

PRINTED IN THE UNITED STATES OF AMERICA

Contents

Contents

Preface

THE PERSONS to whom I am indebted for the many facets of the material in this book are numerous and diverse. The book has been developed over the period of ten years since 1951 when I published my first book, *The Christian Pastor*, under the auspices of The Westminster Press. This book is a sequel to that work. *The Christian Pastor* aimed to deal with the ministry of the pastor in its wider and more comprehensive dimensions, and this present work focuses specifically on his work as a counselor. Therefore, I am especially indebted to The Westminster Press for continuing sponsorship of me as an author. Dr. Paul L. Meacham and Dr. Roland W. Tapp have been to me more than editors; they have been colleagues in the intellectual life and genuine friends in the covenantal relationship of the Christian faith. To them and to all those who work with them I am lastingly indebted.

The book is dedicated to my colleagues in the Department of Psychology of Religion and Pastoral Care at the Southern Baptist Theological Seminary, Profs. Samuel Southard and D. Swan Haworth. These men have been my collaborators and consultants in the making of this book, since the insights outlined here have been wrought out through the processess of teaching theological students side by side with them. They have, during my present sabbatical leave, carried the academic responsibility of the department and enabled me to have the necessary time to complete this work. For their friendship and encouragement in our life together, I am deeply in their debt.

The major portion of this book has been developed through the presentation of lectureships at several theological seminaries affiliated with the American Association of Theological Schools. I first formulated the materials and point of view in the T. V. Moore Lectures at the San Francisco Theological Seminary in San Anselmo, California, in 1957. At approximately the same time and on the same journey I was also privileged to present portions of the material as the Annual Lectures at the Golden Gate Baptist Theological Seminary, then at Berkeley, California.

The material in Chapter IX, along with many ideas presented in other parts of the book, was presented in 1956 as the Samuel Crozer Lectures at the Crozer Baptist Theological Seminary in Chester, Pennsylvania. Part of the material in Chapter I was presented as one of the Cole Lectures at Vanderbilt Divinity School in 1960. The remainder of the material in Chapter I and that in Chapter II was presented as the Whitley Lectures in the Baptist College at Bristol and Cardiff, and at Spurgeon's College of the Baptist Union of Great Britain and Ireland in 1961.

The material, furthermore, in Chapter III and also that in Chapters I and II was used in somewhat different form as the Laymen's Lectures of the School of Theology of Anderson College, Anderson, Indiana. The material in Chapters VIII and IX was developed in the outline form for the Associated Mennonite Theological Seminaries at Elkhart, Indiana, in their lectureship of 1960, and presented in manuscript form at the Alumni Lectures of the Louisville Presbyterian Theological Seminary in Louisville, Kentucky, in 1961.

To the presidents and deans, the faculties and students, of these seminaries who have helped me to come over the parapet of my own culture to an appreciation of wide vistas of spiritual fellowship with them, I am grateful indeed. My experience in dialogue with them has largely shaped these efforts to see

Protestant pastoral counseling in terms of our bonds of shared commitment in the Christian faith, our heritage of learning wrought out of suffering, and our concern for the ministry to the brokenhearted.

But to more than all of these, I am indebted to the anonymous people who have trusted me as a pastoral counselor. They have been my teachers and my friends as well as counselees. The "prophecies in part" here have come from my encounter with their questions and dilemmas. For the privilege of making these generalizations on the basis of this experience as a counselor, there is really no adequate way of saying thank you. Yet I can record my indebtedness here.

W. E. O.

The Southern Baptist Theological Seminary
Louisville, Kentucky

Introduction

THE REMARKABLE DEVELOPMENT of pastoral counseling during the last thirty years has been predominantly, although not exclusively, a Protestant growth. Several reasons lie behind this, and no simple explanation suffices. Protestants tend to start over from scratch every three or four generations. We do not adequately consolidate the communal wisdom of the centuries because of our antipathy for tradition. Therefore, we have accrued less capital in the form of proverbs, manuals of church discipline, canonical laws, etc. We have been, furthermore, in closer contact with the distinctly empirical dimensions of pastoral counseling by reason of our greater dependence upon secular forms of education. At the same time, as Protestants we have tended to draw our theoretical presuppositions for pastoral counseling from the scientific sources that are extrinsic to, although not necessarily hostile to, the theology of the church.

The purpose of this book is to derive both theory and practice of counseling from the intrinsic meanings of the Protestant pastoral heritage rather than to move initially from the extrinsic presuppositions of one or more forms of counseling and psychotherapy set forth by representatives of other professions. Hence, I have chosen the subject "Protestant Pastoral Counseling" with the clear intention of drawing formulations concerning counseling from the basic genius of Protestantism, a vital part of which is the Protestant understanding of ministry.

11

This grows out of my conviction that the time has come for the Christian pastor to prove his own work as a counselor. Then, as the apostle Paul says, "his reason to boast will be in himself alone and not in his neighbor." The Christian pastor must be open, teachable, and appreciative toward persons of other disciplines, but he must have a clear sense of his own selfhood as a pastor before he shall have much to offer inter-disciplinary discussions. Borrowed selfhood will not sustain him in the long pull of the days and years as a counselor. He must have his own individuality under God.

This book, furthermore, is written upon the assumption that the reader is acquainted with the superior and valuable works already written by competent authorities on the subject of pastoral counseling. A minimum knowledge of basic works in allied disciplines on the subject of counseling is also assumed. This book is not another attempt to retrace or review these excellent works which can best be read firsthand. For example, the pioneer work by Anton Boisen, *The Exploration of the Inner World*, originally published in 1937 and republished in 1952 (Harper & Brothers), meaningfully discusses the distinctive task of the minister. Also, a comprehensive and detailed study of the work of the pastor as a counselor was published by Seward Hiltner (*Pastoral Counseling*, Abingdon-Cokesbury Press, 1949). Subsequently Hiltner furnished a conceptual orientation to the task of pastoral theology in his *Preface to Pastoral Theology* (Abingdon Press, 1958). With Lowell G. Colston, he has provided as a necessary sequel to his earlier books *The Context of Pastoral Counseling* (Abingdon Press, 1961). Carroll Wise's *Pastoral Counseling* (Harper & Brothers, 1951) reflects the emerging emphasis of interpersonal psychiatry and, to a greater degree, the influence of client-centered therapy upon pastoral counseling. In 1959, a group of Southern Baptist theological professors produced a symposium on the subject, *An Introduction to Pastoral Counseling* (The Broadman Press, 1959). These men discussed the operational problems of day-to-day pastoral counseling in the context of the church and gave special emphasis to the relation between pastoral counseling and the educational intentions of the church.

Among the interpenetrating influences of the sciences of psychology and psychiatry upon pastoral counseling, one finds three or four profoundly influential volumes. Carl R. Rogers, in his book *Client-centered Therapy* (Houghton Mifflin Company, 1951), has exercised an overarching influence upon the teaching and practice of pastoral counseling. Harry Stack Sullivan's books, *The Interpersonal Theory of Psychiatry* (W. W. Norton & Company, 1953), and *The Psychiatric Interview* (W. W. Norton & Company, 1954), gave further technical assistance and provided fresh theoretical approaches for the study of pastoral counseling. These are all solid contributions to our learning in this field. Three studies have exercised lasting influence on my own thinking and on that of many other research men in the field of pastoral counseling: Martin Buber's *I and Thou* (Edinburgh: T. & T. Clark, 1937), David Roberts' *Psychotherapy and a Christian View of Man* (Charles Scribner's Sons, 1950), and Albert C. Outler's *Psychotherapy and the Christian Message* (Harper & Brothers, 1954). These works deserve the careful attention that will be assumed in the following pages.

The present volume both builds upon this knowledge and seeks to take a new point of departure. At the same time as I recognize indebtedness to these contributions, I am seeking to move on to fresh and even different presuppositions. Pastoral counseling is in peril of becoming repetitious, the next step beyond which is sterility. This can be avoided by asking new questions. Intrinsic within Protestant theology are resources for developing an understanding of counseling which will not later have to be "glued" in parallelisms to this, that, and the other hastily remembered doctrine of theology, like a sort of "harmony" of two different "gospels." Those things which belong together in the beginning do not need to be "glued" together later. Theology, to change the figure of speech, should be the pastoral counselor's original impression rather than a sort of negative afterimage. Careful attention in the beginning to the basic sources of working hypothesis will obviate the necessity for such later parallelistic discussions of "counseling *and* theology." Hence my own intention to move from within the Christian faith itself for an understanding of the theory and practice of Protestant pastoral counseling.

I

Protestant Distinctives
and Pastoral Counseling

SOMEONE has said that "today is a day of beckoning truths"
which demands a "deeper truthfulness." Yet today is also a
day of "proud men drest in a little, brief authority," who on
their own behalf expect a "spurious humility" of their fellows
as they covertly persuade them with the finality of their dogmas. (C. J. Wright, "Protestant Principles and the Future,"
The Hibbert Journal, Vol. LVII, April, 1959, p. 234.) Diabol-
ically enough, one of these dogmas is the *infinality* of everything! These dark aphorisms, when applied to present-day
pastoral counseling, necessitate a deeper truthfulness and a
closer spirit of self-criticism of the "little, brief authority" that
may have accumulated both to the people and the positions
represented in this area of theological concern. Pastoral counseling has hastened into premature orthodoxies of presupposi-
tion and procedure after the first hedgerow break-through into
conversation with the behavioral sciences. We need now to
take heed to ourselves lest these presuppositions become "final
dogmas" to *us*. In reality they may be "cut flowers," beautiful
for a time, but destined, because of their rootlessness in the
deposit of the Christian faith, to wither and fade.

CONTEMPORARY CHALLENGES TO PASTORAL COUNSELING

The appeal for self-criticism on the part of those concerned
in any way with pastoral counseling has been made by several

15

significant and serious Protestant scholars. They have meaningfully and reverently challenged the area of pastoral counseling. Persons, therefore, who have dedicated life and sub-
stance to undivided attention to the development of pastoral
counseling as a discipline should take these challenges to heart
without special pleading or self-defensiveness. The popularity
of a new field should not so enchant us that we forfeit or de-
fault in learning responsibly from constructive criticism. At
least four challenges to pastoral counseling, then, need to be
clearly stated. Within the unique distinctives of the Protestant
heritage the resources for meeting these challenges can be
found.

1. The Challenge of Community

One of the main temptations of the pastoral counselor is
the appeal of solitude in his work. He works alone with individuals, not from a platform with crowds. He is tempted to
be a "lone wolf," separated and isolated from his colleagues
in the ministry, from the fellowship of responsibility borne
along with the lay leadership of his church, and from the historical community of the great cloud of witnesses who have
gone before him in his ministry to distressed persons. If by reason of natural endowment and long years of intensive discipline
in the individual counseling of people the pastoral counselor
accrues prestige, he is likely to be even more of a "prima
donna" than is the exceptionally popular preacher. He may
make decisions that involve others without seeking their judgment. He may assume full responsibility for such matters as
premarital counseling, participation in complicated social situations such as divorce, racial tension, and suicidal risk without conference with his lay leadership. He may make major
policy decisions about the use of his time without collaboration with the fellowship of believers to whom he is responsible
for his ministry. This is what being a "prima donna" means.

This isolationism appears at a deeper and more involved
level in the teaching of pastoral counseling in the context of

theological education today. Richard Niebuhr, Daniel Day Williams, and James Gustafson articulate this challenge with vivid clarity in an interpretative bulletin released during their survey of theological education under the auspices of the Carnegie Foundation and the American Association of Theological Schools:

> A special form of "isolationism" manifests itself in the schools when certain operational disciplines develop a separate existence of their own, not as specializations, but as speciously complete forms of theological education. At one time, in some places, religious education and social ethics moved in this direction. Now a similar tendency appears occasionally in the development of the study of pastoral counseling. In the former instances, theologies of religious education and of the social gospel were excogitated—with doctrines of God and man, of sin and redemption, of church and the world, derived from the special insights or dogmas of the new discipline. Now one hears echoes here and there of a kind of theology of pastoral counseling which appears to be developing in relative independence of the theology of the Bible and the church. Familiar words, such as redemption and reconciliation, crucifixion and resurrection, occur in these specialized theologies, but they have acquired restricted and impoverished meaning in the new context. To be sure, religion and social action were not separated from the rest of theology in all schools, and the separation is by no means the rule in pastoral counseling today, but the tendency in this direction is in some places unmistakable. (H. Richard Niebuhr, Daniel Day Williams, James M. Gustafson, *Theological Education in America,* "Isolation and Cooperation in Theological Education," Bulletin No. 3, January, 1955, p. 2.)

In their later volume, these authors say that this "apprehension is usually shared by the men in the pastoral field, which is a healthy state of affairs" (*The Advancement of Theological Education*, p. 122; Harper & Brothers, 1957).

The coming of age of pastoral counseling calls for putting away this isolationism by entering into durable fellowship with the theological, historical, and Biblical disciplines of the seminary curriculum, by calling upon the wisdom and pastoral comradeship of laymen at the operational level of the life of the churches, and by drawing upon the poetic-prophetic experience of Christian pastors of other eras. (NOTE: Boisen demonstrates this in his *Exploration of the Inner World* through his penetrating studies of John Bunyan and George Fox. Hiltner does likewise in his *Preface to Pastoral Theology*, Abingdon Press, 1958, through his careful analysis of the work of one Ichabod Spencer, a pastor of the nineteenth century.) At the same time, the research men in these older disciplines are challenged in their isolation as "tycoons of the curriculum." The venerability of their subject matter is a challenge to stewardship, not a hiding place for insecure men.

2. The Challenge of History and Identity

Implicit within the challenge of community and the criticism of isolationism is the challenge of historical rootage and clarity of spiritual identity among pastoral counselors. Discussions of redemption and reconciliation, crucifixion and resurrection, we are told, can be carried on apart from the classical meanings of these truths. The accusation of "fadism" is leveled at pastoral counseling by less secure critics. However, the accusation has telling effect if we are not rooted deeply enough in the eternal to survive the ravages of time and circumstance.

This challenge is most clearly and persuasively stated by C. Hobart Mowrer, Professor of Psychology at the University of Illinois, when he says that contemporary clergymen are "in the awkward position of having 'sold their birthright' for a mess of psychological pottage." By judging himself solely by the criteria of other professions, by failing to "tap the potential within the great traditions of religion itself," and by

naïvely and uncritically adopting the theoretical presuppositions of psychology and psychiatry, the minister has lost any
clear confidence in his own identity. Mowrer challenges the
pastoral counselor for having what he calls "a 'trained in-
capacity' and educated reluctance to come really to grips"
with the moral and spiritual roots of mental illness. "In his
own eyes as well as those of others, he is clearly a second- or
third-class operator in this field," says Mowrer. The pastoral
counselor is challenged to dig into the reality of sin, of man's
inescapable responsibility before God as a sinner, and of his
need for forgiveness from sin. Mowrer says that "Protestantism
has, on the whole, handled the problem of guilt very badly and
. . . the gospel of sin, salvation, and redemption is not one of
bondage but of liberation, hope, and strength; and we must,
I believe, return to it in all seriousness." (O. Hobart Mowrer,
The Crisis in Psychiatry and Religion, p. 77; D. Van Nostrand
Company, Inc., 1961.)

Obviously, then, pastoral counselors are being challenged,
even by psychologists, to develop an understanding of counseling that is intrinsic to the distinctive principles of our faith
and that will issue in a clear and confident sense of our own
identity as men of God in Christ. In another article, Mowrer
expresses his challenge in candid terms:

> At the very time that psychologists are becoming
> distrustful of the sickness approach to personality dis-
> turbances and are beginning to look with more benign
> interest and respect toward certain moral and religious
> precepts, religionists themselves are being caught up in
> and bedazzled by the same preposterous system of
> thought as that from which we psychologists are just re-
> covering. ("Sin, the Lesser of Two Evils," *The American
> Psychologist*, Vol. 15, No. 5, May, 1960, p. 303.)

Whereas Mowrer does much special pleading for psychology
as opposed to psychiatry as a helping profession, nevertheless
his point is well taken, and his challenge to pastoral counseling

to move from its own rather than secondhand, borrowed pre-suppositions is well taken. He has ferreted out our shabby insecurity in our own beliefs and foggy lack of clarity in our basic identity. However, he reflects a lack of knowledge of the literature of pastoral care and counseling. As early as 1950 these same things were being said in published books by this author and others.

3. The Challenge by the Sovereignty of Man

Joachim Scharfenberg, a German pastor, rightly challenges contemporary pastoral care and counseling at its anthropocentric point of departure. He asks: "Is it not possible that here the religious consciousness, i.e., certain psychological patterns of behavior and conduct, has itself all unnoticed become the theme of pastoral theology instead of the work of the Holy Spirit?" ("The Babylonian Captivity of Pastoral Theology," *The Journal of Pastoral Care*, Vol. 8, No. 3, Fall, 1954, p. 133.) This anthropocentric approach can resolve itself into the too-easy clichés of pastoral counseling "rules of thumb" in evaluating a given counselee. For example, even though continuities between one's experience with his parents and his concept of God can be identified, and even though records of these continuities are evident in the New Testament long before Freudian theory emerged, we are likely to make a leap of surmise and assume that the person who has never experienced the love of an earthly father can *never* understand the love of God. Then, if this is true, asks Scharfenberg, "must all people who do not enjoy such an experience on the human level be excluded from salvation?" Would not it be more in keeping with the gospel, *when taken from God's point of view,* to say that *any* human father's love is weak, sinful, incomplete, and distorted, and that the gifts of *any* earthly parent are evil as compared with the gift of the Heavenly Father, even the Holy Spirit? Thus, the responsible growth of an individual implies forgiveness of his parents for their trespasses as a vital part of self-acceptance. Inasmuch as the parent has become a part of us, then our forgiveness of him is in part a coming to terms with ourselves. But such forgiveness is not possible apart from having ourselves been forgiven first of all by God. Such a new point of departure relates the self to a Person beyond itself, without which "that self must remain frustrated and unfulfilled." (Doris Mode, "God-centered Therapy," *The Journal of Pastoral Care,* Vol. 4, Nos. 1 and 2, Spring-Summer, 1950, p. 19.)

This challenge by the sovereignty of man is a key challenge not only to pastoral counseling but to the whole of the discipline of theology. Therefore, it is the most profound and valid challenge of those mentioned here. From it ensue the other challenges. If this one were constantly met, the others would tend to come into line. This is demonstrated in the challenges of a minister's competence in pastoral counseling.

4. Challenges to Competence

One of the jagged-edged problems that cuts its way into every discussion of pastoral counseling is that of the competence of the pastor, especially at the point of his equipment and training as a counselor. Prof. Willard L. Sperry, in his book *The Ethical Basis of Medical Practice,* raises this problem in the form that it usually appears:

The minister, unlike most professional men today, is little better than a Jack-of-all-trades. . . . Latterly there has been much interest in the application of newer disciplines in psychology to pastoral care, and some of our larger churches now number on their staffs men who confine themselves to this phase of a minister's work. But the number of these men is not as yet large enough to have created a recognized specialist caste in the ministry. It is a fair question how far competent psychiatrists and analysts can afford to give to such men, in want of full medical training, recognition as professional equals. A little knowledge, even with the best heart in the world, is, in

these areas, a dangerous thing to let loose on a community. (Paul B. Hoeber, Inc., 1950, p. 38.)

This challenge of the minister's competence is based on
criteria that are external to the ministry itself. The question is
not raised by Professor Sperry as to the adequacy of the
minister's training *as a minister*. Rather, his competence as a
medical doctor is questioned. Furthermore, when a minister
actually has full medical or psychological training, the tacit
assumption of Sperry is that this in and of itself will qualify
him to work as a pastoral counselor and meet the articulated
needs which are presented to a pastor. Even casual observation of ministers who are actually trained in medicine, social
work, and psychology reveals that they do not become *pastors*.
They become doctors, social workers, or psychologists. Two
reasons seem to be evident, namely, these just-named professions are not equipped to teach a man to be a pastor—they
either assume that this does not require any specialized training or that, if it does, the minister is already thoroughly aware
of what his role as a minister is. In the second place, the
shortage of persons qualified to function as doctors, psychologists, or social workers is so great that the minister's identity
as a minister gets lost in the shuffle of demand. But, in es-
sence, the demand that a pastoral counselor qualify in competence in another profession is begging the question of the
adequacy of his own education as a minister. Theologians
hereby avoid the hard discipline of developing the minister's
own intrinsic identity by perfecting a kind of intensively supervised, individually taught, and thoroughly informed education that insists that the theological student implement his
explicit role as a minister.

Such has been the effort in the National Conference on
Clinical Pastoral Education, the Association of Professors of
Theology in the Practical Field, and similar regional groups
in America. (See *Clinical Education for the Pastoral Ministry*,
ed. by E. E. Bruder and M. L. Barb; Washington: Advisory
Committee on Clinical Pastoral Education, 1958.) Blizzard's

studies on the role conceptions of the minister indicate that the minister's fundamental insecurity lies not so much in his lack of preparation in other disciplines such as medicine, social work, and psychology as in his lack of clarity of and respect for his own identity as a minister. (Samuel W. Blizzard, "The Parish Minister's Self-image of His Master Role," *The Minister's Own Mental Health*, ed. by Wayne E. Oates; Channel Press, Inc., 1961.)

THE EFFECTIVE RESPONSE OF PROTESTANT PASTORAL THEOLOGY

These four challenges, then—the challenge of community, the challenge of history and identity, the challenge of the sovereignty of man, and the challenge of competence—all necessitate an agonizing reappraisal of pastoral counseling in terms of the theological claims upon the lives of the minister and his counselee.

We have used many bases for critically examining the work of ministers as counselors. For example, we have used the clinical methodology of allied disciplines in the exploration of the inner world of suffering people's struggle with sin and search for salvation. (Anton T. Boisen, *The Exploration of the Inner World;* Harper & Brothers, 1952.) We have used the critical insights of social and cultural anthropology to focus our shepherding compassion on individuals and families in their quest for a lasting meaning in the mass culture and the stratifying culture of our day. (Seward Hiltner, *The Christian Shepherd: Some Aspects of Pastoral Care*; Abingdon Press, 1959.) We have used the intimate and detailed knowledge of the psychotherapists to throw light on the encounter with and content of the Christian faith. (David Roberts, *Psychotherapy and a Christian View of Man;* Charles Scribner's Sons, 1951.) We have applied the skills of psycho-social role analysis both to the role and function of the pastor in relation to stress-ridden persons and to the interaction of these persons with each other. (Wayne E. Oates, *The Christian Pastor;* The West-minster Press, 1951. Also, Samuel W. Blizzard, "The Protestant Minister's Integrating Roles," *Religious Education,* Vol. LIII, No. v, July-August, 1959, pp. 374–380. Also, H. Richard Niebuhr, James M. Gustafson, and Daniel Day Williams, *The Purpose of the Church and Its Ministry;* Harper & Brothers, 1956.)

But all these critical instruments for testing the theses and hypotheses of pastoral care are "outside readings": Like a thermometer on a cold day, seen through the window of the home, they provide real guidance for the regulation of the counseling activity of the pastor within the churches. How-ever, to press the figure a bit farther, we must pay careful attention to the fuel and furnace within if we do not wish the outside reading to become the inside state of affairs in the church. We will borrow the confusion and internal contra-dictions of other professions when we would do well to wrestle with our own until we receive a blessing of clarifi-cation.

We need now to examine critically the pastoral task of the minister in the light of the internal Protestant principles which have given dynamic and direction, warmth and compassion, to Christian pastors in every age who have taken these principles seriously and sought to focus them upon their encounters with people in need. Our purpose now is to focus four salient Protestant principles upon the meaning, purpose, and function of the pastoral counselor. These principles are: (1) the sovereign Lordship of Christ; (2) the responsible dialogue between God as Creator and man as creature; (3) the con-secration of life and the priestly vocation of every believer; (4) the release from the bondage of self-justification into the freedom of the justification of the believer by faith.

As such, then, pastoral counseling is an adventure in pastoral theology. James Smart has accurately defined pastoral theol-ogy as bringing "the whole of theology to a focus upon the point in the church's life where it attempts to deal with human beings not in the mass but as individuals or in intimate groups, family or otherwise." (James Smart, "The Minister as a Pastor," *Canadian Journal of Theology*, Vol. V, No. 3, July, 1959, pp. 182–183.)

Apart from such a centering of the whole of theology upon pastoral counseling, the hard-earned gains of clinical experience, the descriptive data we have accumulated, and the recurrent processes of pastoral visitation and counseling simply provide an opportunity for the pastor to be another Sophist in the Socratic sense of which Plato speaks in *The Republic*. We as pastors become, as he says, men who "learn how to approach and handle" people, "at what times and from what causes they are dangerous or the reverse, and what is the meaning of their several cries, and by what sounds, when another utters them, people are soothed or infuriated." Then, by "continually attending" upon people, we "become perfect in all of this." We "call our knowledge wisdom and make of it a system," "although we have no real notion of what we mean by the principles or passions of which we are speaking. . . . By heavens, would not such an one be a rare educator?" (Plato, *The Republic*, Book VI, tr. by Benjamin Jowett, pp. 237–238; Tudor Publishing Company.) Focusing the whole of Protestant theology upon pastoral counseling can save us from such a fate!

The Sovereign Lordship of Christ

The first Protestant principle that defines and illustrates the practice of pastoral care is the sovereign Lordship of Christ. In this sense, pastoral counseling in all its forms should provocatively challenge all idolatry. As Wilhelm Pauck puts it in *The Heritage of the Reformation*, p. 149 (The Free Press, 1950), the spirit of Protestantism is prophetic. "In the name of the sovereign, creative Lord of history, . . . it protests against all absolutizations of the historically relative and against all tendencies toward the self-sufficiency of man." This, as Dillenberger and Welch say, is the spirit of creative protest, "which springs from the acknowledgment of the sovereignty of God and of the living character of his revelation of himself in Jesus Christ." (John Dillenberger and Claude Welch, *Protestant Christianity*, p. 312; Charles Scribner's Sons, 1954.)

A distinctly Protestant pastoral counseling does not begin with the nature of man. Rather, it begins with the truth about God. The sovereign Lordship of Christ as a trenchant truth about God poignantly accentuates the basic character of man. John Calvin does not mince words when he states this truth:

> The human mind is, so to speak, a perpetual forge of idols . . . stuffed as it is with presumptuous rashness, [the human mind] dares to imagine a god suited to its own capacity . . . it substitutes an empty phantom in the place of God. . . . The god whom man has thus conceived inwardly he attempts to embody outwardly. The mind, in this way, conceives the idol, and the hand gives it birth. (*Institutes of the Christian Religion*, tr. by Henry Beveridge, Vol. I, p. 97; Wm. B. Eerdmans Publishing Company, 1957.)

The contemporary Christian pastor lives in an era of collapsing idols. As Richard Niebuhr has said, "men have become disillusioned about themselves and are becoming disillusioned about their idols." (*The Christian Century*, March 2, 1960, p. 250.) This is a time when we do not always have to shatter men's idols; they are collapsing of their own accord. We have become accustomed to thinking of the prophetic task as an iconoclastic one, one in which we pull down men's idols. We have neglected two basic pastoral dimensions of the prophetic role. These have been ignored and obscured in the prophetic challenge of the Lordship of Christ to the idols which possess and shackle people's lives. We are called not only to cast down every high thing that exalts itself against the knowledge of God in Christ; we are also called to wean immature people from bondage to the idols of the hearthplace, the provincial idols of their birthplace, and the excluding passions of their ambitions. And again, the Christian prophet is called to comfort people in the loss of their broken idols. Life itself is the icon breaker. We are often called, as Isaiah was, to pick up the pieces, "to bind up the brokenhearted," as he put it (Isa. 61:1). Pastoral counseling actively does these two things.

For example, Rachel has her modern counterpart in the men and women today who are unable to journey at ease with their spouses because they insist on covertly worshiping the household gods of their parents. Further, the very purposes of marriage are defeated when the good fruits of marriage and family living in and of themselves become absolute values, idols to which people clutch feverishly. For instance, one of the major purposes of marriage and lasting satisfactions of the family is the procreation of children. But the deification of children is followed all too quickly by child sacrifice, however refined and subtle its forms take. Also, the childless couple can jeopardize their whole relationship to God in their inextinguishable demand for children. Likewise, purity of life and fidelity to each other is a high purpose of marriage, but it also may be the basis for idolatrous jealousy. In the presence of real breaches of fidelity within marriage, the offended one can become self-righteous enough to quote the spurious text in Matt. 5:32 as justification for a permanent spirit of unforgiveness and hardness of heart. As Martin Thornton has said: "The end of man is not purity of heart, but the vision of God. The best way to come to the former is by aiming purposefully at the latter." (Martin Thornton, *Pastoral Theology: A Reorientation*, p. 10; The Macmillan Company, 1957.)

The idolatry of children or of partial purity in sinful people can lie at the root of the difficulties presented to the pastoral counselor. Weaning people from such idols is one of the objectives of pastoral counseling. It takes time, but the purpose is the mature man in Christ who is able to partake of the strong meat that is the dedication of the marriage itself to God. For the chief end of marriage is not parenthood, purity, or any

other such finite goal. The chief end of marriage is to glorify
God and to enoy *him* forever.

The Dialogue Between Creator and Creature

The second Protestant principle from which an understanding of pastoral counseling emerges is the personal dialogue
between God the Creator and man the creature. I set this over
against the philosophical dialogue between the natural and
supernatural which is characteristic of both Catholic and En-
lightenment-oriented Protestant theologians. This principle
seems to me to be necessary for clarifying certain pastoral
problems. For example, much thinking about healing both
inside and outside of Protestantism is posited upon the distinction between the natural and supernatural causes and
effects of life rather than upon the personal dialogue between
God as Creator and man as creature. If a doctor's discovery
of penicillin were unknown to a devoted Christian who prayed
for the first patient whose life was saved by penicillin, the
Christian would assume that a miracle had happened. The
doctor might at least feel unappreciated and at most be left
cynical with his sense of the power in penicillin. Such thinking
is based on the assumption that prayer is a *supernatural* means
of healing and penicillin is a *natural* one. But the whole perspective is changed when we see the doctor, the praying
Christian, the sick patient, and the penicillin as parts of the
total creation and God as Creator mobilizing both the hidden
and the revealed resources of his creation to heal the person
of pneumonia. But more than that—if the patient had *not*
survived, the relationship between Creator and creature still
remains indissoluble. Nothing could separate them in reality,
only in fellowship. In other words, God has not failed us when
a person dies. He has taught us that the difference between
man and God is that of creature and Creator. We learn that
we cannot exchange the worship of the true and living God
for the worship of the dead. This speaks to us at the heart of
the problem of working through grief.

The Consecration of Life and the Priesthood of All Believers

Closely related to the second principle of the personal dialogue of the Creator with the creature is a third principle: the
consecration of all of life and the priesthood of all believers.
T. W. Manson is right, I think, when he says that the priesthood of the believer cannot be separated from the high priesthood of Christ. He defines this high priesthood as Christ's
"complete self-dedication in unreserved obedience to God his
Father and in unlimited love and compassion toward men,
his brethren. This . . . must be normative for any Christian
doctrine of priesthood and sacrifice; and it is obvious that
priesthood so defined is something in which all believers can
and, indeed, must have a part." (Thomas W. Manson, *Ministry
and Priesthood: Christ's and Ours,* p. 63; John Knox Press,
1958.) When all of life is hallowed by God through his having
consecrated it to us and us to it, then he reveals it to us that
he has not made anything common or unclean, nor has any
man's task been made holy in such a way as to leave another
man's task secular. Through his redemption in Christ, "we
are his workmanship, created in Christ Jesus unto good works,
which God hath before ordained that we should walk in them"
(Eph. 2:10, KJV). From this we "may conclude that the priesthood of all believers lies in the fact that each believer offers
himself as a sacrifice according to the pattern laid down by
Christ." (Manson, *Ministry,* p. 64.)

The Protestant principle of the priesthood of all believers
focuses upon the practice of pastoral counseling in at least
three important ways. First, it underscores the mutual burden-
bearing character of the Christian community. The priesthood
of all believers negates the kind of misunderstanding of the
Christian faith which would insist that every man is sufficient
unto himself. Every man is responsible *for* his brother, even
when he has erred. No man need feel that he can live from
birth to death without need of counsel from his brother as
well. The hyperindividualism of Protestants is a violation of

this principle. No one of us is sufficient unto himself. We cannot say that we have no need of each other. To confess the need for counseling is no evidence of a lack of faith. Rather, it may be, although it is not necessarily, the activation of a livelier faith-response in which God leads us to sources of mutual assistance in the Christian fellowship. Such understanding is to the point in pastoral counseling when parishioners say that they feel so guilty and ashamed and weak as to have sought counseling assistance. Furthermore, it is relevant in the development of patience and understanding among Christians. The demonic enters the Christian community when we decide of ourselves that a brother is unnecessary or that we should be rid of him. Institutional relationships can be severed, but human relationships cannot. For better or for worse, relationships are durable. The task of the pastor is to know this and to sustain and reconcile relationships in as much as in him lieth. From the vantage point of the perspective of Christ, the Good Shepherd, no one is expendable.

In the second place, the priesthood of all believers is relevant to pastoral care in that it affirms the duty of all Christians to serve one another in love in all stations in life. The psychologist, the psychiatrist, the social worker, the penologist, the internal medicine expert—can from their stations in life sustain a Christian in his distress. In turn, the Christian has a ministry to render to them. They too have need of a friend, a confidant, a pastor, a shepherd. They are not sufficient unto themselves either. They receive the ministry of Christ also. If, by the grace of Christ, they should become Christians, they would still function as always in their stations in life. Martin Luther, in his *Christmas Book* (p. 50; The Westminster Press, 1948), says of the shepherds that they went to see the child Jesus:

> The Scripture says plainly that they returned and did exactly the same work as before. They did not despise their service, but took it up again where they left off with

all fidelity, and I tell you that no bishop on earth ever
had so fine a crook as those shepherds.

The third way in which the priesthood of all believers
challenges our presuppositions with reference to pastoral care
is at the point of creating a subspecialty of the ministry of
pastoral counseling. This ranges all the way from the requirement of clinical pastoral training for ordination, to the persistent expectation that a minister shall have undergone psychoanalytic treatment, to the minister's "hanging out his
shingle" as a private therapist. Our Protestant presuppositions
about the ministry have uniquely emphasized "the *personality*
of the minister. He comes as a friend and fellow Christian
rather than as a priest or as one spiritually gifted; and it is
through a direct, personal relationship that he seeks to be of
help." (Cyril Richardson, "Church Unity and the Ministry to
the Sick," *Religion in Life,* Vol. 21, No. 1, Winter, 1951–1952,
p. 68.) This is the reason why professors in pastoral theology
have laid such heavy emphasis upon training, self-understand-
ing, and emotional health of the minister.

But these very reasons back us into other equally significant
considerations, sight of which must never be lost: the danger
of creating a specialized "priesthood within a priesthood," the
possibility of developing the concept of a "private pastor" apart
from the continuing life of the churches, and the way in which
the average minister and church member will *use* such hyper-
specialism to avoid responsibility for the mutual burden-bearing character of the Christian fellowship. Indeed and in fact,
each of them has his own burden to bear also, because he too
is a priest. Pastoral counseling is not a specialty for the few
ministers who would ride it as a hobby or declare independence of the church. It is a responsibility of every minister for
which he should be educated in relation to his total task as a
theologian and a pastor. *The private practice of pastoral counseling apart from the life of the church is a violation of the
basic character of the ministry, if not an actual violation of*

professional ethics. Care should be taken in this statement of principle to clarify what is meant by "the church." A broad meaning is used here to refer to the responsible expressions of the church, either in the local congregation, the association of churches—denominational or interdenominational—or the institutions of the churches, such as schools and colleges. Admittedly, all these are filled with human fallibility, but even so they provide a ground upon which individual wisdom can be tested through the work of the Holy Spirit with both the individual and the group. From a clinical point of view, counseling is by nature a *shared* responsibility, whether we admit it or not. The medical psychotherapist, for instance, shares his responsibility with the rest of the medical profession. The minister by the nature of the case shares his ministry as a counselor with the church that ordained and educated him. This is why the caring concerns of the pastor should be taught to laymen by pastors. The meaning of lay leadership in the church is in desperate need of an intensive re-evaluation, away from the purely financial policy management of the church and toward the understanding of the lay leader as having a pastoral task himself. Until we begin asking and answering such questions as these, we have simply thrown our theology out of gear and turned ourselves over to the pushing power of automatic social change.

The Bondage of Self-justification and the Freedom of Justification by Faith

Discussions of Protestant principles usually begin with the doctrine of justification by faith. No discussion of Protestant distinctives is complete without careful attention to the meaning of justification by faith. By reason of the overattached relationship between therapeutic psychology and pastoral counseling, the nonjudgmental and permissive approaches of clinically oriented pastors of today have been interpreted as a loss of prophetic consciousness, as a moral nonchalance, and as a moral relativism. Our usual stance when these interpretations are made is to be defensive. A more creative approach is to admit that sometimes they are true and to dig more deeply into the meaning of the righteousness that comes from God.

Justification begins with the disclosure of God in Christ, who, "without asking a sign of worth, extended his forgiveness to those who trusted him rather than themselves and their activities." (Dillenberger and Welch, *Protestant Christianity*, p. 20.) When Luther grasped that the justice of God had decreed in Christ that "through grace and sheer mercy, God justifies us through faith," he said: "Thereupon I felt myself reborn and to have gone through open doors into Paradise." (Roland Bainton, *Here I Stand*, p. 65; Abingdon Press, 1950.) Therefore, as N. H. Snaith says, justification in the Biblical sense of *dikaioo* is "not so much an ethical word as a . . . vocabulary of salvation." (*A Theological Word Book of the Bible*, ed. by Alan Richardson, p. 118; The Macmillan Company, 1950.) He further says that justification is that "first step in the process of salvation, . . . that immediate setting-right with God which God himself accomplishes by his grace when man has faith" (*ibid.*, p. 119). God has broken the vicious circle of rejection whereby a person moves from one idolatrously human relationship to another, hoping to find complete acceptance "just as he is without one plea." This unreal need for God in a human form—father, mother, teacher, state, or church—is the spawning ground of neurosis. A man is justified before God, not by readjusting his perspective of this, that, or the other human relationship, but by coming upon, as a treasure hidden in the field of life, the transforming good news of the Kingdom that God is not man, that he, in Christ, is eternally and qualitatively different from man. Yet He has taken His stand with man in the event of the incarnation, the Person of Christ, and the indwelling Holy Spirit in the community of faith.

A person comes to his pastor filled with the noisome pestilence of his own self-condemnation. He is made suspicious by possibilities of punishment and reprisals from the fellow human being to whom he would open his heart and make himself known. The pastor is permissive, accepting, and forgiving, not because morals do not matter. The springs of his compassion do not issue in a babbling brook of nonchalant self-indulgence that waters his own desire to do wrong. And acceptance has little meaning until clearheaded judgment has established that something wrong enough to be accepted has been done. The pastoral counselor's mood then is one of patience, not indifference. His own permissiveness gushes forth from the depths of his own specific, clear, and conscious memory of having been justified by faith and that without deserving it, himself. His law is neither the forensic meditations of canonical lawyers through the ages nor a perfectly restored sacred canon. His passion is to fulfill the law of Christ by restoring gently the one overtaken in a fault, looking to himself, lest he also be tempted. He can be kind and tenderhearted, forgiving the brother because God for Christ's sake forgave him.

For the Christian pastor the opposite of sin is not virtue but faith. As Paul put it, "Whatsoever is not of faith is sin." In this sense, faith is the actual establishment of a conscious relationship to God. We are called of God to stand and live in this essential relationship to him, to be confronted by him who speaks to us and requires our response, and in Christ responds with grace and peace. To shrink back from this selfhood is sin. To move out of the bivouac of irresponsibility and hidden hovering in the safeties and blurrings of self-justification is to respond to the call of God by faith. Then, as the writer of I Peter says, we who "were no people" now "are God's people." With this kind of birth of a new identity in Christ through faith, the pastoral theologian is always at work, even at the risk of being thought nonchalant about some of the secondary moral results of such transformation of life.

II

Pastoral Counseling in the Free Church Tradition

THE "FREE CHURCH TRADITION," as it is known in Britain and to some extent in the United States, presents both contributions to and ambiguities for the contemporary Protestant pastoral counselor. (NOTE: Talcott Parsons accurately says that "at the time of the American Revolution the principle of separation of church and state was something of a *tour de force*" and was precipitated by "political expediency . . . and the prominence among the Founding Fathers of a group of intellectuals, typified by Thomas Jefferson, who were deeply influenced by the Deism of the French Enlightenment." [Talcott Parsons, "The Pattern of Religious Organization in the United States," *Symbolism in Religion and Literature*, ed. by R. May, p. 156; George Braziller, Inc., 1960.]) This is particularly true if his own religious heritage stems from the free church tradition. The problems and conflicts he experiences both within himself as a believing Christian and with his congregation as a fellowship of believers are somewhat clarified—if not always alleviated—by an understanding of the issues that his adherence to the free church tradition poses for him as a pastoral counselor.

The free church tradition has many roots. Three of the most important of these roots are: (1) the Radical Reformation of the sixteenth century as distinguished from Lutheranism, Calvinism, and Anglicanism; (2) the development of religious freedom and political democracy in America; and (3) the conservation of the results of the Great Awakening in America. These three sources of vitality furnished strength and sustenance for the churches of the free church tradition. The pastoral counselor of any tradition is enriched deeply by the study of the history of these movements. Personal contact with contemporary Christian communions whose heritage is distinctly that of the Anabaptist movement, or the Great Awakening of frontier America, of course, provides the best understanding. The separatism of many such groups makes this difficult at times.

However, important stress needs to be laid upon the fact that the ideals and professions of the free church tradition are not the private property of any one group of Protestants. By reason of the clear-cut principle of the separation of church and state, which has been characteristic of religion in America, *all* Protestantism has either implicitly or explicitly incorporated many of the ideals of the free church tradition. Likewise, American Protestantism is characterized by a spirit of nonconformity, diversity, and individualism. Even within the more structured churches, such as the Episcopal Church, this is very true. Furthermore, some valid evidence indicates that the Roman Catholic Church in America has been influenced by the ideals of the free church tradition, which grew out of the spirit of nonconformity in Europe and Great Britain. Robert D. Cross has ably demonstrated through the careful comparison and contrast of primary sources that the combined impact of the free church convictions of American Protestants and the constitutional separation of church and state in America has developed an articulate liberal movement within the Roman Catholic Church in America. The leaders of this movement have contended that the church's position about the sovereignty of the church over the state, for instance, is a thesis that arose out of the pre-twentieth-century historical contentions. They contend that the American position of separation of church and state is a "thesis" in its own right, arising out of differing historical conditions. Therefore, "there must be harmony between the actions of church and state so that the individual citizen is not forced to choose between his religious and political obligations." (Robert D. Cross, *The Emergence of Liberal Catholicism in America*, p. 221; Harvard University Press, 1958.)

A full discussion of pastoral counseling in the free church tradition, therefore, is a vital part of this treatise on Protestant pastoral counseling. These emphases and ideals have both tacitly and articulately shaped the practice of pastoral counseling in America. A careful examination of the ideals of the free church tradition in relation to the practice of pastoral counseling as we know it today will reflect many of the ideals of this tradition in the development of pastoral counseling itself.

The ideals of the free church tradition present both advantages and ambiguities to the pastoral counselor as he seeks to clarify his own identity in the pastoral care of individuals and groups. Therefore, the ensuing discussion will attempt to explain what the ideals of the free church tradition are, to point out the advantages that these ideals afford the pastoral counselor, and to explore some of the ambiguities that these ideals create for the pastoral counselor.

Spiritual Nonconformity and Pastoral Counseling

The proponents of the free church tradition introduced nonconformity as a way of life into the religion of the West. In Europe, with heretical precursors of an infinite variety, the Anabaptists arose in nonconformity to the Reformers such as Luther and Calvin. They were "distinct groups" who "through the medium of preaching . . . accepted the gospel of Jesus Christ by faith . . . and separated [themselves] from the life of paganism to bring forth fruits of righteousness." (Gunnar Westin, *The Free Church Through the Ages*, by O. A. Olson, p. 1; The Broadman Press, 1958.)

In England the free congregation movement and the larger Puritan attitude toward life presented a solid stance of nonconformity that made a rich and varied contribution to Christendom in the British Isles. As the English authority, Ernest A. Payne, has said, nonconformity even today "remains a very important factor in the religious life of" Britain. (Ernest A. Payne, *The Free Church Tradition in the Life of England,* p. 170; London: S.C.M. Press, Ltd., 1951.) In America the religious concern of persons like Roger Williams and the rationalism and deism of the more or less aristocratic founders of American political democracy strangely combined to eventuate in the formal inclusion of the separation of church and state in the American Constitution. In a word, from both a sociological and psychological point of view, the free church tradition represents the spiritual patterning of rebellion in the religious life.

The overdependence of contemporary pastoral counseling upon psychoanalytic presuppositions has led to fundamental confusion as to the nature of religious experience and the practice of pastoral counseling. Psychoanalysis, culturally, has had little or no direct contact with the spirit and mood of the free churches. To the contrary, it has grown up in the presence of highly structured ecclesiastical expressions of religion—Judaism, Catholicism, Anglicanism, and American Episcopalianism. As such, psychoanalysis itself became almost religiously fervent in its rebellion against religion as authority. For example, Sigmund Freud, in describing Leonardo da Vinci, said that Leonardo, inasmuch as he had cast away the fetters of authority in his relationship to his father during his earliest childhood, also failed to remain a believer, and so escaped the clutches of dogmatic religion. In this connection, Freud states the truism about religion for which he has become noted: "Psychoanalysis . . . has shown us that a personal God is, psychologically, nothing other than an exalted father, and it brings us evidence every day how young people lose their religious belief as soon as their father's authority breaks down" (Sigmund Freud, *Complete Psychological Works,* Vol. XX, p. 123; London: Hogarth Press, Ltd., 1957). Likewise, Erich

Fromm rejects personal theism on the basis of the authoritarianism of conventional religion. He makes an appeal for a nontheistic, humanistic, and unconventional kind of religion that rebels against the authoritarian structures of conventional religion. He sees authoritarian religion as alienating man "from his own powers" and making him "slavishly dependent upon God." (Erich Fromm, *Psychoanalysis and Religion*, p. 51; Yale University Press, 1950.)

Following the cue of this kind of psychological truism quite uncritically, pastoral counselors have tended to overidentify all religion as a form of repression that always demands conformity to authority. This easy interpretation has been rather gullibly accepted by many pastoral counselors. As a result, the frontier rebelliousness of many free churchmen is completely ignored, if not misunderstood altogether. Religion is not just a means of conformity; it has as often been the means of rebellion against authority. Religious experience has become a form of rebellion against the superficial protections of popular, idolatrous religion, against the use of religion to enforce only dependency and to stifle growth, and against the authoritarian and chaotic forms of irreligion in our day.

One of the major problems the pastoral counselor confronts is the rebellion of his counselees against the superficiality of popular, idolatrous religions. Seward Hiltner has rightly said in his perceptive discussion of "shepherding rebels" that there is an "astonishing lot" of "potential creativity" in rebellion. (*The Christian Shepherd*, p. 126. This is in his conclusion to a chapter on "Shepherding Rebels," pp. 113–126.)

Even groups that hold most vigorously to the spirit of rebellion against the state church, against the crassness of the world, and against the undisciplined laxity of conventional religion run into the other side of the paradox, and tend to become extremely legalistic and authoritarian. For example, a Mennonite asked concerning his church, "Instead of having a teaching relationship to youth, [do] we have an ecclesiastical hierarchy which decides what we are supposed to believe and substitutes this authority for the learning relationship of disciples to each other and to Christ?" (Chester A. Raber, *An Investigation Into the Beliefs of Mennonite Young People*, unpublished master's thesis, Southern Baptist Theological Seminary, May, 1954, p. 2.) Or, more strongly than this, Sören Kierkegaard, the poet-theologian of a century ago, in rebellious opposition could say of the state church of Denmark that they were "a clerical gang of swindlers who have taken forcible possession of the firm 'Jesus Christ' and done a flourishing business under the name of Christianity" (Sören Kierkegaard, *Attack Upon "Christendom,"* tr. by Walter Lowrie, p. 117; Princeton University Press, 1944). Yet, on the other hand, even with his nonconformity, Kierkegaard espouses a Christian faith that "rests upon the assumption that the Christian is in a relationship of *opposition*, that to be a Christian is to believe in God, to love him, in a relationship of opposition" (*ibid.*, p. 149). By a "relationship of opposition" he means essentially one of rebellion and nonconformity to the superficial idolatries of human existence, as well as being opposite as sinner from the holiness of God. This kind of questioning and nonconformity simply does not fit the pattern of shrinking obeisance to authority that some—not all—psychoanalysts insipidly ascribe to all religion.

This spirit of nonconformity also applies to the Christian demand to place the claims of faith in God above those of marriage and the family. Within the context of effective and growing Christian experience, heavy emphasis has been laid by members of the free church tradition upon the necessity of an individual's becoming free of his family if he is to live the life of faith fully. This has been based solidly upon the teaching of Jesus that in behalf of the Christian faith a person should leave house, brethren, sisters, father, mother, wife, children, lands, for his sake and the gospel's (Mark 10:29). He asks concerning himself: "Who is my mother or my brethren? . . . Whosoever shall do the will of God, the same is my brother, and my sister, and mother" (Mark 3:33, 35). Contrary to the psychoanalytic thesis of Freud, Jesus insists that a person's relationship to God does not genuinely come into being until he has "let the dead bury their dead" in the family dominations of his life. Later psychoanalysts have perceived this relationship in a way that Freud did not. J. C. Flügel, for instance, clearly identifies the adult experience of spiritual rebirth as a symbolic actualization of "a more vigorous and independent mode of life, involving greater freedom from the protecting and guarding influence of the parents and especially the mother, as well as the achievement of moral or religious movement or conversion" (J. C. Flügel, *The Psychoanalytic Study of the Family*, p. 76; Hillary House, Inc., 1948).

Nonconformity to the kind of religion that is espoused by parents may equally as well be expressed in fidelity to another form of religion, as in the development of religious apathy or hostility. The pastoral counselor who is alert to this "nonconformity meaning" of religion often sees young people taking a different approach even to their ancestral religion from that of their parents. Thus religion may be a means of establishing autonomy of their parents. Later, after the rebellion has been accomplished, they are faced with the further task of maturity, i.e., relating to their faith as an end in itself and not as a means of rebellion.

Furthermore, the pastoral counselor who recognizes the nonconformity tradition among Christians sees into irreligion in a way which psychological truisms about authoritarianism cannot reveal. For example, a child in a home where religious values and spiritual concern are grossly neglected may rebel against his family by becoming deeply concerned with religious faith. His interests and participation in religious living may very well be a forthright criticism (at a certain stage of his religious development) of the chaotic spiritual disorganization of his home. In homes where atheism or agnosticism is frankly espoused the child may express his rebellion and nonconformity to his parents by developing religious interests of his own. Phillip Polatin and Ellen C. Philtine tell of a discussion between an irreligious father and his seven-year-old son:

> The child came home from private school, where he always had his lunch, and asked thoughtfully why grace was not said at home before a meal as it was invariably said at school. The father, outraged that his son was being taught pious gestures, launched into an explanation that grace was said to God, that in order to say grace one had to believe in God, that he personally did not believe in the myth of the God who sat in heaven or hell but only the joy or misery one experienced on earth, that it was all a fairy tale invented by the churches to keep people submissive and unthinking, and that he had thought this all out and that was why he did not say grace. The little boy sat quietly, his hands folded together before him, and then said: "Do you mind if I believe in God? I like to say grace." (*The Well Adjusted Personality: Preventive Psychiatry for Everyday Use*, p. 210; J. B. Lippincott Company, 1952.)

Polatin and Philtine's interpretation of this instance overlooks the sturdy spirit of rebellion and nonconformity in the seven-year-old boy. At the same time they imply a kind of "maturity" in the father that is belied by his authoritarianism and insecurity.

The advantages of nonconformity and rebellion in emotional and spiritual growth cannot fail to be appreciated by the alert pastoral counselor. Pastoral counseling at its heart should be the creation of a permissive atmosphere in which the negations, the aggressive no, and the rising up of the individuality of the person in freedom can be affirmed.

Yet at the same time the pastoral counselor cannot so overemphasize the advantages of the spirit of nonconformity which characterized the free church tradition that he overlooks the serious ambiguities that are involved in this advantage. For example, the rebellious and nonconforming person may well be motivated by the same spirit of authoritarianism against which he is rebelling. The criteria of his rebellion may become simply new intellectual formulations whereby he forces conformity upon those who follow him or who join with him in his religious group. Whereas the sectarian movement within Protestantism has been continually breaking out of the shackles of authority, nevertheless we have been subterraneanly at the business of building new conformities which in all their subtlety are equally as authoritarian as the structures against which we have rebelled. They simply lack the overt, conscious, explicit order and design. Thus we continue to split the fellowship of Christians into more and more small groups which are at odds with each other.

The price of nonconformity is the risk and result of divisiveness. In this sense the pastoral counselor has the unique responsibility of being a minister of reconciliation between generations of Christians. As such, he is responsible for maintaining the fellowship at the same time that he is an understanding and sympathetic counselor for those who rebel. For example, the pastor of a church in a college town has this dilemma always with him. He counsels with growing college students who are breaking out of the bounds of ancestral traditions and achieving autonomy for themselves under God. At the same time he works with older persons in conserving the values that have been wrought out by their rebellions of earlier years. These people have, at great expense and effort to themselves, established the community against which the young people are rebelling. Although the days of severe clashes between state and nonconformist churches of dissenters are somewhat pale in our memory now, the contemporary pastoral counselor faces the nonconformity of every generation as it rises up against the "establishments" of the previous one.

ADULT FAITH AND PASTORAL COUNSELING

A second characteristic of the free church tradition is, as Ernest Payne again says, an insistence upon "the necessity of personal decision regarding God's offer of salvation to men. We are not born Christians, nor can we be made Christians by others, not even by the church. God has given us freedom, and salvation is by personal faith." (*The Free Church Tradition in the Life of England,* p. 174.) This is the conviction upon which the rejection of infant baptism is based. This conviction E. Y. Mullins calls "the competence of the soul in matters of religion." The heart of religion personally beating through faith comes most clearly into tone here. A person must be a responsible, mature, deciding, choosing self under God before he is accepted as a member of the fellowship of faith. This acceptance is symbolized in his baptism. This is an ecclesiastical statement of a conviction which has been lost in great segments of even the free church tradition of Christian communions. Although this conviction has been stated ecclesiastically, it can be stated psychologically without reference to such experiences as baptism. For example, Gordon Allport says in his Terry Lectures that "to feel oneself meaningfully linked to the whole of Being is not possible before puberty. . . . Since, however, the process of becoming continues throughout life, we rightly expect the full development of sentiment only in the adult reaches of personality." (Gordon W. Allport, *Becoming: Basic Considerations for a Psychology of Personality,* pp. 94–95; Yale University Press, 1955.)

American pastoral counseling, as has been said before, has been greatly influenced by the client-centered therapy formulations of Carl Rogers. The underlying philosophy of this school of therapy is that the emerging self of the individual is competent to make its own decisions, to revise its own directions, and to arrive at a satisfactory and purposeful existence without direction from the counselor. This theory has been interpreted quite passively by some counselors, and more dynamically by others.

Strangely enough, some client-centered therapists are as nondirective as the more extreme Calvinists of the early free church tradition. They did not believe in "the use of means" in persuading people to change their lives; neither do these "latter-day saints" of nondirectivism. Rather, they feel that given friendliness and good company the person will change his own way without the help of others. In an equally ana-chronistic spirit, the more directive counselor of today may be compared with the aggressive missionary of the free church tradition who insists that by aggressive persuasion men should be "won" to Christ. As in the early days of predestinationism and aggressive persuasion in missions, both nondirectivism and directivism can go to seed in behalf of either passivity and the lack of commitment on the part of some pastoral counselors or in behalf of compulsive self-assertion on the behalf of cer-tain other counselors.

The balancing insight that keeps a pastoral counselor from either extreme is an insistence upon personal, adult decision in religious faith and conduct of life. Pastoral counseling in a large measure has grown as a discipline because of the need of church members for something more than religious tradition with which to meet specific stresses of life. People come to the pastoral counselor at points of severe crisis and stress such as acute bereavement, a threatened marital breakup, severe alco-holism, mental illness, family delinquencies, etc. They tell us that they have "been a Baptist since before they can remem-ber." They might as well have said Methodist, Presbyterian, or any other group. They have always held *nominally and tradi-tionally* to the tenets of the faith and have participated socially in the life of the church. But now that the "evil days have drawn nigh" they are without resources, understanding, or an undergirding faith with which to deal with the tangible issues of stress that brought them to the counselor. The pastoral counselor, through the careful application of the discipline of longer-term, formal kinds of counseling, sees these individuals shift from a shallow, superficial assent to a set of articles of faith to a profound, personal rebirth of their very selves. The pastoral counselor continually picks up the wrecks of human life, the lives of persons who have run aground on the shoals of superficial religion. Thinking all the while they were in the depths of the channel of God's grace, in reality they found themselves aground and wrecked.

Pastors whose tradition lies in the free church movement can no longer, however, point to infant baptism as the cause solely and singly of these tragedies. Rather, we have to confess that superficial evangelism, careless and undisciplined indifference at the point of insisting upon converts bringing forth fruits worthy of repentance, and even the mass baptism of children who have been hurried into professions of faith— all these point toward the way in which the competency of the individual's own mature decision-making ability before God has been violated. These point toward the necessity for reaffirmation of adult decision and faith, as well as a more carefully disciplined fellowship *even among churches that do not practice infant baptism.*

A Disciplined Fellowship and Pastoral Counseling

A third salient characteristic of the free church tradition is the face-to-face, disciplined, and "gathered" fellowship of believers upon which it insists. The disciplined fellowship of gathered believers may be identified in three distinct ways. First, the believer who enters the fellowship is carefully instructed, thoroughly examined and tested, and patiently brought to maturity in his decision before he is baptized. This is discipline at the point of entry into the fellowship. Baptism is the symbol of a measure of maturity.

Second, the disciplined fellowship may be seen in terms of the personal, face-to-face, "known" relationship these persons have to each other. They are responsible for and to each other in works of love that include instruction, admonition, mutual burden-bearing in the fulfillment of the law of Christ. For example, the confession of a Baptist group in London in 1612 insisted "that the members of every church or congregation ought to know one another, so they may perform all the duties of love one toward another both to soul and body" (quoted in Ernest A. Payne, *The Fellowship of Believers: Baptist Thought and Practice Yesterday and Today*, p. 26; London: Carey Kingsgate Press, Ltd., 1952). Small-group discipline is lost even in the free church tradition whenever churches become ambitious as denominations, competing with each other within their own fellowships for size, social status, real-estate achievement, and numerical pride. Herein, denominations which owe their heritage to the free church movement have moved away from the church as *Gemeinde,* or fellowship of believers, to the church as *Kirche,* or the organization of believers.

In the third place, the disciplined fellowship implies that the whole membership of the church shall give counsel and guidance to each individual and family within the church. Traditionally this discipline in some of the smaller groups of Christians, such as the Mennonites in particular, was administered through the practice of the Lord's Supper. The Lord's Supper was looked upon as the time and occasion for "righting" relationships within the community, for cleansing the heart in personal confession of sin, and for the discipline of the Christian fellowship according to Matt. 18:15-20, I Cor. 5:7-11, I Tim. 6:5, Titus 3:9. If a person did not bring himself into line with the expectations of the community concerning his attitude and behavior, he was to be driven out, and the church was enjoined to withdraw from him and to flee from him. Even members of his own family were to aid the church in the imposition of "the ban" upon the offending member. (Menno Simons, "On the Ban: Question and Answers," *Spiritual and Anabaptist Writers,* ed. by George H. Williams and Angel M. Mergal, pp. 261-271; The Westminster Press, 1957.)

One underlying conviction is a common denominator of all three of these meanings of the disciplined fellowship: i.e., these Christians perceive the church itself as the counselor of its members. That which the contemporary pastoral counselor individually seeks to do, these churches of the free church tradition perceive as the corporate and individual responsibility of the church as a whole and of each individual member as a lay person. In their conception of the ideal community, which from the practical point of view may even be considered somewhat Utopian, the members of these disciplined fellowships of Christians still dare to believe that the good fruits of which the formal pastoral counselor dreams for his counselee should be brought into being by the local congregation of believing Christians. This poses several painful dilemmas for both the pastor and the congregation of such churches.

In the first place, the congregation itself is usually too large for these persons to know each other well enough to be competent to serve as effectively as the dream calls for. The increase of anonymity, especially in the city church, as well as the increase of the size of the church, makes such discipline difficult indeed to approach, much less to realize. One asks: "Are these expectations built upon the presuppositions of a rural community in which the church is the only institution?" In the second place, the instructions of our Lord in Matt. 18:15-20 suggest a *threefold* step in the admonition of an offender against the fellowship. Usually, however, the first two steps are neglected and the responsibility for instruction and admonition of an individual member is not often dealt with in face-to-face encounter between the offender and the offended. The suggestion is that the person who has been offended go to the offender and seek to win his brother. This would be "two . . . gathered" in Christ's name. In the event that this fails, he is urged, in the second step, to go to the offender with another member of the fellowship. This would be "three . . . gathered" in Christ's name. Only after these two efforts have failed should the matter be brought before the fellowship of Christians as a whole. One asks: Is this what it means when it says immediately after this command, "Where *two or three* are gathered," that the promise of the presence of Christ in the Holy Spirit is given?

In the third place, the real breakdown of discipline comes when the fellowship as a whole no longer feels any responsibility for the behavior of individuals, nor does the individual feel any responsibility to the fellowship as a whole. Then the breakdown is complete. The behavior of a member becomes his private business, to the exclusion of the community.

In these three exigencies, the dilemma of pastoral counseling emerges. For example, an individual member of the church will "hear" that another member is in trouble or engaging in some great offense. Instead of accepting responsibility for personally influencing him, he talks to a third person about him rather than going to the offender. They in turn may take this as an opportunity simply to pass on gossip, or they may come to the pastor himself as a representative of the fellowship of Christians. If, indeed, the pastor is fortunate, the person in distress has already come to him privately and is engaged in a process of counseling with him. But ordinarily, the "respectability maintenance" mechanisms in the community are such that neither the members of the church nor the pastor is in touch with the difficulty. The trouble brews until it breaks forth in the common knowledge of the community. A divorce proceeding is published in the newspapers. An automobile accident involves an alcoholic member. An embezzling church member is arraigned amidst a total business collapse. Or a total tragedy occurs in a suicide.

With the breakdown of the discipline of the community, the crushing load of total responsibility for pastoral counseling falls upon the shoulders of the pastor himself. He has a large membership. He necessarily must promote the complex business organization of the church. The recruitment of new members absorbs the rest of his energies. He may, therefore, be in too-difficult straits to give effective pastoral counseling attention to the individuals in trouble. Furthermore, the same "respectability maintenance" mechanisms that prevented the fellowship of Christians from communicating to him the stress of individuals in need serve also to deem it unwise, unnecessary, and "none-of-the-business" of the minister to be "doing that sort of thing" which is required of a counseling pastor. If a pastor goes very far in spite of other pressures, he may neglect his other responsibilities. Then he is out of keeping with the expectations of his congregation. Predominant among these expectations is the requirement that he participate as a "jolly good fellow" in a multiplicity of social activities as a community functionary. Therefore, the building of an effective counseling ministry demands serious attention on the part of both the church and its minister as to their basic purposes under God as a disciplined community of believers.

SEPARATION OF CHURCH AND STATE AND PASTORAL COUNSELING

Many of the ambiguities and ills that have just been described are persistent side effects of a vitally necessary operation that severed the church from the state. The author of this book readily reveals his own position when he says that the separation of the church and the state is a "vitally necessary operation." At the same time he recognizes the side effects which this has created in the relationship of the pastor to his people. These have been debilitating results of the separation of the church and state, although the gains have outreached the losses. It is well to deal with these negative factors first. Then the advantages that the pastoral counselor in the free church tradition enjoys by reason of his insistence upon the separation of the church and the state will be clearer. The kinds of disciplines that this principle imposes upon the pastoral counselor will be more challenging.

Persons in the free church tradition have always interpreted religious freedom to mean autonomy, not only of family heritages through infant baptism, but also freedom of the church from the state. The nonconformity and rebellion of free churchmen took on a definite political significance at this point. They have tended always to feel as Kierkegaard felt when he said, "To set State and Christianity together by the ears in this fashion makes just as good sense as to talk of a yard of butter, or if possible, there is less sense in it, since butter and a yard are merely things which have nothing to do with one another, whereas State and Christianity are inversely related to, or rather from, one another" (Kierkegaard, *Attack Upon "Christendom,"* p. 127). However, independence of the church from the state required that the free churches become economically independent of financial support by the state. In their beginnings, the churches have remained very small, informal fellowships of believers meeting in homes or rented quarters. Their leadership was predominantly a lay leadership who earned their income by other means than church support. Thus the financial undergirding of the program of the churches was not too relevant to the free church understanding of the work of the minister.

Salaries and real estate were not a problem. The minister was a first among equals who gave of his time without much if any remuneration. But when the size of the churches increased, the ecclesiastical structure became more complex; real estate was acquired; buildings were necessary; and ministers were asked to spend their full time at the expense of the fellowship. Then the whole situation reversed. The time and energy of the pastor was called upon to raise money for the various projects of the church, and great portions of his attention had to be addressed to such matters as denominational affairs, building programs, and fiscal policy.

In this latter instance, among the free churches the memories of the Great Awakening provided an ideal promotional medium in the revival-meeting pattern. Through this medium the size of the churches was increased, even to the extent of competition with other churches of "like faith and order." The pastor was judged on his ability as an administrator of the complex organization of the church and as a recruitment officer for the expanding membership of the church.

Under these stresses and expectations it became very easy for the churches to isolate and restrict their relationship and that of the pastor to the distinctly formal functions of church membership, church attendance, and church giving. The caring functions of the church have, therefore, tended to atrophy or to be relegated to nonchurch agencies and professions. A subtle process of secularization set in as a result. The educational functions of life were relegated to the public schools. The welfare functions of the church were classified with the "social gospel" and rejected. Thus by stress and neglect the "care of the flock" was relegated to the welfare state. More recently, the care and cure of souls has been seen as the function of helping professions, such as social work, psychology, psychiatry, and psychoanalysis, with little or no relation or responsibility to the church. Some free churchmen have tended to see these specialists as lay expressions of Christian ministry, assuming that the individual person dedicated himself to Christ. Others have been more hostile and seen even more empirical kinds of pastoral care as alien to the purposes of the church and its ministry, antithetical to the more "spiritual" approaches of evangelism, somewhat specially defined.

These are some of the painful side effects of the decision of the free church tradition to refuse state aid in the support of the church lest "public authority . . . use their financial powers as a potent weapon of discrimination against various religions or their followers" (Arcot Krishnaswami, "The Status of Religions in Relation to the State," *A Journal of the Church and State,* Vol. 2, No. 1, May, 1960, p. 46). However, the result has tended to be a religion which is

too limited in its conception of its own significance. It is entirely too satisfied with its prevalent compartmental status. . . . The trend is to dismiss it "as an adjectival and peripheral concern." Nicholas Berdyaev says that organized Christianity is "degenerated because it has been relegated to a corner of the human soul and has ceased to be a total attitude toward life, as, of course, it should be" (T. B. Maston, "The Church, the State, and the Christian Ethic," *A Journal of Church and State*, Vol. 2, No. 1, May, 1960, p. 27).

Another untoward side effect of the free church tradition of separation of church and state upon the role of the pastor as a counselor has been the way in which the training of pastoral counselors, particularly in its earliest phases between 1920 and 1945, has been divorced from theological education and from the life of the parish situation itself. Early explorers in the field of pastoral care and counseling support themselves as chaplains in state institutions. If they could not get support this way, they had to turn to private sources of financial support. This was the case in the association of Russell Dicks with the medical doctor, Richard C. Cabot.

It was not until 1945 and later that the larger denominations, such as Baptists, Methodists, Lutherans, and Congregationalists, established chairs of instruction in pastoral theology, pastoral care, and pastoral counseling through the funds of the churches themselves. Since this has been done, however, increasing attention has been paid to the relevance of Protestant distinctives and local church life for the practice of pastoral counseling by ministers.

Even so, ministers themselves in America have begun to enjoy independence from the churches and schools in some instances. Substitutes for state support of the ministry have in a few signal instances been located. For example, in the tax structure of America, foundations have been formed by corporations and individuals for the purpose of giving money, which otherwise would be taxable, to benevolent causes. These foundations have subsidized pastoral counseling centers, training centers, and individual research. Also, some few American ministers have sought to "earn a living" at pastoral counseling on a private-practice basis. They do this by charging fees. However, without additional support from either independent wealth, a foundation, or a group of churches these efforts have usually been financially precarious.

From an operational point of view, probably the most vivid example of the relevance of the problem of church and state for the practice of pastoral counseling is in premarital pastoral counseling. The pastor, in an effort to be nice to everyone, often fails to ask the questions as *to whom he is representing when he marries a couple.* Is he representing the church in performing what he and the gathered community of believers, along with the man and woman to be married, have agreed to be a genuinely Christian marriage? Or, is he a representative of the state, performing a civil marriage, with no regard to the relationship of the couple to the church?

Once he has answered these two questions, his whole approach to pastoral counseling in premarital situations is shaped and conditioned by the answer he gives. For, if he looks upon himself as *always* a representative of the church and *never* a functionary of the state as is true in a pure interpretation of the free church tradition, then he could not with clarity of conviction marry a couple who were not demonstrably participant in the new life in Christ. Furthermore, if he sees himself, not as a priest who exercises the right of decision in these matters alone, but as a representative of the gathered community of believers, then he could not make such decisions as this without involving the fellowship of believers in a disciplined confrontation of the issues at stake. He would necessarily be a catalytic agent activating the processes of the group of the church in such a way that the decision about policy in the marriage of persons would be the common voice of the church. This, it seems to me, would be holding true to his convictions as a participant in the free church tradition. In this he would have to learn what Wittenberg has called "the art of group discipline."

Charismatic Faith and Pastoral Counseling

A fifth dimension of the free church tradition is often over-looked: a common characteristic of free church groups has been their conviction that both the gathered community and the man of God are chosen, led, and equipped "for the work of ministry, for the building up of the body of Christ" through the work of the Holy Spirit. In other words it is a *charismatic* understanding of church and ministry. Whereas other groups of Protestants have held to this also in different manners, times, and places, the participants of the free church tradition have not only held to it; they have insisted upon it.

From this point of view, therefore, the pastoral counselor, is assisted by, is under the tutelage of, and is held responsible to the Holy Spirit. This concept of "giftedness" has undergone a whole spectrum of interpretations. Some groups have held that without evidence of the "gift of Holy Spirit," one's very regenerateness has not been demonstrated. Other interpreters have looked upon this giftedness as talent that was inborn through creation and brought alive in redemption. As these two shades of interpretation blend together, one finds a steady resistance in the free church tradition to more empirical and skilled approaches to pastoral counseling in which method, process of development, and pastoral ingenuity are brought into play. One often hears this resistance expressed in such comments as: "Pastoral counselors are born and not made." "Pastoral counseling is just a matter of using common sense, and being devoted to the Lord." "Pastoral counseling does not require training, just experience." Whereas such remarks as these suggest a spirit of defensiveness and fear rather than one of power and of love and of self-control, nevertheless they do point to a positive conviction on the part of the charismatically oriented free churchman that the work of the Holy Spirit is relevant both in the equipment and in the function of the pastoral counselor. Furthermore, these comments also suggest that apart from this, pastoral counseling itself may be a manipulation of skills and methods rather than participation in a genuinely spiritual relationship to the person who seeks counseling.

However, on the other hand, the charismatic faith of the free church tradition itself may be moved over into pietistic manipulation of people in professional evangelism. The evangelist is likely to assume that the instantaneous experience of conversion is equivalent to, and a substitute for, the continuing pilgrimage of redemption instead of being its point of beginning the new life in Christ. In doing so he is likely to neglect his responsibility for the follow-up of the results of his evangelism. This task is left to other ministers who take more seriously the skills and disciplines of pastoral counseling as a continuing process relationship.

These applications of charismatic conviction to the practice of pastoral counseling are not at all new. They have also been apparent in the practice of Christian preaching. Skill and education in the work of the preacher have both tended to be looked upon with suspicion by persons who believe sincerely that the work of the Holy Spirit is a direct, unsolicited, and unscheduled gift of the Holy Spirit apart from the discipline, training, and education of the preacher.

However, this whole discussion of the relevance of the free church tradition to pastoral counseling, with its emphasis upon spiritual nonconformity, adult faith, disciplined fellowship, separation of church and state, and charismatic faith, has been questioned recently by Joachim Scharfenberg. He criticizes the field of pastoral care and counseling for its anthropocentric point of departure and its neglect of the work of the Holy Spirit. (Scharfenberg, "The Babylonic Captivity of Pastoral Theology," *loc. cit.*, p. 133.) An examination of the work of the Holy Spirit as counselor is therefore in order at this point.

III

The Holy Spirit as Counselor

THE NEW TESTAMENT TEACHING with reference to the Holy Spirit is indispensable wisdom for the practice of pastoral counseling. Especially relevant is the Revised Standard translation of the name of the Paraclete as "the Counselor." This translation of the name is certainly the proper description of the character of God as seen in both the Old and New Testaments. The Eternal God strikes Paul with awe when he exclaims:

> "For who has known the mind of the Lord,
> or who has been his counselor?" . . .
> For from him and through him and to him are all
> things. To him be glory forever. (Rom. 11:34, 36.)

Furthermore, the Messiah in the prophecy of Isaiah is called the "Wonderful Counselor" (Isa. 9:6). This term means that the Holy Spirit brings to fresh vitality the memory of the things of Christ, thereby "bringing to light" the repentance of those who are out of touch with the truth as revealed in Christ. The Holy Spirit brings the hope of forgiveness and the redemption of the world at the same time. (C. K. Barrett, "The Holy Spirit in the Fourth Gospel," *Journal of Theological Studies,* 1:1–15, 1950.) The unity of the Trinity is apparent in the thought of God the Father as the Counselor. The Messiah is the Anointed One sent to heal the brokenhearted and to release the captives. And the Holy Spirit is the gift of the

Father upon the prayer of the Son that we should never be orphans but always have the continuing counsel of the Holy Spirit.

Yet, whereas Scharfenberg and others rightly score all of us, and especially non-Barthians, for not making the Holy Spirit the theme of our pastoral theology, the only comfort we have in the face of the truth he states is that all other branches of theological inquiry are offenders with us. Henry P. Van Dusen rightly observes that most of the books concerning the Holy Spirit are both moldy with age and filled with cries of alarm that the Holy Spirit is "the neglected stepchild of the Trinity." He entitles his work, which actually is concerned with the whole Trinitarian doctrine, *Spirit, Son and Father: The Christian Faith in the Light of the Holy Spirit,* thus giving the Holy Spirit first place in consideration. (Charles Scribner's Sons, 1958.) Hence, I consider it highly necessary both from these competent appraisals of our neglect and from my own memories of desperation in the practice of pastoral counseling, to give more than just passing reference to the Holy Spirit as Counselor.

THE RESPONSIBILITY OF THE HOLY SPIRIT

The Holy Spirit is in truth the Counselor in every interpersonal relationship, and not we ourselves. This is the most basic affirmation concerning the Holy Spirit as Counselor. As the report of the Commission on the Ministry of the New York Academy of Sciences puts it, "The clergyman always sees God as a partner in the counseling process . . . and feels rather hesitant in attributing to his own efforts whatever success may be achieved." ("The Findings of the Commission in the Ministry," *Annals of the New York Academy of Sciences,* Vol. 63, Article 3, November 7, 1955, p. 428.) The pastoral counselor relates himself to the Holy Spirit as Counselor in much the same way as a doctor does to life. Life itself is in reality the therapist, and the doctors are only the assistants. The Christian believes that the Holy Spirit *is* life itself. This affirms that God is sovereign in any counseling relationship. The modern pastoral counselor's rediscovery of the sovereignty of God challenges him to self-discipline. Counseling can become a clever demonstration of power for him. He may "play God" by usurping the autonomy of the individual soul before God. A pastor sometimes creates dependency relationships with people in which they lose his friendship if they do not do what he thinks is right. Or he may fear he will lose their support if he does not do what they want done. This moves very close to demanding idolatry of them, or making an idol of them.

On the other hand, the spiritually secure pastor knows that the life of his counselee is actually in the hands of God, and not his. The Holy Spirit and not he himself is the Counselor. The processes of purpose in this life situation are deeper than his own power to probe. Consequently, he can "rest himself in these thoughts." He does not have to rush to defend God. He does not mistake his own insecurity for the precariousness of a flimsy god's position in the world. He can take people's troubles seriously without overdeveloped and overworked feelings of responsibility that keep him awake at night, worrying about all the problems people have presented to him the day before. Leslie Weatherhead describes this spirit of secure trust in God in telling of the simplicity of the faith of an old charwoman who, during the bombing raids of London, would sit down by her cleaning buckets and go to sleep. When asked how she did it, she replied: "The good Book tells me that the Lord fainteth not, neither is weary, and that he stayeth awake and watches over his own. So there's no use in both of us staying awake!"

THE HOLY SPIRIT AS COUNSELOR OF THE PASTOR

This leads to the second affirmation concerning the work of the Holy Spirit as Counselor. The Holy Spirit, given the opening of a consistently cultivated prayer life in the pastor him-

self, is the Strengthener and Counselor of that pastor. This
applies particularly to the times in which the pastor feels inadequate, weak, and borne down by his own personal problems. The pastor encounters the overwhelming power of the
evil that possesses people's lives. He contemplates the complexity of his task. He is thrust back upon the depth of the
riches and wisdom and knowledge of God. He is prone to ask:
"Who is sufficient for these things?" (II Cor. 2:16). These very
weaknesses and feelings of insufficiency are known by the
Holy Spirit in his work in the pastor himself. As Paul puts it,
"The Spirit helps us in our weakness." These weaknesses to
which he refers apply to deficiencies in authority, dignity, or
power, deficiencies in strength, and even to illnesses of body
and spirit, which plague the minister himself.

Even though the book was published in 1928, H. Wheeler
Robinson's *The Christian Experience of the Holy Spirit* remains one of the most dependable theological interpretations
of the Holy Spirit. At the outset of the book, the author tells of
his own personal experience in a serious illness in which he
and his own spiritual resources had failed for lack of personal
strength. He looked upon the truths of the gospel that he had
preached and sought to practice as demanding "an active effort for which the physical energy was lacking." He searched
his faith and that of others and found the gap in "his own
conception of evangelical truth." He found it in his neglect of
those conceptions of the Holy Spirit in which the New Testament is so rich. (H. Wheeler Robinson, *The Christian Experience of the Holy Spirit*, p. 4; Harper & Brothers, 1928.) The
book that he was empowered to write was nourished by his
rediscovery of the ministry of the Holy Spirit as he confronted
his own depleted spiritual and physical energies. Such may
also be said both in evaluation and remedy of the kind of
spiritual dryness and destitution which comes to the pastor
as he counsels with more and more people. It seems, as St.
John of the Cross says, that these very aridities, rather than
spiritual delights and pleasures, are a sort of necessary prelude

and preparation for a more vivid knowledge of the glory of
God. (Saint John of the Cross, *Dark Night of the Soul,* ed. by
E. Allison Peers, 3d edition, p. 80; Doubleday Image Books,
1959.)

The pastor's main assurance at this point comes not from
any perfection he may imagine himself to have achieved but
from the basic relationship he has with God. This cannot be
shaken, "the Spirit himself bearing witness with our spirit
that we are children of God." The Christian pastor consequently takes a positive and courageous stand in the face of
the tribulations that beset him. He lays hold of every bit of
counseling help he can get in his venture toward maturity.
Sometimes a pastor's problems are of such a deep and wide
nature that they hinder and cripple the work of God to which
he has been led. Such a pastor should not be averse to getting
the best medical and psychiatric help available for himself as
a person. But when all is said and done, he draws the main
strength of his life as a person and as a pastor from his relationship to God through the Holy Spirit. He concentrates upon
and lays hold of his sufferings through the power of the
love of God rather than being desecrated and laid hold of
by the "spirit of slavery," to fall back into fear. He has received, instead, a spirit of sonship, of abiding relationship with
God.

This personal ministry of the Holy Spirit to him becomes,
therefore, the basis of his rejoicing as a counselor. He rejoices
in his sufferings, "knowing that suffering produces endurance,
and endurance produces character, and character produces
hope, and hope does not disappoint us, *because God's love has
been poured into our hearts through the Holy Spirit.*" Furthermore, the very practical question as to the basis of the pastor's
rejoicing over his successes as a counselor is answered also.
Here again, as in the case of the Seventy upon returning with
joy from their healing mission, the pastor's rejoicing is
grounded in his relationship to the Kingdom of Heaven, not in
the fact that the demons are subject to him. For if any man

thinks he stands in this, let him take heed lest he fall. The Holy Spirit is at work in the life of the pastor so that his suffering helps him learn from his own mistakes. The Holy Spirit prompts him to thank God that people are brought from death unto life through his ministry by the power of the Holy Spirit as Counselor.

THE HOLY SPIRIT AND THE ANXIETY OF COMMUNICATION

However, we need to be more specific about the work of the Holy Spirit as Counselor in the interpersonal relationship between a pastor and the individuals who "open up" their problems to him. Probably the main anxiety barrier between the pastor and his counselee is over "what to say." This is the *anxiety of communication*. Much has been said in the literature on pastoral counseling about what to say, how much to say, who should do the talking, and how things that are said can hurt or help people. Some of this writing is classified under the heading of the controversy among counselors as to how directive or nondirective they should be. These controversial discussions indicate great anxiety on the part of pastors about "what to say" in counseling.

In the specific context of the pastoral situation, the pastor especially is anxious about what to say. He knows that he may be held publicly responsible for what he says to his counselee. In the role of administrator of his church, a pastor has to deal with personal problems of church members. The problems are often thoroughly embedded and entangled in the official connections of these people with the church organizations. He, therefore, feels threatened as to what he says to church members. They in turn are exceedingly anxious about how much they can safely tell him.

Although the original setting of Jesus' words in Matt. 10:19–20 was that of the persecution of Christians, nevertheless, the meaning is highly appropriate to the anxiety about communication of which we are thinking here:

When they deliver you up, do not be anxious how you are to speak or what you are to say; for what you are to say will be given to you in that hour; for it is not you who speak, but the spirit of your Father speaking through you.

The deeper a pastor goes into the inner difficulties of people, the less his ethical and spiritual perspective coincides with the popular superficialities, stereotypes, and crass ethical contradictions in the average church community. Therefore, the tension of communicating the gospel at its deepest level is charged with heavy community threat for the faithful pastor. Therefore, the actual context of Jesus' words is not inappropriate today, inasmuch as in some mission fields and in certain social classes and regional areas of our country today a man actually would be delivered up to the councils if he declared the "whole counsel of God" in the things he had to say.

Jesus told his disciples that he was sending them forth as sheep among the wolves. He counseled them to have a shrewdness in love that can strike the balance between sincerity and irresponsible idealism—to have the wisdom of serpents and the harmlessness of doves. He related this directly to the work of the Holy Spirit as Counselor. He told them that they should not be anxious, because the Holy Spirit would tell them in that hour what to say.

Another situation of communication anxiety exists when a pastor and his counselee struggle to understand each other clearly. The depths of feeling cannot be uttered. The power of language fails as they seek to communicate with each other. At these points, the relationship itself becomes a groping kind of prayer. This became especially real as the mother and father of a feeble-minded child came to me with the painful concern of not knowing how to pray. They said that they were speechless as they sought to talk with God about the whole thing. Filled with mingled emotions of love, fear, hostility, and mystery toward God, little wonder is it that the numbness of their grief would cause their prayers to fail for words. Their anxiety about communication brought to me anew the reality of the work of the Holy Spirit as Counselor. "For we do not know how to pray as we ought, but the Spirit himself intercedes for us with sighs too deep for words. And he who searches the hearts of men knows what is the mind of the Spirit, because the Spirit intercedes for the saints according to the will of God." (Rom. 8:26–27.) This was all I could say to them; it was all I needed to say.

Korzybski, the scientific authority on communication, has said that the most profound level of communication is the silent level, when language itself "plays out" and, in awe-struck reverence, we can only point at what we see and feel. At this level, each person "hears in his own language," even as at Pentecost when the Holy Spirit came upon them, people of every race heard the gospel in their own language. When the anxiety of communication is converted into the hunger for reconciliation and understanding, then the work of the Holy Spirit is at the zenith of its power. The pastor in his counseling, therefore, needs to persevere in patience when people begin to misunderstand him and at that point every effort at clarification should be exerted, because at this very point, the work of the Holy Spirit is most often in evidence, relaxing the tension *between* the pastor and his counselee. Understanding comes out of confusion, and peace out of conflict. Just when his counselee is threatening to reject him most is when the pastor is at the point of learning the most himself. For the things that go on *between* a counselor and a counselee are the royal road to insight and spiritual growth.

THE HOLY SPIRIT AS TEACHER IN COUNSELING

This last statement needs to be clarified and made more specific. This can best be done by discussing the revealing work of the Holy Spirit. The Counselor, the Holy Spirit, teaches the pastor and his counselee all things, and brings to their remembrance the things that Jesus has taught. This "teaching" is informative and instructional in the case of little children who do not know the Bible and of adults who have only a smattering of the Biblical content of the Christian message. But the interpretation of the Scriptures and the application of the message in the light of the immediate, personal situation of a counselee is more than the repetition of a word-tradition. The hearts of pastor and counselee often are like those of the two disciples on the road to Emmaus: they burn within them as the Spirit of the living God opens both their eyes to the Scriptures. Here the Creator Spirit is at work also in the life of those who are actually dying to an old self and being brought alive unto a new being in Christ. Old things pass away and all things become new. As one counselee described it, she felt as if she had been found half-dead, and was now alive again. She spoke of the day of the discovery as her birthday, and thought of herself as a new person and living unto God. She thanked her pastor for not having rushed in to do all her spiritual discovering for her. He had restrained his need to tell her what God was about to reveal to her Himself. In a sense she was complimenting her pastor for not grieving the Holy Spirit as the Counselor by hindering his work. She went through many rigors of anxiety and furtive wondering as she groped toward a clear perception of the new life coming to pass within her whole being.

THE HOLY SPIRIT AND CREATIVE INSECURITY

This person's life story suggests that not all stress and strain is bad. Some of it is the creative anxiety concomitant with any great spiritual happening. Paul called the process whereby the Holy Spirit mobilizes this anxiety toward the birth of a new life in an individual before God a "working out" of salvation. The attending anxiety he called "fear and trembling." The pastor quite often is likely to interpret peace as repose, serenity as the absence of tension, and faith as the absence of the stress of growth. This is the farthest from the New Testament teachings concerning the indwelling activity of God the Holy Spirit. When the Holy Spirit is at work within a person, peace is not repose but a tumultuous activity within. The courage of the person is mobilized for either the birth or the growth of a new self under God. Serenity is the inner security of knowing that God is in everything working "for good with those who love him, who are called according to his purpose" (Rom. 8:28).

Faith is the affirmation of the work of God through the acceptance of that inner struggle of the soul. The whole person responds in the effort to become the person which God in both his creation and redemption intends that one be. Faith involves the tearing up of old securities, such as Abraham had in Ur of the Chaldees, and going out not knowing where one goes. In fact, faith in a real sense is the courage of not knowing. Faith is a response to the call of God to a new life. Faith refuses to shrink back from the demands of growth and maturity. Faith moves out beyond the safe confines of "a known way." Louise Haskins said it best:

> I said to the man who stood at the gate of the Year:
>   Give me a light that I may tread safely into the
>   unknown.
> And he replied: Go out into the darkness and put
>   thine hand into the hand of God.
> That shall be to thee better than light and safer than
>   a known way. (Minnie Louise Haskins, "The Gate of
>   the Year," quoted in *Worship Resources for the Christian Year*, ed. by Charles L. Wallis, p. 373; Harper &
>   Brothers, 1954.)

THE HOLY SPIRIT AND THE ANXIETY OF SEPARATION

One cannot encounter this unknownness without some newer and more eternal security than he has left behind. The threat of separation creates more anxiety than one can bear alone. A teen-age boy does not leave home and seek a larger relationship to other people all by himself. He shrinks back from the homesickness, the loneliness, and the raw necessity of having to earn his own living. He hungers for a companion in his venture. A young girl does not leave her father and mother and trust her life into marriage without great trepidation if she feels that she is isolated from all those to whom she has been close until now. A fear-ridden neurotic person does not easily give up his symptoms until he has some more abiding way of coping with his imponderable anxieties. The bereaved person does not readily give up the fantasy that the loved one is not really dead until some new influx of the Spirit of the living God overwhelms the fear of loneliness. A disciple of the Lord Jesus Christ can forsake father, mother, brother, sister, for the gospel, but he cannot endure the isolation alone. What, then, is the work of the Holy Spirit as Counselor in this *anxiety of separation?*

Jesus made it very plain. He was aware of the power of loneliness himself. He reminded himself many times that he was not alone. The Heavenly Father was with him. He could, therefore, sense the aloneness in his followers. He said to them:

> I will not leave you desolate; I will come to you. . . . If a man loves me, he will keep my word, and my Father will love him, and we will come to him and make our home with him. . . . These things have I spoken to you, while I am still with you. But the Counselor, the Holy Spirit, whom the Father will send in my name, he will teach you all things, and bring to your remembrance all that I have said to you. Peace I leave with you; my peace I give to you; not as the world gives do I give to you. Let not your hearts be troubled, neither let them be afraid. (John 14:18, 23, 25–27.)

Jesus' word "desolate" is the same word from which we get our word "orphan." Christ will not leave us as orphans. The gift of the Holy Spirit is the conquest of man's loneliness and

isolation. The importance of all earthly families is lowered.
The Spirit of God reconstitutes the individual as a member of
the family of God. The anxiety of communication is overcome
by the reality of communion in the family of God. Here, God
is our Father, Jesus Christ is our elder Brother, and the Holy
Spirit is the life's blood of our eternally inseparable sonship
with each other in fellowship with other Christians. The
anxiety of loneliness is overcome by the power of the Holy
Spirit. The middle walls of partition between men and God
and men and men are broken down. The gathered community
of Christians is always a reconstituted family of people. We
are bound together by participation in the gift of the Holy
Spirit.

This reality is the daily bread of the pastor's ministry to the
corporate fellowship of his church. He is constantly dealing
with emotionally starved, spiritually orphaned people. Their
parents may well be alive, but they have deserted them, rejected them, or been otherwise unable to give them love and
security. These persons are suffering from a real spiritual
"vitamin deficiency." To them it is a pernicious anemia of the
spirit. Psychotherapists have been known to carry these people
for years as patients. (See Carl R. Rogers, "A Personal Formulation of Client-centered Therapy," *Marriage and Family Living,* Vol. XIV, No. 4, Nov., 1952, p. 360.) The main thing
counselors have been able to do is to provide some of the
emotional nutriment for which the person has an insatiable
craving. I have seen such persons find a new life and a new
meaning in the acceptance, the faithfulness, and the non-
exploitative love and security which they discovered in a
Christian community. Christians will find that they themselves
are depleted emotionally by such persons unless the persons
discover a direct personal relationship to the Living God in
their powerlessness to help themselves. The Alcoholics Anonymous groups are having remarkable success in dealing with
fellow alcoholics this way. Instead of filling this aching, chok-
ing void with wine, the fellowship of the group fills the

alcoholic with consistently firm and patient love. One wonders why some of the alcoholics who make professions of faith in our churches are not able to carry through with their confession. Maybe the people in the churches repeat the same mistakes that their parents made in their treatment of them. After the alcoholic has been converted, the more conventional church member is likely to expect him to be self-sufficient in his own will power and to reject him if he falls.

The Holy Spirit inhabits and animates the church as the body of Christ. We participate in the Kingdom of God in the "betweenness" of Christians in common bond with each other and as they witness to their faith to those who are not Christian. The highly personal and intense encounters of counseling provide wider openings for this break-through of the Kingdom in the work of the Holy Spirit. Yet we need to keep in mind that the Holy Spirit does not confine his work to the church. As H. Wheeler Robinson says, "We shall be nearer the truth if we keep in mind his constant activity as Spirit in the whole extraecclesiastical world, whilst emphasizing the unique and supreme activity of his operation through the historic personality and work of Jesus Christ." (Robinson, *The Christian Experience of the Holy Spirit*, p. 157.)

Another point at which the communion of the Holy Spirit in the fellowship of the church is real to the counseling problems presented to the pastor is in his dealing with grudge-bearing personalities. Separation comes by open hostility at times. People in churches do get to the point where they do not speak to each other. This separation is a strange reversal of the anxiety of communication in that these persons are afraid of what they will say. However, this kind of spirit gnaws away at the communion of the saints. The pastor is regularly "caught in the middle" of this kind of relationship between his people. These persons too often are the main leaders of his church. This problem was encountered early in the New Testament churches, and the teachings found in Matt. 18:15–20 reflect the concern for reconciliation.

Jesus' first admonition was that one should agree with an adversary while one is still in communication with him. His second injunction was to go to the offending brother, pointing out the fault in private, lowly friendship, with no intention to humiliate. If this does not succeed, the next step is to take one or two other friends and attempt again to reconcile the matter. This occasionally clarifies communication in such a way that an understanding is established. But if not, the community of believers as a whole needs to take some kind of action, and only after this should excommunicating procedures even be considered.

The whole spirit of such a ministry is entirely dependent upon the conscious awareness of the presence of the living Christ in the attempts at reconciliation. Such gatherings together for reconciliation are doomed to failure if they are not in his name. The conscious dependence upon the Holy Spirit as Counselor in these times of broken relationship in the churches is the indispensable necessity if progress is to be made. These contextual problems are too many times forgotten when the promise of Jesus was that "where two or three are gathered together in my name, there am I in the midst of them."

Such a gathering of the offended with the offender in forgiveness and understanding is obviously the work of the Holy Spirit as Counselor. Many times in such situations a pastor can effectively serve as a minister of reconciliation simply by encouraging a person who has been offended by another to go to the person face to face and firmly but gently present his real feelings of being offended. In others, a pastor can, if the person has already attempted this, offer to serve as a third person in such a conversation, in which he tries to help clarify the basis of confused communication. Such conflicts are often based upon two things: first, confused communication, in which what was said and done was misquoted, all the facts were not known, or the people were in too great a hurry to make their real desires understood; and second, such conflicts are based upon real disagreements in matters of principle as to how to do things. This was evident in the Jerusalem Conference reported in Acts, ch. 15.

In these instances, a pastor can work through the power of the Holy Spirit to clear up communication and to work out healthy acceptance of basic differences without a breach of fellowship. But often there comes the demonic element of conscious deception of the brethren, jealousy for power, and lust for gain. Then the pastor contends, not "against flesh and blood, but against the principalities, against the powers, against the world rulers of this present darkness, against the spiritual hosts of wickedness in the heavenly places." These are the forces which produce the kind of death-dealing relationships exemplified in Ananias and Sapphira, persons whose hearts the Evil One filled to lie to the Holy Spirit. The tragedies inherent in such relationships are not confined to the New Testament. Too many modern adherents of the Christian faith go to an early grave because of the demonic possession of such "spirits of falsehood."

THE HOLY SPIRIT AND FALSE SPIRITS

False spirits, then, need to be tested. The pastor should be alert not to believe every spirit. What are the false spirits that present themselves to the pastor in his pastoral ministry and which call for the work of the Holy Spirit in testing them? Paul describes these clearly: First, he speaks of the "spirit of slavery," which causes men "to fall back into fear" (Rom. 8:15). This is slavery to the "elemental spirits of the universe" (Gal. 4:3), which take hold of a person who worships the idols of "beings that by nature are no gods" (Gal. 4:8). Herein is the dynamic connection between spirit possession and idolatry: i.e., the observation of days, months, seasons, and years, the practice of rituals as a means of pride, the emphasis of one of the great doctrines of faith to the exclusion of the whole counsel of God, the placing of family loyalties above the maturing demands of the Holy Spirit, and the nursing of an old grudge to the point of idolatry—all these idolatries fill the life with possessing spirits of fear. And what Paul is saying is that these spirits did not come from God, "for God did not give us a spirit of timidity, but a spirit of power and love and self-control" (II Tim. 1:7).

The first letter of John sharply commands the discerning of false spirits from the Spirit of God:

> Beloved, do not believe every spirit, but test the spirits to see whether they are of God; for many false prophets have gone out into the world. (I John 4:1.)

Then the writer moves into the discussion of the character of God:

> Little children, you are of God and have overcome them; for he who is in you is greater than he who is in the world. . . . For God is love. . . . There is no fear in love, but perfect love casts out fear. . . . Keep yourselves from idols.

The Holy Spirit as Counselor is the power of love over fear, and the exorcism of spirits is essentially the casting out of fear through love. Herein are the spirits discerned from one another. Empowered by the Holy Spirit, the pastor is called to this task of discernment and becomes a "son of encouragement" because he is "filled with the Holy Spirit," even as was Barnabas.

THE HOLY SPIRIT AND THE CONVICTION OF SIN

Finally, such discernment of spirits calls for a spiritual conviction of sin, righteousness, and judgment. Basic to all pastoral counseling is the handling of this process of conviction. The question arises again and again as to whether or not the pastor should take a condemnatory attitude toward the sin and unrighteousness of his counselee as he sees it. The impressive thing about us as pastors when we are most con-

cerned with blasting the sinner with harshness and rough-
handed condemnation is that we are usually very anxious
ourselves at the time. Our own guilt fosters this anxiety. We
become more concerned with asserting ourselves than with the
real need of the person for confession and forgiveness. Our
desire to condemn hinders our waiting to see whether the
Holy Spirit is *already* at work in the heart of the person, con-
victing him of sin, of righteousness, and of judgment. Our
anxiety and our judgmental spirit become "works of our own,"
which shut the doors of the Kingdom to our Counselor after
having refused to enter ourselves!

If the pastor has this power to wait, he is less likely to con-
firm the sinner in his waywardness by adding to his need to
defend himself from one more self-righteous person. This
process of conviction is essentially the work of the Holy Spirit,
and not that of the pastor. Modern discussions of pastoral
counseling insist upon a nonjudgmental attitude of accepting
love. *But this does not mean that the conviction of sin does and
should not take place.* Rather, it means that conviction is the
inner accomplishment of the Holy Spirit, not the work of the
pastor. Once the pastor takes such an attitude of judgment, he
becomes intensely convicted of his own need for self-assertion.
In itself, such an attitude is a form of pride as deadly as any
other sin. But this conviction *in him* is also the work of the
Holy Spirit. The atmosphere of the conference with the offending person then changes into a kind of worship in itself
whereby *two sinful persons* confess their faults silently to God
as the Holy Spirit gives them utterance at the level of relationship that is deeper than words. Then, the pastor who is self-
disciplined enough to listen rejoices that even the spirits are
subject to him in the power of the Holy Spirit.

One counselee writes of his counseling experience in these
revealing words:

I needed no man to sit in judgment upon me. Better
than any, I knew wherein I had fallen. The pain of the

load of my own knowledge of the conflict was sufficient
to render conviction leading to the path of wholeness.
Thus, it was in the acceptance of my own role as a
counselee that I was enabled to feel the sharp awareness
of my burden. Aided by the spiritual security and patient
understanding of my counselor, I reached for the depths
for understanding of the One who through a quiet, inner
confrontation brought a source of strength to give meaning to life's suffering. I had become aware of the work of
the Holy Spirit. I marveled at the Christian maturity
such awareness rendered. I became conscious of the
strength from within. With my counselor and this Christian dynamic, I could even face suffering with some
feeling of excitement, for I had learned that only from
the One source can one reap real joy, and the knowledge
of this brought comfort with the mere anticipation of a
further encounter leading to greater depths of spiritual
maturity. Thus, it was, I needed no man to sit in judgment upon me, for who is man in the face of the Lord!

By way of summary, then, we have seen that the Holy Spirit
and not the counselor himself is the center of the burden of
responsibility in the counseling relationship. He is the Counselor of the pastor himself, undergirding him with strength
and guidance. The Holy Spirit is at work always in the "between situation" of the counselor-pastor and the counselee,
overcoming the anxiety of communication. Again, the Holy
Spirit is the teacher and instructor of the counselor and
counselee in both the power of inspiration and the recovery of
memory, in the healing of the truth of the past and in the
solace of the hope of the future. Thus insecurity, separation,
and the power of evil itself can be overcome with the creative
love of God shed abroad in our hearts through the Holy Spirit.
In the arena of this love we can stand to see ourselves as we
really are.

IV

Some Eschatological Dimensions
of Pastoral Counseling

THE PRECEDING DISCUSSION of the Holy Spirit as Counselor raises two fresh issues with reference to pastoral counseling. The first issue is *the quality of hope* by which the pastoral counselor is himself sustained and by means of which he sustains his counselee. The second issue is the way in which the relationship of time, developmental process, and the sense of the end of life and the world affect this sustaining hope in the counselor-counselee situation. Suffering, time, hope—these are involved in the desperate questions of both pastoral counselor and counselee. The prophets asked: "How long, O Lord?" (Isa. 6:11). The apostle prayed: "May the God of hope fill you with all joy and peace in believing, so that by the power of the Holy Spirit you may abound in hope" (Rom. 15:13). The apostle also caught the involvement of this hope in the processes of time, experience, and spiritual growth when he said: "We rejoice in our sufferings, knowing that suffering produces endurance, and endurance produces character, and character produces hope, and hope does not disappoint us, because God's love has been poured into our hearts through the Holy Spirit which has been given to us" (Rom. 5:3–5).

The relevance of these remarks to pastoral counseling does not appear at first glance. We are accustomed to thinking in categories of mental health, emotional maturity, and the like. However, if the pastoral counselor takes the relation of mental health and religion seriously, he will be impressed by what

Margaret Mead, the anthropologist, says in her comment that "probably the simplest cross-cultural model that is relevant to mental health and to religion is the establishment of the ability to hope, or faith, if you wish to call it that." She further says that "the necessary ingredient of hope . . . makes it possible for them to participate in the religious system." (Proceedings, Arden House Conference, 1959, p. 165.) She also points out that societies differ radically in the way in which they enable persons to establish and maintain hope, some in such a way that hope increases with the unfolding of the years, and others with hope decreasing as persons get older.

The religious community is uniquely concerned with the creative nourishment of hope among men, women, and children. The person who seeks the help of other members of the community on any kind of problem does not consciously do so until he has reached a certain measure of despair. When he comes to a pastoral counselor seeking this help, the many meanings of the Kingdom of God to the pastor, to the church that he represents, and to the counselee himself both consciously and unconsciously provide the theological atmosphere in which the counseling takes place. These I choose to call the eschatological dimensions of pastoral counseling. The hopes and fears of the days of men's years have been written into the songs, the religious stories, the events, and the doctrines of Christian eschatology.

The varying motifs of eschatological concern have provided different focuses of concern for pastoral counselors both in history and the present day. An understanding of these focuses of concern enables the pastoral counselor to appreciate the bases of some of the resistances he meets within his own particular tradition as far as his practice of pastoral counseling is concerned. On the other hand, an appraisal of the "eschatological stance" of a given religious tradition enables a pastor to tap the resources of the tradition for his pastoral counseling in unexpected ways.

W. Schweitzer compiled a brief survey of recent discussion

on eschatology with especial reference to ethics. His organization of the material, with some rearrangement of order and emphasis for this new purpose, makes a good pattern for discussing the different kinds of eschatological interpretation in the light of their relevance for pastoral counseling. (W. Schweitzer, *Eschatology and Ethics*, tr. by R. H. Fuller; Geneva, Switzerland: Study Department of the World Council of Churches, 1951.)

Individualistic Eschatology

Many of the Protestant preachers of eschatological truth have restricted their interpretation to individual survival after death, whether they have used the Greek doctrine of immortality or the Hebrew understanding of the resurrection, notwithstanding. The cosmic aspects of eschatology, and especially its relevance to a philosophy of history, are "either left in the background or abandoned altogether." The focal concern is whether or not the individual will be saved from hell and his passage to heaven assured. The distinctly social dimensions of this eschatological concern, as are evident in the New Testament where it appears in such parables as that of Lazarus and Dives (Luke 16:19–31), are often left unattended or positively opposed by individualistic interpreters of eschatology.

The following clinical record focuses the ways in which this kind of individualism may affect the pastoral counseling relationship:

On one occasion I was shaken by the existential question of a counselee. I was preaching in a little church in the industrial area of Louisville. A member of the congregation came up to me after the service and asked if she might make an appointment with me when we might talk together about "a worry" she had. I was to preach at the same church that evening, and I made an appointment with her at seven o'clock, the service being at eight. She came on time. She felt anxious because, she said, she had committed an unpardonable sin. I asked her when she first began to worry about this, and she said about the time she had married and left home some two years before. I asked her what she had done in an attempt to solve this anxiety she was facing, and she told of several different ministers with whom she had talked. I was next!

She said, "Now, I want you to answer me one way or the other, How can I be saved?"

And I said to her, "How have the other men answered you?" and she gave almost by rote answers that they had given. They had explained the "plan of salvation" to her. They had told her the steps that they ordinarily tell emotionally balanced persons to go through in making a confession of faith.

I said, "Have these really met your need?"

She said, "No, I still feel that I can't get the assurance that I am saved."

"Apparently," I said, "this thing is a lot deeper than you seem to think it is. I would like very much to develop a sort of discussion back and forth with you, over a period of time, in which we would gradually work at this and you would gradually come to a solution of your anxiety and to a deepening of your sense of security under God. What would you say if I committed a certain amount of time to you for the next several weeks? Once a week we would sit down and talk together about this, and could you come over to my office at the seminary on next Wednesday afternoon?"

She said: "Oh, yes, I could do that but I'm afraid to. I want to ask you another question. What if I should die and go to hell before next Wednesday, what would you do then?" Now she had asked a basic question. I paused a long time before attempting to respond: "Obviously, you and I are talking about two different gods. The God whom you are asking to save you is a very different God from the God about whom I would talk with you. The God about whom I would talk with you is the God of the Lord Jesus Christ, and I am convinced that that God can take care of you between now and next Wednesday. I don't believe the God you are talking about can. I know the God I'm talking about can. It will take us a good while for you to find out just what kind of God this is. But in the meantime, I think he can sustain you and I will assure you with my whole heart that his ability to care for you doesn't depend upon your ability to feel that you are being cared for." I said, "Now, I'll be glad to see you next Wednesday afternoon if you would like to come by."

She agreed to come by, and with the help of two doctors and myself, found a new perspective of faith in God. In the process of our attempts to agree upon a formal counseling procedure, she had raised the basic issue of her ultimate destiny which, regardless of the particular symbols she was using at the time, was a fundamentally legitimate issue in her life for her to raise with me as a Christian minister. She provoked a lot of anxiety in me as a minister, because I had one picture of Christian hope and she had another. And I had never tried to correlate the simple business of making a second appointment with somebody with the fact that this technique in itself implies a certain concept of eschatology. She caused me to ask that question, and I have always been very grateful to that woman.

This woman caused me to re-examine the nature of salvation. Is it static, accomplished in a moment of time, with no relevance to the process of experience? Or, is salvation a process involving measures of time? Implied in her question, in the second place, is the issue of whether salvation is the achievement of freedom from tension in a sort of lotus-eater's island of existence, or

whether salvation is that sense of quiet courage that
comes to an individual as he participates in that Ulysses-
like encounter with the unknown, in a pilgrimage of fellowship with God.

Probably the most competent exponent of eschatology in
terms of personal, individual salvation was Jonathan Edwards.
Recent studies of the preaching and pastoral care of President
Edwards reflect several characteristics of his approach to persons. First, even though Edwards used what has been called a
"scare theology" of warning men of the terrors of hell and the
threats of total condemnation, he was careful to leave the
weight of initiative upon them in a way that modern exponents
of this eschatology have forgotten in their pastoral practice.
As James A. Stewart says in his introduction to Edwards' *The
Narrative: Being a Faithful Narrative of the Surprising Work
of God in the Conversion of Souls in Northampton and Neigh-
boring Towns and Villages in New England, in a Letter to the
Rev. Doctor Colman of Boston, on November 6, 1736:*

> No public invitations were given by the pastor and
> his fellow workers during this time of revival. Public
> invitations to "come forward and accept Christ as Sav-
> iour" were unknown in the Puritan world. The whole
> sermon was an invitation, with the glorious Gospel of the
> grace of God clearly set forth. They invited the anxious
> and the distressed to meet with them in the vestries at
> the conclusion of the service or during the following
> week. (Page 22; Kregel Publications, 1957.)

Edwards was fearful of plucking unripe fruit. He discerned
the need for personal initiative on the part of his evangelistic
converts. Whereas the invitation itself need not undercut this
initiative, nevertheless, it may, and often does. Thus, evangelism becomes "begging" people to operate apart from their
own convictions. When they move, they may do so to please
us or to get us to leave them alone. Likewise, visitation has

often been used in such ways as to undercut the personal initiative of the individual's powers of decision. Pastoral counseling on religious matters or any others tends to stand or fall upon the person's being motivated to seek help himself. The more initiative is removed from evangelism, the less it is an evangelism and the more it becomes a "scouring of the land and sea" for proselytes, a sort of selling job, a propaganda. Pastoral counseling of today is indeed concerned with the personal salvation of individuals, but has reintroduced the factor of personal initiative on the part of the "seeker."

A second factor in Edwards' preaching and pastoral work further relates individualistic eschatologies to pastoral counseling today. The fear of hell has become somewhat remote for many—although not all—people today. The convictions of preachers themselves are not as clear-cut or explicit as were Edwards' convictions. And, as one writer meaningfully put it, "You cannot be convincing unless you are convinced." However, this does not mean that the deepest meanings and symbolisms of the doctrine of hell are irrelevant today. Nor does it mean that people no longer fear contemporary equivalents of hell. For example, the contemporary drama has made elaborate use of the conception of hell as a vehicle of communication. Jean-Paul Sartre, for example, in his *No Exit*, epitomizes the alienation and estrangement of persons who have been consigned for eternity to inescapable proximity to each other, with no power to relate meaningfully to each other, to communicate satisfyingly with each other. Whereas sophistication in theology has dispelled the impending threat of hell from the pulpit, dramatists find the theme, as such, persuasive.

But more than this, the concept of mental illness itself has taken on some of the proportions of a modern hell. As one counselee put it, "I felt that I had been run through the back halls of hell, but little did I know that it had a basement!" The fear of losing one's mind, the fear of "going to pieces," the fear of one's "unconscious" internalize the cosmic dimensions and epitomize them in our conceptions of mental illness. To the sophisticate, the quest for mental health, maturity, and emotional impeccability amounts to an individualistic quest for heaven.

At one and the same time, we are urged by mental-hygiene preachers to "seek help," to come for help "before it is too late," and also, we are reassured that we are all human, have failings, and should accept our humanity with the courage of imperfection. The individual carries a sense of guilt, not because he failed to commit himself to God, but because he has been "an only child," or because he has never been able to cease "hating his brother," or because he and his father or mother have never been able to get along. Worse than this, he may feel like going to the mourner's bench because of condemnation by the local psychiatrist for not having had a vacation this year! The unpardonable sin would be to have to admit that he had had an ulcer or was suffering from hay fever! What I am trying to say in a somewhat sardonic manner is that the fear of hell and its attendant moralisms is not gone! It has simply quit wearing a Prince Albert coat and begun to wear a more modern garb.

A more serious implication of Jonathan Edwards' individualistic eschatology, however, lies in the careful clinical method he used in his pastoral work. His narratives of "surprising conversions" reflect what he himself called "the endless *variety* in the particular manner and circumstances in which persons are wrought on; and an opportunity of seeing so much will show that God is further from confining himself to a particular method than some imagine." He complained about "some good people amongst us who were before ready to make their own experience a rule to others" (*ibid.*, p. 71). He laid the groundwork for a psychology of religion that emphasizes the varieties of religious experience. A practical result of this has been to correlate individual differences with religious experience, a cardinal principle for pastoral counseling. Furthermore, Edwards, as John H. Gerstner has demonstrated, had a clear-eyed view of the dynamic processes of religious experience. He did not attempt to force a pattern of conformity upon an individual in one short interview. A static transactional preachment of salvation was too superficial for him. He even had a Calvinistic interpretation of regression and "backsliding" in the experience of salvation. (John H. Gerstner, *Steps to Salvation*, esp. pp. 40 ff. and pp. 114–115; The Westminster Press, 1960.)

The spiritual frames of reference in which Jonathan Edwards did his work and those in which the modern pastoral counselor does his are vastly different. Nevertheless, the same kind of individualism, often divorced from the corporate life of the ongoing fellowship of Christians, prevails in both. Likewise, the same sense of imperative urgency tends to impel the pastoral counselor, who likes to think of his work as dealing with "matters of life and death," and not as just matters of personal opinion and doctrine.

The ultimate dimensions of the eternal destiny of the counselee are often missed by the modern pastoral counselor. On the other hand, the salvationism of the individualistic evangelist tends to overlook the worthier and more immediate aspects of the personal life that keep the believer from perceiving the immediate reality of the hope of eternal life held out to him. But in both instances, the communal and cosmic aspects of personal hope and redemption are obscured. And, as Berdyaev has said: "My eternal destiny cannot be isolated; it is linked with the destiny of history, with the destiny of the world and of mankind. The fate of the world and of all humanity is my fate also, and vice versa, their fate cannot be decided without me." (Nicolas Berdyaev, *The Beginning and the End*, p. 235; Harper & Brothers, 1952.) We cannot, as he says, build up "eschatologies of vengeance," whether they are fraught with hostilities toward those we wish to go to hell or with supercilious pity for those we consider "sick" and "unwilling to go for help." When we communicate the sense of doom, we must, as was true of Jesus, be willing to die ourselves that those to whom we communicate it may be spared.

The counselees who come to us as pastors are living in a world that practices "brinkmanship" full time. The impending sense of doom haunts many who wonder not *whether* something awful is going to happen but *when* it is going to happen. Others, like children playing in a rye field, as Salinger's *The Catcher in the Rye* puts it, play with little awareness of what is about to happen. Holden Caulfield says to his sister:

> "You know that song 'If a body catch a body comin' through the rye' I'd like—"
>
> "It's 'If a body *meet* a body coming through the rye'!" old Phoebe said. "It's a poem. By Robert *Burns*."
>
> "I *know* it's a poem by Robert Burns."
>
> She was right, though. It *is* "If a body meet a body coming through the rye." I didn't know it then, though.
>
> "I thought it was 'If a body catch a body,'" I said. "Anyway, I keep picturing all these little kids playing some game in this big field of rye and all. Thousands of little kids, and nobody's around—nobody big, I mean—except me. And I'm standing on the edge of some crazy cliff. What I have to do, I have to catch everybody if they start to go over the cliff—I mean if they're running and they don't look where they're going I have to come out from somewhere and *catch* them. That's all I'd do all day. I'd just be the catcher in the rye and all. I know it's crazy, but that's the only thing I'd really like to be. I know it's crazy." (The New American Library of World Literature, Inc., 1961, p. 156.)

The contemporary pastoral counselor is a sort of "catcher in the rye" who by his personal experience and training *knows* where the precipices of life really are. He works with his counselees, literally catching them if they start to go over the cliff. More than this, he prophetically senses their danger before they do. Hence, his task is prophetic, even in the sense of forecast and prognosis, as much as it is in understanding and diagnosis.

Apocalyptic Eschatology

A large thrust of Protestant eschatology has been quite individualistic. But another prevalent eschatology has been apocalyptic in nature. Apocalypticism confines eschatology to a literal acceptance of the eschatological prophecies of the Old and New Testaments. The basic theological method of the apocalypticist is to separate and isolate eschatology from the rest of Christian teaching in the Bible and the witness of Christian history in the church. The apocalypticist ignores the results of the experience of other Christians after New Testament times, and as C. Penrose St. Amant says, "jumps over history with the intention of recreating the New Testament community as if history since then had not happened." (Personal communication.) However, J. E. Fison cautions, we should "pause before laughingly and patronizingly dismissing the cruder materialistic and millenarian views of the sects." (J. E. Fison, *The Christian Hope: The Presence and the Parousia*, p. 32; Longmans, Green & Co., Inc., 1954.) Underlying these beliefs, says Fison, is the commitment to the rendezvous of God's own choosing rather than our own.

When we take the apocalypticists seriously, we readily see that they usually focus their pastoral rule and the context of their pastoral counsel in the *disciplined community*. The eschatological hope shapes and fashions ready maxims and "standard operating procedures" that are in effect "holding operations," "freezing procedures" pending the consummation of the ages that will call a halt to the besetting difficulties of the times. For example, the apostle Paul could challenge the Thessalonians who gave up the responsibility of earning a living while they awaited the immediate Parousia: "For even when we were with you, we gave you this command: If any one will not work, let him not eat" (II Thess. 3:10). Likewise, Paul's teachings concerning marriage in I Cor., ch. 7, cannot be understood fully apart from his eschatological dualism, i.e., the separation of more immediate concerns of life from the ultimate ones in the approaching *eschaton*. From this point of view, constructive marriage counseling will be consistently modified by the pastor who sincerely holds to the imminent return of Christ. As one person said: "I was always afraid when I was having sexual relations with my husband, because my father, a pastor who believed in the soon return of our Lord, always taught us that we should not be doing anything that we did not want Jesus to find us doing when he returned!" Also, marriage has been relegated to an unimportant place by many apocalypticists and as an evil thing by others, a thing to be done away with.

Such teachings have been formalized by the apocalyptic communities into manuals of discipline. One finds evidence of this in the pastoral epistles of First and Second Timothy and Titus. These letters themselves were instruments of pastoral counsel and care. They were sent to edify the readers in sound doctrinal health. They aimed to clarify the position, duties, and qualifications of the Christian leader. They were efforts to "comb out" lines of relationship in such a way that the fellowship of Christians might live in order, dignity, and spiritual health. Sherman E. Johnson compares them with the Manual of Discipline of the Qumrân sect described in the Dead Sea scrolls. The life of communal sharing, severe penalty for dishonesty, i.e., "stains on one's repentance [for] not [being] honest in resolving the stubbornness of his heart," and the use of group discipline for both the accused and the accuser are remarkably paralleled in the scrolls. (Sherman E. Johnson, "The Dead Sea Manual of Discipline and the Jerusalem Church of Acts," *The Scrolls and the New Testament*, ed. by Krister Stendahl, pp. 129 ff.; Harper & Brothers, 1957. Also, *The Dead Sea Scriptures*, ed. by T. H. Gaster, p. 42; Doubleday Anchor Books, 1956.)

Contemporary Anabaptists, like most apocalyptic communities that have survived for more than one or two generations, have in some instances rigidly enforced a set of rules for living. These community rules tend to take the place of the original eschatological sense of immediate expectancy out of which the rules were first devised. These rules and patterns of discipline, such as social customs, types of dress, manners of speaking, pacifism, refusal to take oaths, refusal to own insurance, etc., have become the basis of pastoral guidance and counseling. In turn, the rebellion of the youth of each new generation has tended to provide the need for private counseling of the youth. Within the community this is done by patient pastors, who have sought to enable the youth to "internalize" the commands as personal choices. Many times it is done on the outside of the community by those in other religious groups to whom these alienated ones have gone.

The basic defect in the presuppositions of the apocalyptic eschatologists both from an ecclesiological and a pastoral point of view lies at the point of their failure to take into consideration the transmission of their faith from one generation to another. They did not take into account the processes of life as well as the end situations of life. They did not take seriously the process in conversion itself. Their sense of urgency was so great that little time remained to waste. They did not consider the changes that occur in an individual's own spiritual perceptions as he moves from youth to early adulthood, middle age, later maturity, and old age. They did not think much about the side effects of social change that take place when a person is faithful to the precepts of frugality, hard work, simplicity, and purity of life which they espoused. They became property owners and rulers of men through these virtues.

The processes of education, for another example, tend to make marginal men of the children of the apocalypticists. A major task of pastoral counseling is cut out for the minister who seeks to meet the personal religious needs of some of these children. They often feel that they have gone beyond the point of no return to the religion of their early sectarian home. Yet they wistfully feel like a "lost sheep of the house of Israel" and cannot find a security such as the disciplined community previously afforded them. At these very points of isolation, pastoral counseling of a longer-term, more intensive variety is indicated uniquely in ways that other professions of counseling have neither the tools nor the ground of communication for performing. Yet, such a counselor himself needs a kind of eschatology that will embrace the realities of personality development, social mobility, and cultural isolation. Other approaches to eschatology have come to grips with these realities.

ECCLESIOLOGICAL-SACRAMENTAL ESCHATOLOGY

The apocalypticists concentrate upon the time-boundness of life and fix themselves upon one point or end in time. But the ecclesiological-sacramental approaches to eschatology see the church as the overcoming of time by eternity. Eternity broke through into time in the incarnation of God in Christ. In the sacraments, the break-through of eternity into time occurs again, again, and again. As Florovsky of the Eastern Orthodox Church says, "The present time acquires an eschatological significance without weakening the expectation of the age to come." (Quoted by W. Schweitzer, *op. cit.*, p. 13.)

The sacramental system of the liturgical churches carefully enfolds the "developmental eras" of individual personality from birth to death. The Christian year and calendar embrace the rhythms of time. The sacraments recapture, particularly the Eucharist, the Christian memory of the past acts of God that transcend time. The developmental tasks of parenthood, puberty, vocation, marriage, illness, and death are presented with the claim, demands, and resources of the Christian community. Yet at the same time *The Book of Common Prayer* repeatedly emphasizes the coming of Christ in its apocalyptic connotations:

O God, whose blessed Son was manifested that he might destroy the works of the devil, and make us the sons of God, and heirs of eternal life; Grant us, we beseech thee, that, having this hope, we may purify our-

selves, even as he is pure; that, when he shall appear
again with power and great glory, we may be made like
unto him in his eternal and glorious Kingdom; where
with thee, O Father, and thee, O Holy Ghost, he liveth
and reigneth ever, one God, world without end. Amen.
(P. 117; Oxford University Press.)

The practice of confession in the ecclesiological-sacramental
eschatologies creates an "end-situation" that relieves guilt and
remorse through absolution. The confessional becomes the
priest's means of maintaining contact with his parishioner, just
as the revival meeting and personal visitation afford this opportunity in the tradition of the eschatology of individualism.
Counseling becomes a by-product of the confessional, or even
a form of confession in itself.

The ministry of confession has always been taken seriously
by those who embrace the sacramental interpretation of life.
We too often overlook the relational dimension of this ministry, and thereby deny ourselves the learning that such ministers afford us as they rely upon the breaking through of the
Shekinah of the Lord in the experience of confession. Furthermore, we often attribute "playing god" motives to these priests
when we have not carefully studied what they actually say and
do. This realization came forcefully upon me as a Baptist when
I recently heard Canon Theodore Wedel of the Cathedral of
Washington call attention to "the order of confession" that is
used in the Greek Orthodox churches. A full account of the
private litany used by the priest comments for itself upon the
present discussion.

The Priest: Blessed be our God, both now and ever, and
unto the ages of ages. Amen.
The Penitent: I have sinned, O Lord, have mercy. O
God, be merciful to me a sinner.
The Priest: Let us pray to the Lord.
O God our Saviour, who through thy prophet Nathan
didst grant to penitent David forgiveness of his sins, and

didst receive Manasseh's prayers of repentance, do thou thyself in thy wonted loving-kindness receive thy servant N., who repenteth of the sins *he* hath committed, overlooking all that *he* hath done, O thou who forgivest offenses and passest over transgressions. For thou, O Lord, hast said, I desire not the death of a sinner, but rather that he should turn from his wickedness and live, and, that sins should be forgiven even unto seventy times seven. How beyond compare is thy greatness, and thy mercy is without measure, for if thou shouldest regard iniquity, who should stand? For thou art the God of the penitent, and to thee we ascribe glory, to the Father, the Son, and the Holy Ghost, both now and ever, and unto the ages of ages. Amen.

The Penitent: Father, Lord of heaven and earth, I confess to thee all the hidden and open sins of my heart and mind, which I have committed unto this day. Wherefore I beg of thee, the merciful and righteous Judge, forgiveness and grace to sin no more.

The Priest says kindly to the Penitent: Brother, inasmuch as thou hast come to me and to God, be not ashamed; for thou speakest not unto me, but unto God, before whom thou standest.

The Priest then questions him in detail about his sins, after which he says: My spiritual child, who hast confessed to my humble person: I, a sinner, have not power on earth to forgive sins; God alone hath that; but through that divinely spoken word which came to the Apostles, after the resurrection of our Lord Jesus Christ, saying, Whosoever sins ye remit, they are remitted, and whosoever sins ye retain, they are retained, we are emboldened to say: Whatsoever thou hast said to my humble person, and whatsoever thou hast failed to say, whether through ignorance or forgetfulness, whatever it may be, may God forgive thee in this world, and in that which is to come.

May God who, through Nathan the Prophet, pardoned David when he confessed his sins, the God who pardoned Peter weeping bitterly for his denial, and who pardoned the sinful woman weeping at his feet, and the publican and the prodigal son—may that same God, through me a sinner, forgive thee all things both in this world and the world to come, and set thee uncondemned before his terrible Judgment Seat. Have no further care for the sins which thou hast confessed, depart in peace.

(The grace of the All-holy Spirit, through me, the unworthy Priest, hath loosed and absolved thee from all thy sins, AMEN: AMEN: AMEN.)

May Christ our true God have mercy upon us and give us peace, forasmuch as he is good and loveth mankind.

(This material was taken from an article by Nicolas Zernor, "The Sacrament of Confession in the Eastern Orthodox Church," in *Theology*, March, 1940, pp. 203–209.)

Pastoral Counseling in the Context of the Kingdom of God

Both the individualism and the utopianism, both the overemphasis upon apocalypticism and the easy acceptance of the sacraments have been challenged by more serious attempts to reappraise eschatology in terms of the Biblical meanings of the Kingdom of God. Let us focus the remainder of this discussion of the eschatological dimension of pastoral counseling upon implications of the Kingdom of God for a psychology of personality and the practice of pastoral counseling. This will accentuate clearly the eschatological dimensions of our task as pastoral counselors.

The discussion of the doctrine of the Kingdom of God in relation to the processes of pastoral counseling to the psychology of personality, and the larger context of pastoral theology is highly necessary. Otherwise, these fields may move on shallow and haphazard theological assumptions. Thus they may become simply another "tools" course in the theological curriculum. The doctrine of the Kingdom of God is a Biblical teaching. As such it provides the rightful theological context for a pastoral counselor. By squaring and plumbing pastoral practice, furthermore, with an adequate Biblical theology, we can avoid creating a "gnosis" kind of theology that will use the same words current in classical theology without regard to the historical rootage of meaning in Biblical revelation. These two justifications necessitate the examination of some of the implications of the doctrine of the Kingdom of God for pastoral counseling.

The psychological realities involved in the doctrine of the Kingdom of God are both wide and deep. They are some of the same realities with which the pastoral counselor continually wrestles. However, he does so in a much different spiritual climate. Particularly is this true when the pastor counsels with people who are desperately searching for a meaningful existence in the presence of what Tillich has called the "threat of destruction" or "nonbeing."

Some clarification of terms is necessary here. The terms "the kingdom of God" and "the kingdom of heaven" are used interchangeably in the Biblical account. At least four basic meanings are implicit in the concept. First, the Kingdom of God means the eternal, ultimate sovereignty of God, the divine *rule* or reign of God. Second, the Kingdom of God means the rule of God among men in an established covenant relationship. This may rightly be called the *realm* of God among men in so far as his sovereignty is acknowledged and his will is done. Third, the Kingdom of God means the complete, final, and perfect triumph of God's rule in the age to come. Fourth, all these first three concepts are coalesced into one meaning of the Kingdom of God as rule and realm, present and future, as time-bound and yet existing in the eternal now. All these imply a depth dimension of the meanings that perdure in man's racial conscious and unconscious experience of himself as man before God. The minister as a counselor, by his very presence, activates an encounter of his counselee with these realities whether he ever says so or not.

THE KINGDOM OF GOD AND THE PSYCHOLOGY OF LOYALTY

Jesus' interpretation of the Kingdom of God was rooted in the Old Testament doctrine of the sovereignty of God. The claims of the first commandment that men shall have no other gods before the Holy One of Israel, to use Isaiah's appellation, were the explicit claims of the Kingdom of God as Jesus preached it. The Kingdom of Heaven is the one treasure which, when one has found it, is worth selling joyfully all one has in order to buy the field in which it is hidden. It is the pearl of great value, which is worth all that one has (Matt. 13:44–45). The Kingdom of God is first in the search of man, and everything else is subordinate to it (Matt. 6:33).

Some would interpret the concept of the sovereignty of God in his divine rule of the Kingdom of God as shallow authoritarianism. But this mistake cannot easily be made by one who is profoundly acquainted with the Biblical message concerning God's rulership. The Biblical concept of his rule rests in the vision of the *power* of God, which ordains, maintains, and orders the multiuniverse of his creation, and yet sustains the life of man in God's providential care and divine wisdom. The power of God is always evident in his *deliverance* of his people from bondage, his release of people from blindness, lameness, leprosy, deafness, death, and poverty. The Old Testament catches the spirit of this sovereignty in the repeated song of praise of God who by his mighty outstretched arm delivered the Israelites from slavery. The New Testament benediction to the Lord's Prayer says it: "For thine is the kingdom and the power and the glory, forever. Amen."

The primacy of the Kingdom of God severs all lesser loyalties that would take first place in the disciple's life. The idolatry of material security requires a man's soul of him. No profit derives from gaining the whole world and losing one's life. The binding power of family loyalties must be broken in behalf of taking up one's cross and following daily after the Master. The worship of any one driving desire to the exclusion of the wholehearted commitment to the Kingdom, be it material security, sex, or hostility, is an adulterous infidelity against the prior claims of the Kingdom. The hope of the Jews for the political overthrow of Rome at the advent of the Messiah blinded even the disciples to the secret of the Kingdom that was at hand in the imminent death, burial, and resurrection of Jesus.

These idolatries have been discussed in different semantic and philosophical categories by contemporary psychologists and philosophers of loyalty. Whitehead would call this the "absolutizing of the finite." Josiah Royce dealt with the need for an enduring and sustaining loyalty in his *Philosophy of Loyalty.* William James spoke of the *habitual center of one's personal energies.* C. G. Jung presents the idea of the complex as a separate organization of the personality, growing *as if* it were independent of the whole life, with an organization of its own and a central locus of loyalty. The *gestalt* interpretation would call this an *unassimilated mass* or an unintegrated part of the life, which was unacceptable to the rest. Gordon Allport, in his new book, *Becoming,* calls the finite loyalties to which man gives his heart the "proximate strivings" of his life. The common denominator of these teachings is that the center of life's loyalties must be great enough to encompass the whole of the life. If not, the lesser loyalty throws the whole life off center, out of kilter. It becomes eccentric, in the strictest meaning of the word. The apex of a person's loyalties sets the slant of all the rest of the relationships of his life. Just as water cannot rise above its own level, apart from some outside force, neither can the quality of a person's life rise above the supreme devotion to which he gives his loyalty. This supreme loyalty is, for all intents and purposes, his god. The Kingdom of God, which is always at hand, subordinates the worship of separate psychic desires, such as economic security, sexual gratification, unbridled aggression, and hostility to the primary demands of the Kingdom of God. These idols distract and distort lives. Pastoral counseling is primarily concerned with bringing people out of bondage to the idols that possess them.

THE KINGDOM OF GOD AND THE DEMONIC

The realm of the demonic is opposed to the Kingdom of God. The power of the Kingdom of God is a separating power, separating the children of men into a Kingdom of God and making the kingdom of evil known for what it is by challenging its power. When the loyalty of men to their idols deepens, to a certain extent it blinds them. The psychologist would say that they are so fixated to father, mother, brother, sister, wife, husband, son, or daughter that they no longer have any insight! Furthermore, the same kind of idolatry can be focused upon a certain church, a state, a philosophy, or a deceased leader. Nevertheless, the idol exerts possessing power upon the person. This is what the psychologists would call compulsiveness in interpersonal relationships. As Paul Tillich says:

> The demonic blinds; it does not reveal. In the state of demonic possession the mind is not really "beside itself," but rather, it is in the power of elements of itself which aspire to be the whole mind which grasp the center of the rational self and destroy it. (*Systematic Theology*, Vol. I, p. 114; University of Chicago Press, 1951.)

The power of the Kingdom of God with its ultimate claims upon the ultimate concerns of men is clearly seen in Jesus' response to the charges that he was in league with the demonic. By the finger of God he cast out demons, and he could say: "The kingdom of God has come upon you." The power of the Kingdom of God separates the children of darkness from the children of light, weans them from their idols, and frees them from the possessing power of the demonic. For the demonic is the finite's claim for ultimacy. The means of grace is elevated to the dignity of grace itself. Even the life of the church may be the compulsive element in religious living that is broken only in a confrontation of the claims of the Kingdom of God upon finite man. The pastoral counselor, through the medium of his own awareness of what is really important, is usually at work in bringing hope to those who have accepted their bondage as a fate. In fact, they may have so completely resigned themselves to such a fate that they think of themselves as happy and ask only to be left alone.

THE PSYCHOLOGICAL REALITIES IN ESCHATOLOGY

Another aspect of the doctrine of the Kingdom of God that has far-reaching implications for the pastoral counselor is the eschatological character of the Kingdom of God. Several aspects of eschatology have already been discussed. They are generally, but not specifically, applicable to pastoral counseling. *But the problem of time and the set end to the existence of man and the universe is specifically relevant to pastoral counseling.* Rudolf Bultmann considers the eschatological and apocalyptic teachings of the New Testament concerning the consummation of the Kingdom of God as mythological ways of describing the fact of man's finitude in a "three-story" universe. He seeks to demythologize the teachings by cutting them loose from their time-bound framework in order to get the heart of the message for our day, unencumbered by the mythology. But Cullmann in his concept of "redemptive history" feels that time is real, that it is an integral part of God's revelatory and redemptive intentions toward man, and that the attempt to remove the time-conditioning character of the Biblical revelation is foreign to the Bible itself. God moves history through meaningful periods of time. These crises are days of salvation. In them the Kingdom is at hand. The time is fulfilled. The anxiety of decision comes upon man in the shortness of time. (Oscar Cullmann, *Christ and Time;* The Westminster Press, 1950.)

Anton Boisen in his book *The Exploration of the Inner World* identified the desperation of this "shortness" of time in the illnesses of psychotic persons. Patients confronting a disastrous sense of failure in life interpret life as *having* come to an end. For instance, a patient with whom I conferred wrote the following words:

> I existed before God existed and knew Adam and Eve when they were in the Garden. . . . As long as I can resist the atoms that come swirling like a black cloud from the planets the world will not come to an end. This is the twentieth century, and time is running short.

This man was seen in 1945 just before the advent of the atomic bomb. He is one of many mental patients whose despair is a matter of life and death. Life has come to an end for them. They cannot tolerate the despair of being finite, having to move from one era in life to another and finally to accept the fact of death. Their illness is the result.

Each stage in man's pilgrimage presents him with a set end to that era in his life. If he genuinely accepts the finality of that end, he moves into a deeper grasp of the meaning of life. If he shrinks back—to use the Hebrews' word for the antithesis of faith—he becomes anxiety-ridden and symptomladen. If he assumes that he is an exception to the ends set for every man's existence, of which death is the supreme example, then as Kierkegaard has said, he has willed to become infinite. And "infinitude's despair is fantastical and limitless." Such a person becomes lost in possibility for having renounced the necessity of the end of his own personal life.

The descriptive symbols that acutely psychotic patients present are often eschatological in nature. They include ideas of the end of the world, the impending disaster of a cosmic conflict, and the breathlessness over the shortness of time. C. G. Jung's concept of the racial unconscious would provide a working hypothesis for saying that these symbols arise from the archetypal depths of personality. They apply to every age and not just to the one in which the New Testament was written. In every impending world crisis, such as the possibility of world destruction by the hydrogen bomb, even the most sophisticated theologians begin to take almost literally the eschatological passages referring to the consummation of the Kingdom of God.

The question may be asked: Does the collapse of the validity of a meaningful eschatology have any connection with mental illness? For example, the various discussions of the mental health of the prophets, such as Ezekiel, and of Jesus all leave out any reference to the obvious fact that the prophets and Jesus lived in a milieu when eschatological interpretations of personal and cosmic history were intensely valid. C. G. Jung is right when he says that "Christ's biography and psychology cannot be separated from eschatology." To do so is to distort the true understanding of him and to agree with those prosaic souls who thought Jesus to be beside himself. In truth, the removal of the hope from a person's life more often than not renders him mentally sick. But Jesus was filled with hope even on the eve of his own crucifixion. (C. G. Jung, *Answer to Job;* Pastoral Psychology Press, 1952 and 1955, p. 72.)

If, then, the presence of an abiding meaning in personal and cosmic history is related to the "ongoingness" of a person's emotional health, then such an eschatology must be pertinent for pastoral counseling especially. An interesting therapeutic commentary on the importance of the end-situation for counseling of any kind is found in the work of Otto Rank, a psychoanalyst who broke away from the original Freudian school. He took issue with Freud's timeless approach to psychotherapy, in which the interviews went on *ad infinitum* as if the person were completely infinite and free of time limits. Rank devised what he called the end-setting in therapeutic procedure. He and the patient set a time as to when the final hour of the therapy would come. He sought to mobilize time and circumstance at the point of the patient's anxiety over the end of the relationship. Rank said that the patient would approach the "last hour" as if his end had really come! The pastor's living situation with people in the natural habitat of the community provides many end-situations that facilitate his pastoral counseling when properly used. The epochs of the Christian year, especially Easter, can be jointly agreed upon as the "final hour" for a given counseling process. Students have the end of the school year with which to cope. Older people have retirement as an end-situation. Exploration of the eternal meaning implicit in these "ends" may bring the counselee to the gates of a new life beyond which there is no turning back. Or, in other instances, they may go away sorrowing because they prefer to *act as if* time and the days of decision are unreal. The more they do this, the nearer to illness they are and the more likely medical ministries are needed to deal with specific syndromes of disease. The patient's refusal or inability to participate in any drama of history with a consummatory passion is in itself a sign of illness.

All this suggests that in pastoral counseling the problems of time and timing are basic. For each counselee the same approach may succeed once and fail at another time for the definite reason of readiness or propitiousness of the moment. Kelman quotes Hippocrates to the effect: "Life is short but art reaches far: the *favorable moment* is transient, experiment is deceptive and decision difficult." (Harold Kelman, " 'Kairos' and the Therapeutic Process," *The Journal of Existential Psychiatry*, Vol. 1, No. 2, Summer, 1960, p. 234.) Kelman says that the therapist can capture the reality of the "crucial time in the history of an illness when it might turn for better or for worse," which he designates as "the kairos." He recognizes modern New and Old Testament scholarship for giving "the notion of kairos new meaning" and says that it is essential and important for psychotherapy. Especially helpful is it in shortening psychoanalytic treatment through a wiser use of major and minor *kairoi* in the history of the patient.

The orthodox analyst, in accepting a patient for treatment, has a way of delaying the great decisions of life—marriage, parenthood, divorce, vocational change, religious commitment, etc.—until "analysis is finished." Yet one is forced to ask if the side effects created by this do not offset the value of the treatment. Pastoral counseling, when it has clearly defined its own identity, underscores the power of these *kairoi* to thrust the person through the entry into a new life by faith in God. The pastoral counselor challenges the efficacy of a psycho-analysis which requires that the real end-situations of life be ignored. At the same time, he appreciates the importance of the *kairoi* in life to such an extent that he is willing to wait on God's own time even longer than the psychoanalyst would take. This in itself necessitates some consideration of the time element in pastoral counseling.

THE KINGDOM OF GOD AND THE SEARCH FOR MEANING

The impending end of a given epoch activates the "impera-tive" in human personality. Man must have meaning to his life if he is to live it and live it well. Of course, many persons live shallow lives with a bare minimum of meaning. But the crises of existence through which even these persons must go as they reach adulthood and move toward old age will weigh them in the balances and thrust their meaningless existences in their faces. Then they will wonder what happened, what the meaning of all this really is. If there is no better meaning taught them, neurotic, psychotic, psychosomatic or antisocial symptoms will fill in the empty, meaningless, aching void.

The Kingdom of God is at hand in man's personal dilemma as he stands between the threat of meaninglessness and the imperative need for meaning. The Kingdom of God is present reality for man's search for meaning and as such is the gift of the good pleasure of the Father to his children. The King-dom is the end goal and as such is the primary passion of man's search for a continuing meaning in life.

V

The Time Element
in Pastoral Counseling

THE WRITER of Ecclesiastes tells us that "to everything
there is a season, and a time to every purpose under the
heaven: a time to be born, and a time to die; a time to plant,
and a time to pluck up that which is planted; a time to kill,
and a time to heal; a time to break down, and a time to build
up; a time to weep, and a time to laugh; a time to mourn, and
a time to dance; a time to cast away stones, and a time to
gather stones together; a time to embrace, and a time to re-
frain from embracing; a time to get, and a time to lose; a time
to keep, and a time to cast away; a time to rend, and a time to
sew; a time to keep silence, and a time to speak; a time to
love, and a time to hate; a time of war, and a time of peace.
. . . I have seen the travail, which God hath given to the sons
of men to be exercised in it. He hath made everything beautiful in his time: also he hath set the world in their heart, so
that no man can find out the work that God maketh from the
beginning to the end." (Eccl. 3:1-8, 10-11.)

In both the art and science of music, time and timing is
vital. This is equally true in the art and science of pastoral
counseling. In a counseling relationship, the pastor is always
engaged in perceiving the work of the Eternal in his appropriate relationship to time. The pastor's awareness of the
appropriateness of a given moment for decision, delay, or
demand is a good gauge of his effectiveness as a pastor, and
particularly as a pastoral counselor. The time factor in pastoral

101

counseling provides a symbolic screen upon which to project an understanding of counseling and the effectiveness of the pastor as a counselor.

For instance, some pastors' ministry consists of innumerable, superficial, brief, and passing relationships to a large number of people. On the other hand, other pastors are so completely unaware of time that they will spend great quantities of time with a very few individuals and allow the total "oversight of the flock of God" to go lacking. Furthermore, when a pastor is confronted with his responsibility as a counselor, the time factor is the issue upon which he tends to hang his whole case as to his responsibility for more intensive counseling with individuals. For instance, he is likely to take the attitude that "the pastor has too many other things to do" to spend more than one conversation with a troubled individual. On the other hand, in his hyperidealism, he is likely to say that "all of the administrative demands of the pastoral tasks" get in the way of what he is really called to do, namely, counsel with individuals. Thus he needs to evaluate the time factor in his total pastoral task and then to see his counseling ministry in that perspective.

The Time Factor in the Total Pastoral Task

Samuel W. Blizzard describes how the minister faces basic ambiguities in performing the many roles, traditional, neo-traditional, and contemporary, which are expected of him by his people. The most troublesome roles to the minister are those in which he functions as a pastoral visitor and counselor as over against those in which he functions as an organizer and an administrator. Yet organization and administration require more than three-fifths of the total workday of the pastor. (Samuel W. Blizzard, "The Minister's Dilemma," *The Christian Century*, April 25, 1956.) Blizzard notes that his "material . . . regarding the expectations of parishioners is inferred from the data that we have regarding how ministers spend their time . . . [and] it is best to stress the fact that the data that we are collecting is self-image data from the minister." (Personal correspondence.) In other words, this is the minister's picture of himself, not an actual study of what the parishioners themselves expect of him. For instance, one of the reasons why parishioners say they do not bring their personal counseling problems to their pastor is that he is "too busy." However, this is what *they* say to him. In talking to chaplains, medical doctors, social workers, etc., parishioners are more likely to say that they did not feel their minister would understand or be concerned about what happens to them. Here the time factor in the total pastoral task may be used as a screen for a breakdown of communication, a lack of motivation for counseling help, or resentment at the thought that it may be needed.

Recent discussions of the minister's own mental health likewise have turned around the time factor in his pastoral relationships within his total tasks. Some persons suggest that more and more ministers are breaking down mentally because of overwork. The whole problem of the minister's own mental health is thereby reduced to the time factor in his total pastoral task. This is a severe oversimplification of his problem which obscures the more dynamic facts that we know about mental illness. More extensive study probes more deeply than this simple interpretation of the pastoral task. One rather needs to raise the question as to ministers' ability to organize their work and to use their time efficiently. They often prefer to do more tangible tasks, to "get results," and to see things happen. They, like many other professionally trained persons who have moved from the lower classes of manual labor to the middle-class professions, feel guilty if they are not "busy about many things."

Therefore, when we begin to consider the specific task of pastoral counseling as it is performed by the parish minister, we need to probe deeply the minister's conception of himself and his controlling purpose and function in life. These factors determine the way he plans and spends his time. He orders his interpersonal relationships to people accordingly. Time is the only thing that a minister has to give away. One measure of his effectiveness as a minister is his stewardship of time in his total task. One justification for teaching pastoral care and pastoral counseling in the seminaries is to enable the pastor to plan his counseling ministry in such a way as to be more effective in helping individuals and thereby to release more time for his other functions of preaching, sermon preparation, and the general administrative oversight of the flock. This necessitates his facing up to the time factor in pastoral counseling as it is related to his total task.

THE TIME FACTOR IN THE SPECIFIC FUNCTION OF PASTORAL COUNSELING

By its very nature, pastoral counseling is defined in terms of a multiple conference relationship. It extends over a period of several weeks. Its objective is spiritual growth and the achievement of insight through a series of carefully regulated conversations between a pastor and a parishioner. In other words, pastoral counseling is a more intensive, more durable, a more highly defined, and more formal relationship between a pastor and a given individual. This "process" relationship presupposes that the deepest changes in personality occur when the revelation of God springs up within the counselee's own internal frame of reference rather than when it is projected into his consciousness by another person. The process of pastoral counseling also presupposes a "depth" view of personality. Both the deepest problems and the surest solutions of those problems spring from "the hidden parts" of man in which he is made to know wisdom, not by the pastor, but by the indwelling activity of the Holy Spirit. The atmosphere in which this takes place does not happen quickly. It comes to pass over a period of trying and testing of relationship between pastor and parishioner. This takes time. For instance, a person who is basically suspicious and has learned bitterly *not* to trust anyone does not just automatically in a moment's time start trusting people when he is told to do so. The feeling of trust does occur spontaneously in human relationships. But ordinarily it takes time to come to pass. The longer, more linear, and durable process of pastoral counseling often brings this into being. When it does so, it is no less a miracle than if it happened in a moment.

The same could be said about the experience of conversion. The first birth of man takes a normal span of time of nine months. One might grin sardonically to himself and ask what it would be like if the medical profession, in order to improve their statistics and increase the number of paying patients, decided to step up and shorten the processes of birth! This makes about as much sense as the stepping up and shortening of the process of conversion by pastors in order to increase the size of their churches and their budgets. Pastoral counseling very specifically offers a more profound kind of evangelism, one that relies more heavily upon the realities of spiritual conception and maturation within the life of man through the creative activity of the Holy Spirit.

In the light of the above definition and illustration of pastoral counseling as a process relationship, pastors then can be divided into two groups. The first group of pastors perceive counseling as giving advice. These pastors usually make time for only one very brief contact with a person about a given problem. They pride themselves on using "common sense" in their counseling. By this they really mean that all human problems are rational and can be "answered" rationally, quickly, and authoritatively. The fact of the matter is that *some* human problems are rational and can be answered quickly with "common sense." But a pastor needs a settled awareness of the deeper, irrational, contradictory, and conflicting nature of man to know when he is dealing with this kind of problem and when he is not. This first kind of pastor does not fall into the prophetic and apostolic tradition of pastoral care. Rather, he is likely to devise a set of formulas and rules of thumb whereby he "answers" problems that are presented to him. He, in the interests of time, deals quickly with problems. Much research could be done on the time element as it is related to authoritarianism. When an advice-giving pastor confronts the tempestuous and chaotic surges of deep distress of a modern Job, he is likely to answer him in much the same way as Job's counselors answered him. He depends on the magic of words. Zophar the Naamathite, Eliphaz the Temanite, and Bildad the Shuhite, are still with us. They still depend upon the magic of words, posited upon the assumption that "saying it solves it." They expect this magic to relieve them of the responsibility of taking the time to hear a person out, to participate with him in his search for a deeper revelation of the helping power of God. But Jobs of our day reply in the words of the Job of the Old Testament!

> Ye are all physicians of no value. Oh that ye would altogether hold your peace! And it should be your wisdom. Here now my reasoning, and hearken to the pleadings of my lips. . . . Hold your peace, let me alone, that I may speak, and let come on me what will. . . . Though he slay me, yet will I trust in him: But I will maintain mine own ways before him. (Job 13:4–6, 13, 15.)

The ministry of reconciliation is a matter of life and death as man struggles in his mortal encounter with the eternal God. Job knew that the dread which gripped his counselors could make him afraid. The deepest encounters of the processes of pastoral counseling are threatening to the minister. His own sense of fear frightens his counselee. The neat rationalisms of the "easy answer" approach to pastoral counseling do occasionally solve the time problem for a busy pastor. But they often actually involve him in many situations in which he will waste more time than he has saved with his "pat" solutions. For instance, he is likely to become involved in long and heated discussions with people who reject his answers. Likewise, in an attempt to "settle" the person's problems "right then and there," he often will use two, three, and even four and five hours at a sitting—or standing—with one person, thereby wasting valuable time. If he had scheduled another appointment, after having asked for time in which to think about the problem, he could have done more good in less time. Five thirty-minute conversations with a person may serve him better than to talk with him three hours at one sitting. A pastor may do him triply as much good and save at least a half hour!

The second group of pastors are those who develop a disciplined use of time in multiple-interview encounters. Such a pastor encourages the person, through the processes of spiritual maturity and insight, to lay hold of and to deal with his own problem. But he is not left alone. The pastor gives him spiritual fellowship and assistance in the pilgrimage of growth. He is not alone. For a time, counseling pastors assumed that if they simply listened to a person that this in itself was what was needed and all that was needed. But more recently, pastors are discovering that their willingness to listen to people's troubles in and of itself is a symbolic way of saying things to the person that words cannot. A nonverbal kind of communication is going on. The symbolic act of scheduling a second interview, for instance, may say to the person many different things: "I am not too busy to take your problem seriously." Or it may say, "I think your problem is serious." Or it may say, "I know you came for my 'answer,' but I am treading water until I can think of one." These are just a few of the things that scheduling a second interview can mean to the person.

On the other hand, the pastor may hit resistance in the scheduling of a second interview. The person may be an extremely demanding and passively dependent individual who insists that if he is the kind of pastor he ought to be, he could just settle the whole matter right there. A passive-aggressive person may forget to show up for the second appointment. An openly hostile person may simply "tell the pastor off" for suggesting that he needs help. In other words, a more intensive pastoral counseling is not just a matter of listening to people, although this is a very great and important part of it. The non-verbal communication going on within the context of the total relationship is in itself a healing light or a threatening irritation or both. The pastor has to listen to this with what Theodor Reik has called "the third ear."

The pastor must clearly define a mutually acceptable and mutually understood counseling relationship for what it really is. What is it? It is a process relationship of several interviews in which the pastor and parishioner explore together the deeper ramifications and the larger and longer purposes of the parishioner's life itself. This becomes an existential encounter once it is established. A process of precounseling, however, must precede it in the uncontrolled and undefined and often confused relationships of the pastoral situation. Too much so-called nondirectiveness on the part of the pastor in this construction of a defined counseling relationship can actually break the contact because the parishioner finds it meaningless.

This task of precounseling usually happens in the first interview. The pastor is still faced with the responsibility of knowing how to make the best use of *one hour* in pastoral interviewing. Unlike many social workers, psychologists and psychiatrists, the pastor has to do his own "intake interviewing." The first interview tends to be exploratory. Usually a third or more of the time in a first interview is required to "hear the person out" as much as that amount of time will permit. Several questions need to be asked on a first interview: (1) How long has the trouble been upon the individual; when did it start? (2) What attempts have been made to solve the difficulty, and especially to whom else has the counselee been for help? (3) How did the person decide to seek out the pastor? (4) What are the various alternatives of which the person has thought as possible solutions? If, in the process of the first interview, one sees that a longer term relationship is indicated, he may suggest this as one additional alternative and frankly explain what the process of counseling has to offer as well as what its limitations are. If the person sees and accepts the validity and wisdom of this procedure, then a second interview is more easily scheduled.

In both instances, that in which one interview is used and

that in which a multiple-process relationship is initiated for pastoral counseling, the use of time symbolizes the pastor's concern and his understanding of the person. To a great extent also the establishment of such a relationship is a form of evaluation and judgment of seriousness. The relationship tends to be made or broken in the first interview. The pastor's firmness and gentleness in interpreting his limitations and his strengths to help the person make the difference. A careful management of the time relationship, then, is the pastor's mode of communicating his concern and understanding of the counselee.

Certain technical problems are involved in the use of time in pastoral counseling. For instance, one of the first questions asked is about *the length of an interview.* An interview kept within the scope of an hour tends to be most effective. The pastor may shorten it for the person who is unaccustomed to formal office situations, such as young children, relatively uneducated persons, and persons in much physical pain. He may lengthen the interview a bit for the person who has traveled a long distance or has some other great handicap in coming for a conference. *The number of interviews* varies in terms of the basic need of the person. However, as we shall see a bit later, the social and structural limitations of the pastoral relationship prevent him from spending elaborate numbers of interviews with any one person. It may be that we shall sooner or later define pastoral counseling in terms of the five-to-ten interview situation in which we deal with more or less specific problem areas of the individual's life, such as bereavement, vocational choice, marital choice, and the making of a basic religious decision as to one's relationship to Christ. However, more and more pastors are being thrust into deeper, longer-term, and more formal types of relationships. But the more time one uses in any given relationship the more important it becomes that he shall have had intensive and extensive clinical pastoral training under careful and mature supervision. When pastors accept such responsibility, they obligate themselves for training commensurate with the responsibility they accept.

Even a full year of clinical pastoral counseling education in and of itself is not sufficient. But when a pastor has intensive psychotherapeutic training, he soon goes beyond the point of no return in the kinds of ecclesiastical support he can secure. As yet, the church has not developed a clearly defined role, much less financial support for the pastor as a private psychotherapist.

The Time Factor and the Changing Meanings of the Pastoral Situation

The technical problems involved in the pastoral use of time in counseling raise some deeper issues as to *the quality and meaning* of the relationship of pastoral counseling. This changes at different phases of pastoral counseling in terms of the time encounter. A pastor's relationship, in one respect at least, derives some of its meaning, direction, and purpose from the amount of time that he is able to use with a given individual. A rough guide is somewhat as follows:

One interview. A pastor has to be more time conscious and more directive. In a one-interview situation he depends more upon the short cuts that his experience has taught him. He gives information; he gives support; he points out other resource people upon whom the counselee may call; he may guardedly answer questions quite directly; he may even give opinions. He should give these in an atmosphere of tentativeness. He should carefully leave the relationship "open" in the event that the person wants to come back to him. Too often pastors have confused openness and honesty with people (who are in as full a possession of their powers for living as he is) with "directiveness" in counseling. The actual fact of the matter is that the pastor does not have a counseling relationship in a one-interview situation if the way we have technically defined it here is correct.

Two to six interviews. Here the pastor is usually involved in short-term crisis or situational counseling. It is largely supportive and reflective, and intensely pastoral in nature. The immediate depths to which second- and third-interview relationships can go is amazing, especially when the counselee has been in classes that the pastor has taught or in worship services that he has conducted. The pastoral role is more significant in some areas of the country than in others. It strikes the deeper and more unconscious mechanisms of the personality more quickly and more certainly in some areas of the country than it does in others. For instance, one can detect a "New Haven bias" in the Richard Niebuhr report as to the degree of confusion and perplexity in people's minds as to the role of a minister. The pastor in a clearly defined religious culture quite often finds a depth-dimension in his relationship to a counselee on the second or third interview. A professional psychotherapist would need several more interviews in which to elicit such response.

Seven to fifteen interviews. The quality of relationship here varies also in terms of the clarity of the role of the counselor. However, if a relationship sustains this long, one is justified in saying that the pastor is involved in a more intensive kind of pastoral counseling. Deeper dynamics and mechanisms of identification, projection, transference, etc., tend to become active. The more aggressive and authoritarian the pastor is, the more likely these are to be set into motion. Likewise, the social situation of the pastor begins to strain a bit. The counselee is likely to want to involve him in social relationships, such as invitations to dinner, requests for a visit at his home, ministries to members of his family who may be sick, etc. Here the basic limitations of the ordinary pastoral relationship for a more or less professional psychotherapeutic endeavor begin to emerge. The social role of the pastor's wife is also brought into play. (This is one unique factor in the Protestant minister's task: he is usually married and his wife knows and is called upon to respond to his counselees, both men and women.) Likewise, the community as a whole begins to ask tacitly: "What is the meaning of all of this going and coming?" The pastor may assure the counselee of confidential treatment of all that he or she says to him. On the other hand, the pastor himself has no assurance of the same kind of confidential treatment from the counselee. The counselee may talk rather vividly and avidly of what goes on in the interview sessions. This in itself must be handled both strategically and tactically in such a way as to contribute to, rather than detract from, the pastor's other functions.

Eleven and above interviews. If the pastor has been faithful and effective up to this point in counseling, he begins to see more unconscious psychological material emerging in the counseling conferences. The counselee may begin to deal with dream material, to involve members of his own family in the drama, to make referrals to the pastor of other people with whom he is related, and to become almost a member of the pastor's family if he has been permitted to involve the pastor socially in the earlier stages of the relationship. If he decides to end the relationship, the pastor has a very definite problem as to what sort of durable relatedness he can offer the counselee in the normal interactions of community living.

THE TIME FACTOR AND THE PASTORAL USE OF COMMUNITY RESOURCES

Obviously, the above rough guide of the shifting meaning of the pastoral counseling relationship in terms of the time factor suggests that the pastor has more than one reason for asking for the help of other community resource persons for more professional types of counseling. Therefore, the time factor in pastoral counseling becomes a very real issue as an indication for referral. A referral system is indispensable for any effective, formal pastoral counseling. One of the reasons that pastors do not have time to do their pastoral ministry is that they insist on doing it all themselves. They do not evaluate the resources of their church and community for giving assistance to individuals. They have failed to build a detailed knowledge of their community as to the agencies, professional and private practitioners, etc., who could help them in their task. Occasionally, pastors call long distances by telephone to ask their former teachers in pastoral care to see one of their parishioners. Occasionally the professor can suggest someone in their own home city about whom they did not know. In one instance, the person to whom I referred the pastor was only a few doors down the street from him!

The amount of time that most pastors can legitimately give to one individual begins to be strained when they go beyond the tenth interview. Pastors often use more interview time than this, sometimes wisely and sometimes not so wisely. However, when they do so, they defy their own limitations in dealing with a person's problems. They are likely to create undue guilt problems in their counselee, particularly if he is a more depressed kind of person. Such a person has to be reassured again and again that the pastor has the time that he really does not have! If the counselee is a passive, dependent individual, the pastor creates hostility problems for himself in that the counselee may use the time poorly and lean dependently on the pastor as a crutch. The counselee, in many instances, will feel the need to give the pastor something. He brings him gifts, offers services, and may even seek to pay for the "services." These actions are highly symbolic and may obligate the pastor in strange and embarrassing ways. On the other hand, their symbolism may often involve forms of worship of God to which the pastor is only incidental. Therefore, we know that when a pastor goes beyond the tenth or eleventh interview with a person he is moving out of a distinctly simple pastoral context and into a highly complex type of relationship. Great sensitivity and responsible maturity are imperative.

Some Theological Dimensions of the Time Factor in Pastoral Counseling

As we plumb the depths of the time factor in pastoral counseling, the more the eternal issues of man's destiny emerge. The pastoral necessity of doing more formal types of counseling raises some fundamental theological and ecclesiastical problems. What is the purpose of the church and its ministry? What is this pastoral relationship like, essentially?

Can a pastor "break" his relationship with a counselee, or is it, by its intrinsic character, a durable, eternal relationship? We have said that the pastor does not "discharge" his counselees. Instead, in terms of his purposive relationship to the church, he hopes that they will become members of the lasting fellowship of the Christian community. Several observers have noted how in a few instances a pastor does a very effective job of pastoral counseling and in the process of it loses rather than gains a new member. They may join someone else's church! On the other hand, at certain stages of pastoral counseling, the counselee may join his church as a demonstration of appreciation to him. This makes it absolutely necessary that the pastor have a synoptic and synthesized view of his theology and church polity in relation to his pastoral counseling practice. His doctrine may become a whetstone upon which the spiritual understanding of his counselee is sharpened.

Furthermore, the persistent tendency of counselees to involve the family life of the pastor indicates something definite about the intrinsic nature of the Protestant minister's role as a family man. At the same time, this presents a real conflict when the pastor begins to perceive himself in a role identity similar to that of the psychologist, psychiatrist, etc. These kinds of counselors are "private" in a way that the pastor is not. This same conflict is raised in terms of the traditional role of the pastor as a visitor in the home when it conflicts with the newer concept of pastoral counseling in which the person is expected by the pastor to come to see him in his study.

In such involvements, the anxiety of the pastor mounts. If he cannot break this relationship, what is the inherent meaning of his time-bound encounter with the counselee? In addition to all that has been mentioned, the counselee transfers deep feelings of love and hate to him, and he in turn develops basic feelings about the counselee. For instance, pastors quite anxiously discuss with professors in great detail the times that members of the opposite sex, and sometimes members of the same sex, begin to interpret their relationship to them as a more distinctly erotic or sexual relationship. One rarely hears a pastor discuss quite so freely his own feelings of love for his parishioners! These are feelings that he carries on in the private soliloquy of his soul at worst, and at best in the I-Thou encounter he has with God in prayer. His anxiety over these feelings may cause him to retreat from a relationship. He may break a relationship at its most crucial point and just at the time when he was on the verge of breaking out of his role as pastor, counselor, etc., and into his role as a fellow human being, a fellow sinner, a fellow child of God, one whose limitations his counselee accepts and affirms even as he has learned to accept and affirm the counselee's limitations. On the other hand, he may continue a counseling relationship past a time of redefinition because it meets his own needs.

As has already been noted, Otto Rank says that within the therapeutic relationship there is an "end-setting" which may be used either redemptively or destructively. In his therapy, he agreed upon the limitations of time that both he and the counselee were suffering and jointly set an end to their relationship in its formal aspects. He likened this end to a death-birth in which an old restricted self died and a new and more potential self was born. The pastor does not have to set ends in his relationships quite so rigidly. Natural life has itself set ends in the great crises of human existence: birth, choice of a mate, religious conversion, the choice of a vocation, illness, old age, death—these are ends that are set within the habitation of man.

The time factor in pastoral counseling has its deepest relevance when the pastor realizes the tremendous sense of the eschatological dimension of life with which even the untutored tend to live in the face of these great crises. The processes of judgment are wrought out here, not in the petty moralisms the pastor can deliver. And we are persuaded that all of these are set within a larger context of the eschatological dimensions of the whole creation, as it groans and travails together. Hence, the high relevance of the more recent re-emphasis upon man's finitude. God *has* set the bounds of our habitation, and the binding of time thrusts us into the ultimate concerns of our existence. As the Moffatt translation of Deut. 29:29 puts it, "The hidden issues of the future are with the Eternal our God, but the unfolded issues of the day are with us and our children for all time, that we may obey all the orders of this law."

No matter how much of a pastor's time a given person shall require, that person necessarily shall have reached a certain level of despair before he seeks pastoral counseling. Many times his personal defenses against the stresses of life are largely shattered. He lives from day to day in the nameless intuition "that years of life can be pressed out of him," by the catastrophes and prolonged duresses under which he lives. He senses that time has run out or is about to run out. Harold G. Wolff cites abundant clinical evidence in which such persons simply "stare out into space and die" for the lack of hope. Wolff calls it "give-up-itis," with which, in spite of our pseudo sophistication, large numbers of those both in and out of the church suffer. The task of the pastoral counselor is so to mobilize the resources of time that eternity may break through to proclaim a "hope that does not disappoint" to those who sit in regions of despair. For, as Wolff again says, "Man is capable of enduring incredible burdens and taking cruel punishment when he has self-esteem, hope, purpose, and belief in his fellows." (Harold G. Wolff, M.D., "What Hope Does for Man," *Saturday Review*, 40:42–45, January 5, 1957.)

Regardless of how much or how little time the pastor has with a given person under stress, his unique identity as a man of hope, as a son of encouragement should remain constant. This ministry of hope is the meeting place of time and eternity in the Good News of Jesus Christ.

VI

Pastoral Counseling as the Ministry of the Church

PASTORAL COUNSELING takes place within the context of the Christian fellowship. Much—not all—of its uniqueness comes alive within this event. The pastor is related to his people, not only as a representative of God, but also as a symbolic personification of the corporate intention of the church toward the individual. The pastor performs his ministry of reconciliation, not only of man with God, but also of the individual man with the body corporate of the specifically defined community known as a local church. Herein the stresses of human relationships are brought to him for his counseling attention. The covenanted fellowship of a church shares beliefs, commitments, purposes, practices. The interacting field of the responsible Christian fellowship, therefore, gives pastoral counseling its meaning as the work of the body of Christ. The pastor of a church through his counseling activates the whole purpose of the church, which is "the increase among men of the love of God and neighbor" (Richard Niebuhr, *The Purpose of the Church and Its Ministry*, p. 83; Harper & Brothers, 1956). But more than that it is the proclamation of the death, burial, and resurrection of Jesus Christ. In a very real sense, the church *is* the counselor. The minister, by reason of the role conferred upon him by the church, implements the counsel of the church.

These somewhat categorical assertions can be illustrated. Specific examples challenge some misconceptions of pastoral counseling that may have tended to grow in the popular mind. For instance, the distinctive character of pastoral counseling is symbolized in the way in which a minister is supported financially. He is not paid for individual services that he renders to individual people. He is not paid by an individual. He is supported by the church. His income symbolizes the corporate good will of the church toward the individuals to whom he ministers. Expressions of appreciation are received as acts of worship of God in the church by the church. They are not received as "attempts to pay off" the minister for "services rendered." When we apply this fact, and I think it is a fact, to the historical development of the neotraditional role of the pastor as a formal counselor, we get some very interesting results.

For example, as has been said in a previous chapter, the discipline of pastoral counseling is an outgrowth of the clinical pastoral training movement. This movement was initiated by Anton Boisen and Russell Dicks in the late twenties and early thirties. However, they initiated it in the context of a hospital. Anton Boisen has been primarily supported by state funds as an employee of the state. Russell Dicks as a chaplain was paid by Richard Cabot, an individual. The insights they discovered and the role that they fulfilled were posited upon a certain independence of financial support by the church itself. The Council for Clinical Training and the Institute for Pastoral Care for two decades were largely responsible for the training of theological students in pastoral care and counseling in its more recent perspectives. They were able to do this teaching because their instructors were supported by state and federal institutions. These men worked over and above their regular duties as chaplains in institutions in order to do the sacrificial tasks of teaching theological students. They have usually been loyal to the church, but it has been an independent loyalty, not an economic necessity. However, the contributions that they have made to pastoral counseling have been from an extra-ecclesiastical frame of reference. Only recently has the church, through its teaching agencies—the seminaries—begun to accept responsibility commensurate with its desire to control such teaching. Likewise, increasingly have agencies such as The Council for Clinical Training begun to accept responsibility commensurate with their desire for support from the churches and seminaries. The closer alliance, therefore, of the movement with other professions than with the church itself is not accidental but directly related to their separation from the church.

Another example from the history of pastoral counseling in its more recent expression is that, in the absence of theologically trained instructors in the field of pastoral care and pastoral counseling, ministers have turned to other professions for their guiding images of themselves as counselors. They have turned to psychologists, psychiatrists, and psychoanalysts, and to a much lesser degree, social workers. However, as representatives of the church, doing their counseling in the context of the Christian fellowship, their role is radically different from that of any of these professions in terms of the way they are supported. They do not have a private, fee-taking, direct, service-rendered relationship through which to control their encounter with their counselee. Rather, they are supported on a public, philanthropic, and, at best, stewardship basis by the voluntary contributions of a voluntary society. This relationship, both from the point of view of the use of money and of time, is radically different from that of the professional counselor. It imposes limitations, and yet offers resources that the private practitioner does not encounter.

The distinctive factor whereby a pastor counsels in the context of the Christian fellowship challenges both his conception of the church and his conception of himself as a disciplined, trained professional person. There are some evidences that a subprofession of pastoral counseling is beginning to emerge within the context of the Christian community as a whole. The civilian chaplaincy movement is an illustration. The predominant function of the chaplain of a general, a psychiatric, or some other specialized type of hospital is that of pastoral counseling. But only feebly have the churches accepted any responsibility for the financial support of these chaplains. There has been mild effort at this point in the American Protestant Hospital Association. An even fainter evidence of interest is recorded in the support of chaplains in state and federal institutions. A few churches, such as the Marble Collegiate Church in New York City, have established counseling clinics. However, as in this instance, the relationship between the clinic and the church is parallelistic rather than integral. Some churches, on the other hand, have begun to add members to their staff who have been specially trained in pastoral counseling. Great confusion exists here as to the separation of this function of formal counseling from that of the preaching task of the minister. Even more serious confusion arises when persons from other disciplines and other professions who have had little or no theological education are added to the staff of the church.

However, the main thrust of the life of the churches is in the direction of the equipment of all their clergy for a more limited and yet more competent kind of function as pastoral counselors. An exceptionally large percentage of the seminaries in the American Association of Theological Schools have added full-time professors in the field of pastoral care and pastoral counseling since 1945. The returned serviceman saw his chaplain as a personal counselor and came back from the war expecting this kind of service from his minister. The returned chaplain who had functioned in this role without training came back to his seminary demanding this kind of equipment. Therefore, the local parish minister began to receive training in pastoral counseling along with the rest of his theological curriculum. The content of the field of pastoral care began to be defined in relation to the rest of the theological curriculum. Thus all of us have been and are being thrust into deeper consideration of the unique characteristics of pastoral counseling when it is done in the context of the Christian church. The more experience we have accrued, the more case studies we have been able to interpret, the more tentative conclusions to lasting questions we have been able to draw, the more we have had

to face up to the determinative power of a pastor's conception
of the church upon his role and function as a pastoral counselor.

The Pastor's Conception of the Church and of Himself as a Pastoral Counselor

A mutually challenging and cleansing relationship exists between the pastor's basic ecclesiology and his pastoral function
as a counselor. A polar tension is at work here that will never
be settled. However, if it is accepted, explored, and understood, it will provide effective stimulus for continuing growth
for the pastor and his work as a counselor in the context of the
Christian fellowship.

The whole problem of divorce and the remarriage of divorcees is a case in point. When an Episcopalian minister asks
me, a Baptist minister, what I do with reference to the remarriage of divorced people, two issues are at stake. First, I
know that his question is a rather academic one as far as his
practice is concerned. He may be personally interested in what
I personally would do, but when he gets involved in an actual
decision about a particular couple, he would not ask me. He
would necessarily have to ask his bishop! Likewise, I notice
that my own ecclesiology is at stake. I may say to him that I
am a Baptist minister and that I decide on an individual case
and do what I think is right under God. But when I do this, I
have forsaken my basic ecclesiological belief that the local
congregation have already through their popular mores developed a set of opinions of their own which exercise a shaping
and even determining influence upon what I do. Then I confront the fact that my counseling ministry with an individual
divorced couple must necessarily be augmented by a small-
group, two-way communication—educational ministry with
the leadership of my church. When I do this, I am thrust back
upon my role and function as a teacher and as a preacher
among the people whom I represent. If I take these responsibilities seriously and hold closely to my doctrine of the auton-

omy of the local church, then I will come somewhere near the position that one former Presbyterian minister in my home city reached.

Dr. W. A. Benfield, formerly pastor of the Highland Presbyterian Church in Louisville, Kentucky, studied the position of his denomination on marriage, along with the lay leadership in his church. Through the processes of teaching and group discussion the whole church arrived at a position with reference to the marriage of any persons, divorced or not, who seek the services of the pastor. *First,* the services of the church are used at the time of marriage without charge being made or honoraria being given by the participants in the wedding service. This is based upon the principle that the church seeks to express its interest in its members and help them to realize that marriage should be identified with the church as a holy, sacred relationship. *In the second place,* the church officers have adopted, and the church is supporting a policy whereby the ministers officiate at a marriage ceremony only when the man and woman to be married are Christians. They feel that a Christian minister necessarily is obligated to express the purpose of the church in marriage through the fulfillment on the part of a couple of a meaningful relationship with God. *And in the third place,* the church and its officers are supporting a policy whereby people to be married in the church are required to spend an extended measure of time and means going through a clinical program of instruction, counseling, and spiritual fellowship. This program is designed to make the position of the church meaningful at the time of marriage and to help couples understand and be committed to the full nature of the Christian faith and of mature marriage. Here we have a consistent pattern of premarital guidance and counsel provided by the church and implemented through the pastor.

Another example of the inseparable relationship of pastoral counseling to the context of the Christian fellowship in which it takes place is that of counseling with reference to problems of birth control. The Catholic church perceives itself as the custodian of the family. It exerts forensic authority over its members as to whom they shall marry, how the children shall be reared, and how the processes of conception and parenthood shall be controlled and guided. Protestant churches are somewhat hesitant to discuss these matters. The Catholic Church, on the other hand, has discussed them openly, freely, and persistently *within the presuppositions of its faith.* The sexual ethics of Protestant people have for several centuries moved along untouched by the radical theological presuppositions of the Reformation with reference to human life as they are applied to the intimate encounter of men and women in sexual relationship. As a result, our people go on suffering an intolerable dilemma between Catholic authoritarianism and marriage and family relationships with reference to the procreation of children and the meaning of the sex act, on the one hand, and secular humanism on the other hand. Secular humanism assumes that each individual is a "good" unto himself apart from the sovereignty of God as Creator in the corporate fellowship of an ethically defined community.

Subterraneanly at this present time, for example, discussions are going on in the law courts and in the canonical courts with reference to the meaning of artificial insemination. Prof. Joseph F. Fletcher in his book entitled *Morals and Medicine* (Princeton, 1954) has rejected the authoritarian supernaturalism of the Catholic Church with reference to artificial insemination and affirms the personalistic and humanitarian legitimacy of artificial insemination. However, he falls short of the unique genius of Reformation theology in the life of the church by taking the other horn of a Catholic distinction between the natural and the supernatural. He comes up, in my opinion, at least, with a naturalistic answer in opposition to supernaturalistic answers proposed by the Catholic tradition.

The essentially Protestant distinction, as has been said in Ch. I, is not one of setting the natural over against the supernatural. This particular distinction was unknown to those who wrote our Bible. The Reformation marked a reaffirmation of the Biblical distinction between God as Creator and man as creature, between the Creator and his creation. All of creation is to be brought under the sovereign rule and purpose of God. For instance, the rhythm method of birth control is dependent upon a knowledge of the calendar as surely as the use of other methods is dependent upon the knowledge of diaphragms. One is as much a creation of man as another, and man in turn is always a creature himself. To submit either to a childish dependence upon ecclesiastical authority or to a superficial carte blanche acceptance of the discoveries of medicine in either instance may ensue in immaturity and irresponsibility. Avoidance of the chief purpose of man, which is to glorify his Creator and to enjoy him forever, results in the use of all of the created implements for man's happiness for finite and self-centered purposes.

The Protestant understanding of God is the foundation of our understanding of the church—man's ordered relationship to his fellows under God in Christ. Therefore, our pastoral counseling in intensely intimate problems happens in the context of the basic beliefs and commitments of that covenanted community.

A more immediately recognized expression of this basic point of view comes into focus when we challenge certain superficial ideas about pastoral counseling which say that our basic responsibility is to individuals and that the administrative task of the pastor is odious to us. Pastors and seminary professors do a great deal of looking down the nose at the supposedly inferior task of administration. This particular attitude is neither Biblically nor clinically defensible. The apostle Paul was just as concerned about expressing his pastoral ministry through raising money for the destitute people of Jerusalem as he was in helping a runaway slave with his problem with authority persons! The contemporary pastor does his counseling in an administrative context. His pastoral care of the whole flock of God through his administrative oversight accentuates the dynamic, interpersonal character of pastoral counseling. Pastoral counseling may be eased in its weight or increased in its difficulty in direct proportion to the pastor's insight, commitment, and ability as an administrator. And we tend to reject our responsibility at this point because we have equated this, as Niebuhr says, with "a nontheological smattering of successful business practices." (*The Purpose of the Church and Its Ministry*, p. 84.) We owe some of this to the fact that professors of church administration have not kept up with their research in the most recent conceptions of group life, leadership, and business administration, but have drawn their cue from a few tycoons from another generation. We owe much more of it to shallow thinking about the intrinsic nature of the church and the purposes of its ministry.

Several integral relationships bind pastoral leadership and pastoral counseling together. *First,* the tension that the pastor must bear as he weighs the needs of the individual against those of the corporate community can never be removed. This is the tension between the "one" and the "ninety and nine." A pastor ceases to be a pastor at heart when he ceases to feel this tension. He cannot be debonair or doctrinaire about either a given individual or the whole destiny of the church of which he is pastor. For instance, a psychiatrist interviewed a certain counselee whom a pastor referred to him. The counselee had developed a certain "unheard of" practice in his sexual relationships with his wife. How did this come to the attention of his pastor? Did the wife tell him? Did the husband tell him? No. The *father* of the wife told him. The father was a deacon in the church of which the counselor was pastor. How did the father tell him? He told him that his daughter was no longer living with her husband because he, the father, had forbidden her to live with him and forbidden the husband to come near the house at the risk of being shot. Then the husband came to the pastor, confessing the particular sexual perversion about which the father had already told the pastor. The son-in-law had been to a psychiatrist. The psychiatrist had said, and rightly so, that this was not an unusual thing. No, it was not unusual *to the psychiatrist in his context.* But it was *desperately* unusual to the father of the girl, who happened to be a deacon in the church for which the pastor was responsible.

The psychiatrist had the safety of a private office and a detached relationship. He had the individual, even apart from his family, totally at heart. But the pastor had not only the individual, but also the family; he had not only the individual and the family, but also the care of the whole church at stake. The psychiatrist said that he did not see that this particular act would do any harm. But just because he did not see, it does not mean that someone could not have been shot! The pastor was much more anxious than the psychiatrist. The psychiatrist could have interpreted the counselee as being immature, "having a lot of problems of his own," or have made some other highly individualistic interpretation of his reaction. He indeed might have been all of these. But the anxiety of the pastor grew out of the fact that he had a more complex and different kind of responsibility from that of the psychiatrist. He could not but take this seriously. This is the kind of insight that the social worker would take into consideration in a clinic setting. It reflects the structural inadequacy of the work of a private psychiatrist as a ground on which he and the local pastor can stand together in meeting all the needs of the family and community as well as those of the individual. This particular instance actually worked out in a much more effective manner by reason of the fact that the psychiatrist and the minister involved both had the courage to stay with each other until each understood the other's "frame of reference" and could profit from their combined picture of the needs of the individual and the community.

Another task of pastoral counseling in the context of the church is integrally bound by the tension the pastor feels between the permissive attitude suggested by research and counseling and the authority that he carries as an administrator of his flock. The pastor cannot cease to feel the tension between authority and permissiveness. He cannot settle this tension on either side of the dilemma. He must find a higher and more creative synthesis. This tension is intrinsic to being a pastor. For instance, a pastor on a routine pastoral visit was told by one of his church leaders that her husband and another woman of the community, also a very active church leader, were engaging in illicit sexual intimacies. The pastor became agitated and overexerted his authority. He told the accused woman that she should resign her positions in the church. He could not be permissive long enough to bring the very inflamed relationship under control. He could not be permissive long enough to "hear all of the story" of any of the participants. He felt that he had to handle the situation all by himself immediately. As a result, he exercised administrative authority and made a decision for the person with reference to her church offices. He then was put into the embarrassing position of realizing that the woman had to explain to other people why she was not doing the work they expected her to do. When they did ask her, she told them to "ask the preacher—he knew why." Then he had mass resignations from first one and then the other who themselves had been involved in various types of indiscretions and feared exposure from the pastor as a result. The end result of this confusion was that the pastor gave up the church in sheer desperation. His very opportunity as a counselor was jeopardized by his basic failure as an administrator.

Both of the foregoing illustrations point out the impossibility of separating counseling problems from pastoral leadership problems. The pastoral counselor does his work in a dynamic, and even threatening, field of interpersonal relationships. When we compare his social function with that of people of other professions, we are being quite unrealistic when we easily equate it with that of the psychologist or the psychiatrist. The pastor's social function corresponds in some respects to that of a social worker who does both social case work and social group work. But even from the standpoint of group work, the pastor does not deal merely with the problems of small groups. He works more in the context of what Maxwell Jones has called the "therapeutic community." He must be aware of the ways in which authority and community structure can be pressed into service to help the individual to bear his burdens, and at the same time he is expected to bear his own burdens well.

The loss of controlled anonymity in the parish context is

both a help and a hindrance to effective individual counseling. The pastor necessarily has to have keen insight into the varieties of relationships to which he has access and to which he is at the same time subject himself. Thus he can lay hold of the resources of the parish context and work realistically within its limitations.

THE RESOURCES OF THE CHRISTIAN FELLOWSHIP FOR PASTORAL COUNSELING

The complexity of his responsibilities so overwhelm a pastor that he is prone to overlook the basic resources that the very complexities themselves afford him. The church itself affords him some rich assistance in his task as a counselor. Many times problems that would require innumerable individual interviews if one were working in isolation from the community can be met in an even better fashion by a careful and wise mobilization of the total resources of the community of Christians. Many pastors will have representatives of the other professions within the lay membership of their church—doctors of all the specialties, lawyers, public educators, and social workers from public assistance agencies. Some of the most effective pastors have been those who have either formally or informally built themselves a "professional advisory committee" composed of representatives of the great disciplines just named. These people belong to this committee, not by the demands of the ecclesiastical organization, but by reason of the professional skills that they have and the advice, guidance, and judgment that they can give to the pastor upon his specific request.

In my own city the laymen of the various churches of the Louisville Council of Churches have formed subcommittees to work as liaisons between the churches and the various institutions of the community. Mr. George Stoll, a Methodist layman, has led this movement for the last sixteen years. He has written a report of this type of activity in his book entitled *Laymen at Work* (Abingdon Press, 1955). Russell Dicks has emphasized the work of the pastor as a teacher of his people in the arts of pastoral care. In his little book, *You Came Unto Me,* he has given a guide for the study of pastoral visitation. One reason visitation is such a chore to both pastors and laymen is that it is a meaningless task to them. Some training of selected individuals in this matter will equip the pastor with resource people upon whom he can rely.

In discussing the purpose of the church and its ministry, Professor Niebuhr has pointed out that the pastor is a counselor of counselors. Many of the people in a pastor's community are already depending upon each other for emotional aid and guidance. The pastor does not need to perceive himself as just a "counselor" to whom everyone must come. He cuts off the resources of the natural forces of helpfulness within the community itself should he insist on being *the* counselor. However, if he perceives himself as the pastoral guide of a purposeful fellowship of people who have a creative and redemptive intention toward each other, he can mobilize the resources of the whole community in both the prevention and the cure of some highly personal problems.

When the pastor takes this view of the over-all life of the church, he begins to evaluate the group life of the church more seriously. He is challenged by the effective work of small group movements such as Alcoholics Anonymous. He is forced to reassess the meaning of his educational program. He no longer turns this program over in a negligent fashion to some person to bear alone as a Director of Religious Education. He becomes a pastoral educator. Blizzard pointed out that only about one twentieth of the time of the pastor is spent in teaching. Teaching differs basically from preaching in that it is two-way communication in which people can ask questions and challenge the teacher. Some types of pastoral counseling can be done better on a group basis than on an individual basis. The group, in turn, becomes the ground of communication on which the pastor can stand as he establishes rapport with individuals who otherwise would not have come to him.

But there are also resources from without the walls of the church as the church and its pastor come into dynamic encounter with the non-Christian community. Many of the representatives of other professions are frankly not Christians. However, if they are good professional people, they have a fundamental respect for the religious persuasion of those with whom they work. But the actual care of such people, especially when these counselees are also members of a local parish, is at the same time in the hands of the pastor of the church. Regardless of how many other people are caring for a given individual, that person still needs a pastor. The pastor does not find out what his own real ministry truly is in its fullest expression until he has had the privilege of being a *pastoral* counselor to a person who has *already* greatly profited from competent psychiatric or psychoanalytic help.

The Christian fellowship has a basic responsibility to bear the Christian witness to members of the other helping professions. They themselves need pastoral care. No man is sufficient unto himself. And even when rejection by another professional person shuts us out, the all-encompassing character of the Christian witness of the love of God draws a larger circle that takes them in. If we do not have Christian persons in the other helping professions, it is not ours to "hurl the cynic's ban" and carp at their lack of religion. We need to ask the question, "Where were we as pastors when they were making their decision to enter these professions?" We also need to ask the question, "Are we not ministers of reconciliation in relation to them, also?"

Furthermore, governmental agenices offer resources from outside the church upon which we may draw to help people. American Protestant pastors' emphasis on the separation of church and state quite often allows the institutional and personal services of governmental agencies to the members of our own churches to go unused; or these resources may be used on bases that do not take into consideration the spiritual values and moral principles of the Christian faith. The strengths and weaknesses of the principle of separation of church and state have been seen clearly in the development of chaplaincy services for inmates of state and federal institutions. Christian ministers who become chaplains in these institutions may lose their perspective of the relevance of the church for what they are doing. This loss of perspective is often caused by the sheer neglect of the chaplains by the local churches of the community. On the other hand, the contrary effect is more often the case: chaplains in state institutions and the military appreciate the meaning of a church fellowship in a fresh and vital way not apparent among pastors of churches. The reciprocity between local churches and other institutions of the community was never meant to be stifled and negated by the principle of separation of church and state. We cannot keep two organisms of society separate by destroying, neglecting, or impoverishing one or the other.

A Case Record from 1673

We often mistakenly assume that the full activation of the life of the church in the care of disturbed and sick people is a "new thing." This very newness accounts for much superficial, "passer-by" kind of concern on the part of some ministers for the distresses of others. However, both our assumptions of "newness" and our spiritual superficiality are challenged by the following case record, dated 1673, published by E. B. Underhill in *The Records of a Church of Christ*, in Broadmead, Bristol, England. I am indebted to Mr. Hugh Wamble, a graduate student in church history at the time, for calling this to my attention. These are clinical notes recorded by the church clerk in what we today would call the "minutes" of the church. I am reproducing here the case record, just as it was recorded by a church clerk in 1673.

Sister Mary Skinner was, after further speaking with her, and satisfaction received, added to this congregation on the sixth day of the second month, 1673.

Sister Bird, on the Key, deceased 22nd of second month, 1673, and left by will, to one of the brethren, five pounds, towards stock for the congregation.

Upon the 23rd day of this second month, 1673, a sad providence fell out to this congregation, which was this: —Our brother, John Fry, a bachelor, fell distracted. First it came upon him in a way of despairing, that he was lost and damned; then he brake out in bad language to all the brethren that came near him, calling them very bad names, and immodest expressions to some women, raving and striking them that came near to hold him, and when they were forced to bind him on the bed, he would spit at some, and use such vile and grievous words, it was consternation of spirit to all that knew him, it being so directly opposite and contrary to the whole frame of his former way and temper.

And being thus sorely assaulted and pressed by the devil, as all that beheld and heard him could not other- wise judge, he did also (and that which is worse than all) break forth into such dreadful and horrible expressions, against the whole Deity, at some times with such blas- phemous words, that it made the hearts of all that heard it to ache, and the hair of their heads, as it were, to stand on end: and their spirits to be so pressed thereby hardly able to contain, or to be in the room to hear it, being so astonished at what the Lord had suffered to befall this brother; that had the testimony of all, good and bad, that he had a very lovely, humble conversation, and judged that he walked close with God, as was attested by a godly judicious doctor of physic (Dr. Ichabod Chauncey had been chaplain to Sir Edward Harley's regiment, at Dun- kirk, but on the passing of the Act of Uniformity became a physician in Bristol. He was prosecuted under the 35 Eliz, and banished the realm in 1684, but returned to Bristol in 1686.—Palmer's Noncon. Mem ii, 352.), a member of another congregation in this city, that had lived several years tabled in the house with him, having a grave woman to his mother-in-law that kept his house, she being a sister named Fry, in fellowship with us. This doctor whilst he tabled there, observed him all along to be a very sober, practical Christian; reading and praying after the work of his outward calling (when his journeymen were departed, and his servants had left work), until the tenth and eleventh hour most nights.

His distraction broke in upon him upon the fourth day of the week (called Wednesday), and grew higher and higher, into great raging, as aforesaid. Physical means were used, but all in vain. Most persuaded he should be carried into the country for help. But some of the brethren desired the church might seek the Lord, by fasting and prayer to the Lord, to heal and deliver him.

Whereupon, the second day following, being the 28th day of the month, the congregation kept a day of prayer, in our brother Fry's house, and in the room where he was in the bed bound; but his raging was so great in the beginning of the day, that we thought we should not have been able to have continued in the room. Yet, notwithstanding, a brother began the work of the day by him, and the day was, by the Lord's assistance, carried on, and a gracious answer of prayer was given by the Lord, as we did seem to apprehend, insomuch that the spirit of rage left him in a great measure, that it ceased by the evening of that day, before we parted from him. Praise only be to the Lord!

Upon that day seven night, being the 5th day of the third month following the church came together again into the same place, and kept another day of prayer to the Lord for him. For, although the Lord did so graciously answer the church's former prayers, that in a great measure the spirit of raging left him, yet a great spirit of fear remained in him. But on this day also, the

Lord did mercifully incline towards us, and gave a gracious answer to his people's seeking him in his own way; so that very observably the spirit of fear left him, that he was not so much in horror and frightful apprehensions as he had been. And means were used physically for his recovery, as blooding, purging, and leeching, to draw the distemper from his head; according to our prayers, that if the Lord pleased to have us use outward means, that he would direct to it, and bless the means; which he compassionately answered.

But when he began to come to himself, and his poor thin body, that had been plucked down, began to receive some refreshment, we had great fears his distemper would have come on again with its former violence. For though those fits ceased for above a month, yet he could not arrive to any comfort or faith, and could hardly be prevailed with to go to prayer himself; he lay under such despairing thoughts still, that it was all in vain, no promise did belong to him, etc. But he lay under reflection upon himself, what a wretch he was for what he had in or by fits uttered against, or of, the Lord. By which we perceived he remembered much, if not all; so that he was filled with such shame, that he would hide his face from every one that came to see him, or hang down his head, or not speak. He was so filled with a spirit of shame, after the spirit of rage and spirit of fear had left him, that they could not yet prevail with him to go but to a near neighbor, nor hardly to see a person that came in.

Therefore the church appointed another day of prayer for him, and so came together again, upon the ninth day of the fourth month following, anno 1673, at his house, to seek the Lord, as it were to perfect the work of his recovery, to take the spirit of shame from him, that he might go about his lawful calling forth of doors. For which the Lord gave a gracious answer of prayer also, to

admiration. For the very next day after this, he was emboldened to go forth about his business in the city, as he
did formerly; yea, he went from house to house, about his
occasions, to his customers, for the space of four or five
hours, and returned. Thus the Lord cast, as it were, three
spirits, visible, to be seen, out of him: viz., a spirit of uncleanness for rage and blasphemy; secondly, a spirit of
horror and fear; and thirdly, a spirit of shame, and, as it
were, dumbness. Oh, the condescension, mercy, grace,
favour, and faithfulness of the God and Father of our
Lord Jesus Christ, that he should answer prayer, and
hear such poor, vile and unworthy ones as we were! O,
nothing in us, nothing in us! Not for our sakes did he
this wonderful thing in our day, but for his own name's
sake; having engaged himself to do for us whatsoever
we ask in the name of our Lord Jesus Christ. Laus Deo.
Sola Deo gloria. Whom, to this day, near three years
since he recovered, the Lord hath kept in his former
glorious frame of spirit; and he usually exercises in
prayer, in the congregation, on fast days, as formerly, and
hath been very well ever since in his body. Magnified be
the Lord!

At the very outset of this case, we are impressed with the
fact that this is a *church* record and not just the record of an
individual pastor. Recently I visited this church in England
and asked who the pastor in 1673 was. I learned that the Rev.
Thomas Hardcastle had come to the church in 1671, having
been ejected from Bramham in Yorkshire. An engraved plaque
in the vestibule of the church states that "he was imprisoned
seven times for religion, and died suddenly, August 29th,
1678." It is likely, then, that at the time of the illness of Brother
Fry the pastor was in prison and the church members themselves were doing the pastoral work under his supervision from
the prison!
It appears that the whole church was involved in the care of

Brother Fry. Members participated to the limit of their vision in an intelligent concern for him. The gathered community accepted responsibility in the total task of pastoral care. Decisions were corporate ones and not the isolated acts of a professional pastor. This points to the conclusion that pastoral care today, if theologically sound, should involve the active witness, instruction, and concern of the whole church. Short of this, pastoral care becomes just another "specialty" one more step removed from the central meaning of the witness of the church to "the whole counsel of God" in the redeeming grace of Jesus Christ. The processes of pastoral care are little more than the sewing of a new patch on an old garment unless the purpose of the church as a whole is both enlightened and implemented toward the healing witness of the ministry of love to the disturbed, spirit-possessed, and internally shattered folk such as Brother John Fry.

In the second place, we notice that the Broadmead Church was not totally agreed as to how to care for Brother Fry. "Most persuaded he should be carried into the country for help. But some of the brethren desired the church might seek the Lord, by fasting and prayer to the Lord, to heal and deliver him." The remainder of the church gave at least assent by silence. The smaller group knew that the Lord had said that some healings come only by prayer and fasting. They chose to submit themselves to these disciplines. The disciplines of pastoral care today are listening, prayer, fearless relationship. As fat and bloated as some of us are from overeating, fasting could well be added with something better than "waistline vanity" as a motive. Great numbers of people are not going to give themselves over to such disciplines for the sake of distressed people within or without the church. But the intensive disciplines of committed prayer, study, attention, and suffering are met by commensurate response from the Lord of Life who has deigned to express his healing grace through those who bring themselves into submission to his purposes.

In the third place, we observe this group of Christians turning trustingly to the medical resources they had at hand. They consulted Dr. Ichabod Chauncey, and "means were used physically for his [Brother Fry's] recovery." They prayed "that if the Lord pleased to have us use outward means, that he would direct to it, and bless the means; which he compassionately answered." Here we find the antithesis of modern "faith healers," who look upon any use of medical means of healing as something different from, other than, and even opposed to the healing work of God. God is neither restricted *to* nor *away from* the knowledge of one of his creatures in his healing of another of his creatures. For both the doctor and the patient, the disease and the medical knowledge of the disease and its cure are a part of the creation of which God is sovereign. In neither instance has God made anything common or unclean. Such attitudes are the groundwork of our intensive co-operation with medical experts in modern pastoral care. Such co-operation is not substitution for the power of God but an evangelical outreach of the church to encompass that which the Creator—God—has made available. It is an outreach that seeks to bring that co-operation into the orbit of his sovereign grace, doctor and all, just as did the Broadmead Church.

In the fourth place, the Broadmead record shows that the people of the church carefully observed the behavior of Brother John Fry. They were almost uncanny in the detail with which they noted his "way of despairing," his muteness, his unprecedented change of personality from his usual pattern of life, and the progressive phases of his illness. They discerned the spirits qualitatively, using the primitive psychological concepts at hand, namely, spirit-possession, with a generous mixture of down-to-earth common sense. They traced the process of his illness in terms of the three spirits which had possessed him: "the spirit of uncleanness," "the spirit of horror and fear," and "the spirit of shame."

In the fifth place, we sense the deep self-searching going on in the lives of those who did the ministering. Without self-examination and frank admission of our own sinfulness, weakness, and fears, no real helpfulness comes to others. This *is* prayer! And this group of Christians admitted that they could hardly stand it; they wanted to run! They had trouble staying in the same room with Brother Fry. They were tempted to rebuke, to extort, to condemn, but they did none of these! What did they do? First, they admitted their own anxieties, fears, and self-righteousness. Second, they listened and observed Brother Fry with prayerful, sustained, and fearless attention. They stayed by him. Third, they accepted him with an unconditional love. Fourth, they took his bad behavior as a part of his total disturbance, overlooked it, and did not judge him harshly. Finally, they believed in his fundamental integrity and trusted both his and their lives together into the hands of God. These four expressions of faith, hope, and love were, in my opinion, the secret of their healing power.

Again, the Broadmead group did not feel that *they* had healed Brother Fry when he finally came back to himself. They attributed the act to God and to his faithfulness to keep his promises. This is the hallmark of all pastoral care—Jewish, Catholic, or Protestant—that we are—or should be—averse to attributing any results to our own efforts. In fact, this is the fundamental distinction between the religious and secular approaches to counseling, i.e., the essential humility of the counselor who attributes results, not to his own efforts, but to the co-operative response of God to his discipline and prayer. This puts many faith healers, however pious, into the secular camp. It puts many faithful doctors into the religious camp. It puts many pastoral counselors—preening our feathers with a sense of personal accomplishment—to shame! For as the Broadmead record says: "O, nothing in us, nothing in us!"

Finally, the Broadmead record does what many pastoral and medical records today fail to do; it gives us a three-year follow-up. It says that Brother Fry through "the Lord hath kept in his former glorious frame of spirit." Whether only symptoms or the real causes were dealt with, the three-year follow-up is reassuring as to results.

VII

The Protestant
Pastoral Counselor

BY WAY OF SUMMARY of what has been said thus far, let us say that basic Protestant distinctives are essential and not peripheral to Protestant pastoral counseling. Furthermore, within Protestantism, the free church tradition has contributed additional dimensions of nonconformity, diversity, small-group discipline, and individualism, which are also integral to an understanding of Protestant pastoral counseling. The Holy Spirit, in deed and in fact, is the counselor, and the church and its pastor incarnate the intentions of God, even though they are earthen vessels. All pastoral counseling is cast within a framework of progress, hope, and consummation that we have chosen to call the eschatological dimensions of pastoral counseling. Time is taken seriously in pastoral counseling, and serves as a basis for identifying different kinds of counseling pastors and the unique identities shared by all pastors as counselors. The specific church in which a pastor serves is itself inseparably involved in his work as a counselor. All this converges, however, upon the Protestant pastor himself who articulates the purpose of the church and its ministry. The objective of this chapter is to concentrate upon the identity and the interpersonal competence of the Protestant pastoral counselor.

A BROTHERLY CALLING

The Protestant pastor as a counselor, contrary to both psychoanalytic and Catholic presuppositions, participates in the

139

life of his counselee as a brother-man. He is related responsibly to "siblings" in Christ, and not as a father-figure is related to children in an "over/under" relationship. This describes the Protestant pastor's identity as it actually is in society, and not just as some Protestant pastors see it or particularly as many parishioners want to see him. Many failures in interpersonal competence as pastor and people interact with each other may be traced to an unawareness of this brother-man-ness, or to a refusal to accept the fact, even though they may be aware of it.

Flügel is right when he says that the Christian faith as communicated in the teachings of Jesus is a brotherly faith and not a fatherly-motherly one. Jesus could say that he no longer called his disciples servants but friends. He could say that no man could have greater love than to lay down his life for his friends. He urged his disciples to "call no man father." He enjoined upon them that they love one another as he had loved them. (Flügel, *The Psychoanalytic Study of the Family*, pp. 144 ff.)

The Reformation brought a new identity for the pastor as compared with that of the Catholic priest. The Protestant pastor fulfills his identity as a father in relation to his own children in the home, not in relation to his parishioners. He functions as a fellow Christian along with them, one whose time has been made completely available to the fellowship of Christians by reason of the church's support of him. He is, as has been said, a member of "the other laity." The higher liturgical groups move heavily in the direction of defining their ministry as a fatherly relationship. Nevertheless, one who listens closely to the conversations that parishioners have about their parish priest finds them calling him by his first name! Even so, one is moving more closely to the Catholic definition of the ministry and further away from the distinctly Protestant definition when he introduces the concept of a father-child relationship into the pastoral identity.

Furthermore, the brother-man identity of the Protestant pastor as a counselor challenges the easy clichés of psychoanalytic interpretation of the role of the minister. Very often we hear that the minister is a father-figure to his parishioners. This would imply that "transference feelings" which occur within the pastoral counseling relationship are distinctly those of a child to his father. However, these concepts were devised in a culture which was predominantly Catholic. Likewise, they were devised in the afterglow of a nineteenth-century conception of leadership, namely, the "great man" theory of patriarchal power. Furthermore, they were devised by Freud in his advanced years, and quite definitely oriented to the relationship of an exceptionally old man to people who were much younger. They were developed in the context of the rebellion of a child against the parent, much of which Freud suffered in relation to his own students, as well as in relation to his patients.

However, several criticisms need to be made of this easily accepted maxim among pastoral counselors. First, in those cases where the *parental* bond is continued between a pastor and his counselee-parishioner, it should be remembered that the research of Marvin O. Nelson and Edwin M. Jones indicates that the religious concepts of sixteen persons of the Protestant faith were more closely related to the "mother concept than the father concept." They say that "in the total group means as well as in the means for the subgroup, the God concept had a higher positive correlation with the mother concept than with the father concept." ("An Application of the Q-Technique to the Study of Religious Concepts," *Psychological Reports*, 1957, III, p. 297.) The pastor needs to be aware of the real immaturity of some counselees who expect him to give them motherly care and tend to dissociate him from fatherly authority.

A second criticism of the easy acceptance of the father-identity of the pastor as prompted by easy acceptance of psychoanalytic truisms is a cultural criticism. Schlesinger, Whyte, and Riesman have called our attention to the movement of our culture away from "the great man" theory of leadership and over to the societal or group theory of leadership. They speak of this trend in terms of "the decline of greatness," and "the emergence of the organization man," and "the lonely crowd." The patriarch as a leader "fades away," and "the bright young man" emerges as leader. One has difficulty in refuting this when he sees the collapse of patriarchal figures in political life, such as Stalin, Chiang Kai-shek, Syngman Rhee, and others. Even the holy glow on General Eisenhower's patriarchal leadership has been gradually transmuted into the familiarity of calling him Ike, and the 1960 political campaign posed on both sides of the national political scene a "young sibling" type leadership. In Mr. Kennedy's victory, brothers appear in cabinet and executive offices at the same time. In the context of the life of the church, therefore, the perishing of the patriarchs in an age of "great men," is followed by the emergence of "an accent on youth." Consequently, the major emotions of the pastor-parishioner relationship are more those of competitiveness between younger people in the church than they are the rebellion of the younger against the older ones.

This cultural observation is relevant to the development of pastoral counseling in this country. In its initial stages the field was developed by young men rebelling against the old methods of pastoral care (or lack of method.) They developed a more disciplined, professionally validated, and empirically sound approach to pastoral counseling. However, the movement itself has been characterized by intense sibling rivalries, with few, if any, father figures against whom to rebel. Nevertheless, the writings and verbal interpretations that pastoral counseling experts place upon these kinds of interaction are invariably psychoanalytic interpretations, i.e., the sibling across the way is rebelling against "an authority figure," presumably a "father-figure"! Nothing could be farther from the truth. This is not rebellion, but competition between siblings. Furthermore, the young pastoral counselor finds himself in competition with other young professionals, and compares himself with psychiatrists, social workers, etc., in a competitive sort of way. So competition, not rebellion, is the prevalent emotion, status threats and not authority problems the key to a clear interpretation of conflict.

Protestant pastoral counselors, therefore, will be more in touch with reality by de-emphasizing the father-figure dimension of Catholicism and psychoanalysis and exploring the distinctly Protestant understanding of the "brother-man relationship." The Protestant pastoral counselor deters men who bow before him and say that the gods have come to them in the form of man. As a brother-man he confesses that he is a man of like passions with them, that he is a brother in the faith as well as in sin. The liturgy of confession of the Greek Orthodox Church, which was quoted in a previous chapter, poignantly underscores this. The priest himself says that he, too, is a sinner. He eases the tension of overconstructed transference relationships in which the pastor tries to relate himself, for example, to women counselees as a father to a daughter when actually he is only a few years apart from them in age. Furthermore, he would be much more effectively and realistically related to them if he saw them and enabled them to see him as a brother-man to a sister-woman as the Pastoral Epistles advise. Both brother-man and sister-woman are responsible to and for each other in Christ. Thus the love that develops between them can be a durable kind that does not call for "breaking" the relationship and "discharging" the patient. Such slavishness to developing and breaking transferences is inappropriate to the pastoral identity, even though it is admirably adapted to the psychoanalytic identity. Rather, as we shall see later, the pastor is counseling in the context of a durable fellowship. People rightfully expect unbroken relationships of the Christian community. Relationships must be so perceived and established from the beginning that they can be maintained durably. A father-child relationship cannot be so maintained. A brotherly relationship can. A pastor is not counseling in the context of a choice of patients, a fee-taking structure, and a purposefully broken relationship upon having "completed the treatment." Whatever treatment is offered by the Christian fellowship should be established with the clear view in mind that it is eternal; it changes its form but not its reality.

THE PASTOR AS A FAMILY MAN

The Protestant pastor functions as a counselor within the context of his identity as a married man. He is usually a married man with children. Roland Bainton in his discussion of the life and work of Martin Luther says that "the influence of the man on his people was deepest in the home. In fact, the home was the only sphere of life which the Reformation profoundly affected. This profound effect is symbolized in the fact that the Protestant pastor himself is a married man." (Bainton, *Here I Stand*, p. 384.) This distinguishes him radically from the celibate ministry of the Catholic Church. A part of his total counsel to the community is the witness he bears to his people through his own home. The rectory, the manse, or the parsonage quite often provide both the time and the place for certain kinds of counseling done by the Protestant pastor. The shaping environment of his home gives an air of informality and social involvement to his counseling which inevitably must be taken into consideration when he activates his role as a pastoral counselor.

When the pastor assumes the role of counselor, his relationship to his wife and family participates nonverbally in his relationship to his counselee. The pastoral counselor wisely refrains from discussing confessional confidences with his wife. However, he may discover that his wife definitely needs to know certain information by reason of her own responsible involvement with the life of the counselee. Furthermore, he may also discover that his wife serves as something of an "intake interviewer" for persons who are "testing her out" as to whether or not the problem they have in mind is the kind that should be called to the pastor's attention. Likewise, his wife will be called upon to give supportive help to disturbed counselees who call when he is out of the city or for some other reason is not available. For example, the report of one pastor's wife is pertinent:

A pastor's wife said that one of her husband's counselees called her while her husband was out of the city. Upon having discovered that the pastor was away, the counselee asked the pastor's wife if the pastor had discussed her problem with her. The pastor's wife assured her that he had not. Then the counselee proceeded to catch her up on what she had told the pastor, and to seek some emotional reassurance and comfort from the pastor's wife. In fact, this was such an extended conversation by telephone that the pastor's wife had to neglect certain needs in the home in order to talk with the person!

Obviously, furthermore, the fact that the pastor's children often know their father's counselees is another shaping factor. For example, one pastor said:

An employee of the local post office went on periodic alcoholic binges. He would call me when he was drunk, but never when he was sober. I scheduled interviews with him. We developed a durable relationship. On occasions he would call when I was busy talking with someone else in the home. I noticed my sixteen-year-old son answer the phone on one occasion. The drunken man on the other end of the line asked him if, inasmuch as I was busy, my son would mind talking with him. My son took the matter quite seriously and carried on an extended conversation with him. He became of great interest to my son, and the alcoholic conversed with him even when not drunk. They formed a deep friendship.

Furthermore, when it is known to a counselee, even in a very formal and highly structured situation of pastoral counseling, that the pastor is indeed a pastor, the counselee tends to feel obligated to respond in some way to the pastor's family. This is especially true when the counselee is a participant member of a church. For example, on one occasion I was counseling in a family-relations center in our city. Although I was functioning in an implicitly pastoral capacity, I was not explicitly the pastor of a church. The counseling was done at regular appointment times in a downtown clinic. Inadvertently, the counselee with whom I was conferring had discovered through another member of her own church that my youngest son was a patient in the hospital. She felt the need to visit my wife and son and to let my wife know of her concern for our son. One could interpret this as an expression of overtones of anxiety and guilt because of transference of feelings toward the counselor. However much of this may have been present, I prefer to see the situation as a typical expression of her cultural pattern of involving the pastor and his family in the ongoing process of the pastoral care and counseling relationship.

Basic appreciation for the family dimension of a pastor's counseling points up a growing conviction that the pastor's identity as a married and family man is integral and not accidental to his relationship as a counselor. However, the role of the minister's wife herself needs the kind of close scrutiny that we find in the excellent research work of Wallace Denton in his book *The Role of the Minister's Wife* (The Westminster Press, 1962), which is the first research-based volume on the identity and function of the minister's wife.

Furthermore, the research being conducted by William O. Douglas of Boston University School of Theology under the auspices of the Lilly Foundation promises help in more accurately identifying the ways and the means whereby the pastor's wife is involved in his work as a counselor. Remarkably enough, Denton discovered that the parsonage "has been able to retain more of its traditional functions than many other homes in our society, thus contributing to the minister's wife's sense of worth and value and averting a sense of uselessness characteristic of some housewives in our industrial society"

(Denton, *op. cit.*, p. 146). He also notes that the minister's wife's role expectations "in smaller communities are more clear-cut and insistent than in larger communities" (*ibid.*, p. 149). The minister in the larger, more urban community develops a distinctly formal and more professional kind of pastoral counseling than does the minister in the smaller and more informal community in which his family is so intimately involved in every aspect of his work. Yet, in both instances, the possibility of inflammation in interpersonal relationships arising due to the wife's suspicion of the minister's work as a counselor and her resentment at having to carry the kinds of disciplines that she does are very high. In fact, more than one training center for ministers and pastoral counselors effectively involves the wife in the process of training the pastor.

The growth of tenderness in the Protestant pastor should be a normal result of his being happily and creatively married. This is most important. The caring aspect of a pastor's being is nourished and cherished by his having "been turned in his heart" to his wife and children. Whatever gentleness he has bears witness to his counselees through the tacit and non-verbal actions of his relation to his family. For example:

A woman parishioner called her pastor and asked him if she could see him that evening. It was five o'clock then. He had had a long day and had not seen his children all day. He asked her if it would be at all possible for her to see him the next morning at nine o'clock in his office rather than to come by his home that evening as she had suggested. She immediately agreed to do so. He gave as his reasons for this request that he had not seen his children that day. She understood and said she would see the pastor the next day as scheduled. On the next day the pastor saw her when he himself was in a much more relaxed and refreshed frame of mind. He saw her under conditions of appropriateness in his office. During the conversation she expressed gratitude that he had guarded his time with his children. One of her complaints was that her own husband left the whole care of the children on her!

This last instance demonstrates that the pastor in a Protestant parish is, by reason of his identity as a married family man, constantly under the pressure of demands to ignore his responsibility to his wife and children. Therefore, as a pastoral counselor, he can "structure" his relationships to people in such a way that the factors of time, initiative, privacy, and a clearly defined role can be used to minister more effectively to their real needs as counselees. At the same time doing so protects his family from too much outside interference and exploitation. Nor does he thoroughly jade his energies by trying to meet too many demands in one day.

THE PROTESTANT PASTOR'S SOCIAL CLASS IDENTITY

The socially dynamic characteristics of the Protestant pastor's role, particularly as he does his work in America, tend to coerce him into an overidentification with one or two social classes. He is directly dependent for his livelihood upon the people with whom he counsels. This coerces him too much. The only employee that many people have is their pastor. Therefore they feel they have a right, even apart from the corporate decisions of the fellowship of the church, to decide for him in too many instances what he should be doing and how he should be using his time. The second coercive factor that overidentifies the pastor with a certain social class is that he is a married man, ordinarily with children. His decisions "to please or not to please" his congregation are often determined by his responsibility to meet both the needs and the desires of his wife and children. The wishes of his congregation and the desires of his family for him to live at a certain level of economic affluence make it necessary for him to spend most of his time working directly with the persons in the community who are most economically capable of supporting the church and its program, which of course includes his salary. This limits the amount of time that he can spend with people who are outside his congregation, and especially those who are not sufficiently affluent to contribute economically to the support of the church. This in turn makes him somewhat of a prisoner of one or two social classes. For example, if he depends entirely upon a highly regimented industrial or rural class of people who usually are in the lower middle class, then his development of the more formal aspects of pastoral counseling tends to be limited by the values of that particular group. Furthermore, the high degree of superficial respectability required by persons in the upper middle and lower upper classes who attend church tends to involve him in a kind of "chummy" social informality. It is very difficult to break through this informality in establishing more serious kinds of counseling relationships.

However, the Christian pastor who has a will to win can, by seriously studying the literature on the rapidly emerging class structure in our allegedly classless society, develop some real ability in breaking through the protective devices of the various social classes with whom he works. Seward Hiltner, in his book *The Christian Shepherd*, has called for a systematic scrutiny of "the actual operations of class" structure in the life of our churches. An understanding of social class structure provides the pastoral counselor with a "knowledge of the pressures that class puts on persons and the assumptions that it gives them [as] an important preliminary to being able to establish contact with many sorts and conditions of men" (Hiltner, *The Christian Shepherd*, pp. 95–96).

The specific problem of initiative in pastoral counseling shows the relevance of the social class factor to the processes of pastoral counseling. How much initiative should the counselor take toward the counselee in establishing a relationship? How much initiative can the counselor expect of the counselee in longer-term counseling? Milton Mason discovered in a field study of a semi-rural community in Kentucky that the rural community expects its pastor to visit. They do not expect to "come to see him" when they are in trouble. (Milton Mason, *Social Status Characteristics in Pastoral Care in a Semi-rural Community*, an unpublished doctoral dissertation, The Southern Baptist Theological Seminary, 1951.) Hollingshead and Redlich aptly observe that, even in the highly structured identity of the psychiatrists of the New Haven, Connecticut, community, the persons under treatment who came from the lower two classes rarely sustained a counseling relationship beyond the second or third interview. The very presuppositions of longer term and more extended counseling and psychotherapy seem to be based upon the types of expectancy and value structures indigenous to the upper classes. The lower-class person is more action-centered. He sees less need for verbal communication. He tends to settle things with few words. (A. B. Hollingshead and F. C. Redlich, *Social Class and Mental Illness: A Community Study;* John Wiley & Sons, Inc., 1958.)

The minister who has been trained in longer term types of pastoral counseling has two alternatives when he is working with the less educated, lower classes of people. First, he may have to use many other forms of pastoral care to accomplish the same objectives that longer term counseling is designed to accomplish. In the second place, the pastor, as is most often true, will likely assume that his role as a counselor is not possible in such a situation. This grows out of his over-attachment and overidentification with the particular social class out of which he has come or his extreme need for approval by the social class into which he has moved by reason of his education as a pastor. Or, in the third place, he may develop skill in patiently defining and redefining his relationship to individual counselees and to his church as a whole. In such ways they are gradually educated to the means whereby a pastor may be more deeply meaningful in the more formal kind of pastoral ministry known as counseling.

THE PROTESTANT PASTORAL COUNSELOR   151

The pastor's capacity to combine his teaching function with
his counseling ministry is the basis on which this last more
optimum alternative stands or falls. Yet it in turn rests quite
heavily upon the social class identity of the pastor himself.
The kind of home in which he grew up and the kind of cultural
binding he feels to the social class out of which he emerged
through the processes of education shape his abilities with a
silent but heavy hand. Many Protestant pastors, particularly
in the churches of the free church tradition, have come from
the lowest and lower classes. We tend to derive our self-
concepts from this heritage. As a result we tend to judge our
role and function as pastor quite heavily on the basis of the
presuppositions of the social classes out of which we ourselves
came. Therefore, social class understanding is not only a part
of the professional training of a good pastor. It is also a part
of his personal insight into himself and control over the energies with which he has been endowed in life. This training
should equip him to clarify his own role at most given times
with the persons to whom he is ministering.

This clarification is necessitated by the basic confusion that
exists in the master and working roles of the Protestant pastor
as he attempts to do his work. This confusion is heavier and
calls for greater efforts at clarification at the point of the
pastor's working role as a counselor. This greater degree of
confusion as to the nature of pastoral counseling is caused by
the relative newness of the more formal conceptions of counseling that are being developed in the pastor's mind. Furthermore, congregations are by lethargy and intent kept ignorant
of the kinds of education that are given their pastors in theological schools.

ROLE CONFUSION IN PROTESTANT PASTORAL COUNSELING

The Protestant pastor's role as a counselor is often confused
and undefined because of his involvement with his counselees
as neighbor and brother-man in both the informal and formal

relationships of the pastoral community. The pastor has a certain role in the person's life that may or may not be clear to him when that person, in the exigency of a moment, calls upon him for counseling help. This role is undefined in the confused and anxious mind of his counselee. The pastoral counselor must develop a great deal of canniness in clearly understanding himself and in communicating simply to the counselee the exact nature of his responsibilities as a pastor at any given moment. Whereas this responsibility for clarification rests upon all counselors, it rests more distinctly upon the shoulders of the Protestant pastoral counselor than any other. For example, the Protestant pastoral counselor does not have the kind of control either institutionally or professionally over his relationships as do other counselors, such as doctors. The doctor has a definite schedule: the patient always takes the initiative toward him; he can accept or reject the patient as one whom he is qualified to treat, or he may terminate a relationship to a given patient through referral or discharge. This quite clearly defines his role, as compared with the work of the minister. The Protestant minister, more often than not, does not have the institutional and clerical control on his relationship comparable to those of a Catholic priest or Hebrew rabbi. Even in the most liturgical situations, the Protestant pastoral counselor does not have as much explicitness of authority, the distinct clerical garb, or the forensic structures with which to define his relationship to his counselees as does the priest and rabbi.

Therefore, the Protestant pastor must be alert and capable of understanding the difference between a *confused* interpersonal relationship, an *informal* relationship, and a *formal* relationship. His approach, technique, and resources in dealing with these varied kinds of relationships will be radically different. Therefore, it is imperative that this concluding section of the theoretical presuppositions of the Protestant pastoral counselor in action include a careful discussion of these three kinds of relationships.

The Confused Relationship

The confused or unclarified relationship is one in which a pastor is seeking to discharge his formal responsibility as a pastor, and particularly as a pastoral counselor, in an informal, uncontrolled, undefined, unclarified situation. Usually this is because he does not understand the difference between a formal and an informal relationship. It may be because he rejects the more formal aspects of being a pastor. Or it may be due simply to neglect if he fails to clarify his relationship in conversation with his parishioner, ordinarily assuming that the relationship is clear. As a result he may attempt to communicate with his counselee through the overcast of confusion covering the relationship.

This confusion can come about in several ways. First, the time factor may be out of control. The person presents a problem under the hurried circumstance of the moments just before a morning service is to begin. The pastor hurriedly attempts to deal with a major difficulty that simply cannot be dealt with in a short preoccupied moment of divided attention. This confuses both him and the counselee. He would have done better to have given brief support, affection, and encouragement and to have rescheduled a time later in which the whole matter could be dealt with more leisurely. Secondly, the place factor may be out of kilter. The pastor may be standing on the corner of the main street of the city. He does not have the privacy that is needed, nor does he have the undivided attention that is required. He would do better to schedule the conference at a later time when he can see the person in the privacy of his counseling room. The privilege of a visit to the pastor's home or study to confer privately about a serious problem is in itself a form of encouragement, and at the same time brings clarity and control into the relationship.

A third way of clarifying a relationship is to be sure that the degree of initiative and responsibility are fairly evenly balanced. One of the hallmarks of the pastoral ministry is that we have the right to take initiative toward people, to go to them, and to express concern about them.

However, we must respect the privacy and the individual freedom of a person in the process of taking initiative. Our objective should be to stimulate their own initiative in such a way that they will want help with whatever degree of initiative we take toward them. In other words, we are confusing our relationship to people when we take full responsibility for all the initiative, and relieve them of the health and strength that comes to them when they are stimulated to be wholesomely concerned about their own destinies. The more typical example of this is when a person asks us to go to see a third person. The relationship is likely to become inflamed and confused if some form of welcome on the part of the third person is not sought. Likewise, it would make for a clearer relationship if the person who requests that the pastor visit the third person would suggest to that person that he come to the pastor or, at best, ask him if he would mind if the pastor visited him. A part of the great skill of being an effective Protestant pastor is in knowing where the line of balance for the initiative between the counselor and the counselee lies. This problem has been dealt with at length in books such as Professor Hiltner's volume on pastoral counseling and the *Introduction to Pastoral Counseling* under the editorship of this author, but suffice it to say here that the confused relationships of Protestant pastoral counselors often are to be attributed to a lack of clarification of the problem of initiative.

The fourth factor in confused relationships that needs clarification is the role in which the minister himself is functioning. The minister is caught up as family member and as neighbor and as personal friend and brother-man in relation to those whom he serves as pastoral counselor. He has anonymous relationships, such as contacts on buses, trains, planes, and in the open community. He has diffuse social relationships in the market place contacts, the recreational and social functions of the community, and the host-guest relationships of his own home. He has personal-friend relationships by reason of the fact that the church is a durable fellowship. These people are his friends. He has family relationships to his wife, his children, to his own siblings, and to his mother and father, as well as to the in-laws and more distant relatives. All these informal relationships are woven into the web of his formal functions as a minister and can be very easily confused with them.

Therefore, a pastor needs to know when and when not to activate the more formal dimensions of his task as a minister, particularly at the point of "structuring" or defining a counseling relationship. When he does this well he demonstrates skill in clarifying both in his own mind, and in that of his parishioner, the exact character of their relationship. They may jointly choose that the minister be related in an informal, supportive way as a friend or explicitly agree that the more distinctly social aspects of their relationship be kept to a minimum while the more serious work of counseling is in process. This is usually done in an exploratory interview in which a "plan is made" and a covenant based on trust and mutual understanding is carefully defined. This evaluative interview is a necessary prelude to any long-term counseling relationship. A spirit of reciprocity and rapport must be developed between the pastor and the counselee if any clear-cut progress is genuinely to be made in further counseling interviews. The pastor himself may, on the basis of a mutual sense of clarity between him and his counselee, decide that a longer-term series of counseling conferences between them is indicated. On the other hand, the pastor may define his role less formally and request referral of the counselee to another counselor who will perform the more detailed and formal functions. Such a counselor may be more detached and thus able to offer more privacy. He may be in a fee-taking relationship and thereby able to give more time on a less guilt-producing basis. He may be less involved in the ongoing life of the counselee and in such a role that he can terminate the relationship at an appropriate time.

In summary, it should be said that the failures of communication between pastor and parishioner, pastor and church, pastor and counselee's family, and pastor and the other professional people in the community are caused by the pastor's lack of clarity as to his own identity as a counselor.

The Professional Freedom of the Protestant Pastoral Counselor

In spite of all of the limitations and ambiguities present in the role and function of the Protestant pastor, when all has been said and done he nevertheless has much individual freedom to develop his work as a counselor in its disciplined and professional connotations. He has not only a call to the ministry but his call implies a discipline and a sense of profession that are important to his identity as a counselor.

As Daniel Jenkins says, we have been too reluctant to understand and accept the professional dimensions of the work of the minister. Enough has been said in this book about the responsibility of a pastor to God, about the involvement of the pastor with his church in so far as he functions as a counselor, and about the distinctly commercial aspects of his role to dispel any of the more popular connotations that surround the word "professional." Nevertheless, this word needs clarification in the sense that it applies to the work of the Protestant pastor as a counselor. What do we mean by "professional"?

In Morris L. Cogan's "The Problem of Defining a Profession" (*The Annals of the American Academy of Political and Social Science,* January, 1955, pp. 105–117), one is painfully disappointed at the nebulous discussion of the ministry's ethical bases for professional identity and action. But he is genuinely helped by Cogan's own definition of a profession in another article:

A profession is a vocation whose practice is founded upon an understanding of the theoretical structure of some department of learning or science, and upon the abilities accompanying such understanding. This understanding and these abilities are applied to the practical affairs of man. The practices of the profession are modified by the knowledge of a generalized nature and by the accumulated wisdom and experience of mankind, which serve to correct the errors of specialism. The profession, serving the vital needs of man, considers first its ethical imperative to be altruistic service to the client. (Morris L. Cogan, "Toward a Definition of Profession," *Harvard Educational Review*, Vol. XXIII, Winter, 1953, pp. 35–50.)

Furthermore, Cogan's summary of the literature on the topic in the sixfold criteria of Abraham Flexner in 1915 serves as an excellent guide for the minister's understanding of himself as a disciplined as well as called servant of God:

(1) Intellectual operations coupled with large individual responsibilities, (2) raw materials drawn from science and learning, (3) practical application, (4) an educationally communicable technique, (5) tendency toward self-organization and (6) increasing altruistic motivation. (Abraham Flexner, "Is Social Work a Profession?" *School and Society*, Vol. 1, June 26, 1915, p. 904.)

A more recent study of professional competence as it is related to quackery and charlatanism has been made by William J. Goode. With a clear sense of history, he outlines the characteristics of a profession in his article, "Encroachment, Charlatanism, and the Emerging Profession," *American Sociological Review*, December, 1960, Vol. 25, No. 6, pp. 902–933. He aptly observes that "in the process of institutionalization the most severe skirmishes would occur between the new profession and the occupation closest to it in substantive and clientele interest." He also points to the history of some professions in which rival training organizations using different standards limit the profession's growth through internal competition. Finally, Goode identifies the historically constant factors in the emergence of a new profession: (1) The profession determines its own standards of education and training. (2) The student goes through a more far-reaching adult socialization than the learner in other occupations. (3) Professional practice is often legally reorganized by some form of licensure. (4) Licensing and admissions boards are manned by members of the profession. (5) The legislation concerned with the profession is shaped by the profession. (6) The occupation gains in income, power, and prestige ranking and can demand higher caliber students. (7) The practitioner is relatively free of lay evaluation and control. (8) The norms of practice enforced by the profession are more stringent than legal controls. (9) Members are more strongly identified and affiliated with the profession than are members of other occupations with theirs. (10) The profession is more likely to be a terminal occupation. Members do not care to leave it, and a higher proportion assert that if they had it to do over again, they would again choose this type of work.

We as ministers become too moralistic when we use the word "professional" as if it were an obnoxious thing. We need to measure our own work as ministers, especially in the context of the local ministerial association, by these standards.

In the first place, the Protestant pastoral counselor is professional in the sense that he has committed all his time to the work of being a pastor. He has disentangled himself from other pursuits. He thrusts himself upon all the risks involved in being dependent upon the church and the role of its ministry for his economic support and his identity as a person. This has called for singular decisiveness on his part. If he remains in the ministry and functions competently, this commitment of his time thrusts upon him the responsibility of developing a clear-cut sense of purpose and identity. As Nelson Foote and Leonard Cottrell have said, "There is an inseparable relationship between identity and interpersonal competence."

This particularly applies to the more distinctly professional aspects of being a minister.

In the second place, interpersonal competence is characteristic of the ministry as a profession. Nelson Foote and Leonard Cottrell aptly describe several aspects of interpersonal competence. These can be applied to the work of the pastor as a counselor in terms of his professional characteristics: He has *intelligence,* which involves a breadth "perception of relationships among events," the ability to "symbolize experience" and to interpret life with "meaningful generalizations." The intelligent person is "articulate in communication." He is skilled in "mobilizing the resources of the environment and experience in the services of a variety of goals." (Nelson N. Foote and Leonard S. Cottrell, *Identity and Interpersonal Competence,* p. 53; University of Chicago Press, 1955.) He has *empathy,* which means that the professional person can "perceive" situations from other people's standpoints. Thus he can anticipate and predict their behavior. Pastoral counseling requires the capacity to "take the role of the other" and "the absence of this is a sign of misunderstanding." (*Ibid.,* p. 54.) He is *autonomous,* which means that the professional person is capable of clarifying his own conception of himself. He maintains independently a "stable set of internal standards by which he acts." He is "self-directed and self-controlled in his actions." He has "confidence in and reliance upon himself," "maintains a reasonable degree of self-respect," and "has the capacity for recognizing real threats to self" and can mobilize "realistic defenses when so threatened." He has *judgment,* which means "the ability to adjudicate among values, or to make correct decisions; the index of lack of judgment (bad judgment) is mistakes, but these are the products of an antecedent process in which skill is the important variable." (*Ibid.*) Referral, consultation with other people than the counselee, even acceptance of responsibility for counseling in the first place, all call for judgment. He demonstrates *creativity,* which means that the professional person has "demonstrated the capacity for innovations in behavior or real reconstruction or any aspect of "his environment." He has the ability to "develop fresh perspectives from which to view all accepted routines and to make novel combinations of ideas and objects and so define new goals, endowing old ones with fresh meaning and inventing means for their realization." (*Ibid.*, pp. 55–57.) The pastoral counselor, particularly in his guidance of his counselees, is capable of inventing or improvising new roles or alternative lines of action in problematic situations and to inspire such behavior in others. Many of his counselees are uncreative persons and continually find themselves in dilemmas and impasses. They are at their wit's end. They are shut up to a rigid adherence to one solution to their problems. A part of the professional competence of a pastoral counselor is to provide the creative kind of relationships in which innovations, inventions, and the discovery of new alternatives is a daily event. In short, this creativity engenders *hope*. When a counselee says: "There is nothing else I can do," often the very process of counseling itself *is* that "something else" that opens new avenues to hopeful existence.

A third characteristic of the pastor as a professional person, as Seward Hiltner has said, is that he has the capacity to define and clarify his responsibilities in terms of basic principles and not just techniques or means. This is one of the efforts of this whole volume. Some emphasis has been given to pastoral counseling as technique, but much attention has been given to the development of the pastor's conception of himself and his understanding of the basic principles upon which his work as a counselor stands. Similarly, this applies to the relationship of a pastoral counselor to his counselee. He is not simply manipulating the person toward a chosen end of his own, but is working with the person in the development of basic principles for living. For example, the care of bereaved persons is based upon the principle of "working through" the various stages of grief. This is the principle; clinical technique grows out of it. Furthermore, marital conflict is a process of deterioration of trust, communication, and covenant. The technique of marriage counseling grows out of a detailed understanding of this process of deterioration.

A fourth characteristic of the pastoral counselor as a professional person rests in his equipment and training. The Protestant Reformation itself shifted the emphasis from the structure of the church to the authority of the Bible as a basis for a pastor's calling. At the same time the identity of the pastor shifted from that of a priestly conveyor of the sacraments of the church to that of a person equipped and trained in the Word of God. The Geneva gown symbolized a minister as a scholar whereas the priestly cassock symbolized the minister as an administrator of the sacraments. Similarly, the Protestant pastoral counselor neither depends upon his "personage" nor the institution of the church for his professional competence as a counselor. He must have submitted himself to the disciplines and training that equip him as a counselor. These disciplines include both the classical and the neotraditional types of training in the pastoral ministry. The Protestant pastoral counseling movement in America has rightly concentrated much attention and energy upon the development of professionally valid forms of clinical pastoral education for the minister. The processes of accreditation, qualification, and authorization of the pastor as a counselor are of great importance to Protestant theological educators.

Finally, the identity of the Protestant pastoral counselor is both challenged by and challenges the calling of other professional people. He is related to the doctor, the psychologist, and the social worker as a brother to a brother, and not as a child to a father. Little wonder is it, therefore, that much of the literature on the interprofessional relationships of the pastor to other disciplines is of an entirely competitive order. Competition itself, immature as it often is, is more desirable than the obeisant and obsequious servility of many pastoral counselors toward the dicta of other professions. Overidentification reflects latent hostility. Such servility is only one step removed from the disdain expressed by many pastors who reject their roles as counselors. Even here their contempt is the sidelong glance of envy. The Protestant pastoral counselor will continue to have a "second-rate citizen" conception of his identity as long as he looks upon his relationship to any other profession as a father-child type of identity. The maturity of the Protestant pastoral counselor requires that he look upon his own work as both calling and profession. He must see his colleagues in other professions as brother-men who have similar problems of professional identity. Their solutions are not necessarily superior to his own, even though he can learn much from them. Rather, on a reciprocal basis of brother-to-brother with other professional people, both may learn new insights that are equally valuable in improving their professional identity. The urgent need in Protestant pastoral counseling today is fellowship with other professions, not capitulation to other professions. In this sense the ministry has a base from which to challenge the other helping professions. Whereas we have been weak in developing our conception of profession, they in turn have tended to lose their sense of ministry in their profession. Therefore, we can challenge them to the same kind of commitment and responsibility to God for the works of their hands that they expect from us as we continue to refine our conception of our own profession. Then we can pray together with them that the eternal God will establish the works of our hands and that his beauty may be upon both of us.

VIII

Protestant Pastoral Counseling as Spiritual Conversation

Protestant pastoral counseling is conversation with a Christian intention. When the King James Version of the Bible was published, the word "conversation" had a richer meaning than it does today. Today we think of conversation as an informal interchange of thoughts by the spoken word, to speak between each other, to talk to each other. But "conversation" in 1611 meant one's life, his manner of living, his "way of existing," to use Paul Tournier's phrase. Conversation had at least three connotations. In the first place, this "way of life" referred to one's spiritual history, his autobiography of sin and rebellion. For example, Paul, in Gal. 1:13 refers to his pre-Christian life in which "beyond measure I persecuted the church of God and wasted it." He calls this his "conversation in time past," as it is translated in the King James Version. In Ephesians, this same phrase, "conversation in times past," refers to the time before their redemption in Christ when Christians "walked according to the course of this world."

In the second place, overtones of the extra-Biblical meaning of the original Greek word *anastrophē* emerge in other uses of the word that the King James Version translates "conversation." In the Septuagint and especially the Apocrypha, the more classical meaning of the term is "a turning back," or a "wheeling about," a metaphor for the total change of direction in one's way of life. This appears in Eph. 4:22, where Christians are enjoined to "put off concerning the former conversation the old man. . . ." They are to be renewed in the spirit of their minds, to "put on the new man, which after God is created in righteousness and true holiness." Radical personal change takes place.

As we probe the meaning of "conversation" in its classical sense a bit further, we see, in the third place, that the word was used to refer not only to one's spiritual past, and to the transformation of his life in Christ, but also to the ultimate ends toward which the life of the Christian moves. For example, the King James Version translates Heb. 13:7: "Remember them which have the rule [or, which are guides] over you, who have spoken unto you the word of God: whose faith follow, considering the end of their conversation." The Revised Standard Version is much clearer: "Consider the outcome of their life."

Seen from these three perspectives, pastoral counseling should be understood as spiritual conversation in its classical meaning. As pastoral counselors we are fellow participants with people as they consider their autobiographies of alienation, estrangement, rebellion, and wasting of the purposes of God. We live with them in the crucial moments of decision when they "wheel about" and change their whole manner of life. We reflect with them, as those whose "conversation is in heaven," on the outcome of their lives. We search for the pulse of the hopes that nourish their daily behavior and the ultimate meanings that sustain them in the afflictions of the present moment.

Therefore, pastoral counseling is not *just* talking with people. Pastoral counseling is not *just* listening to people. Pastoral counseling is not *just* focusing on specific "problems" that must be "solved." Pastoral counseling includes all of these, but it is not *just* any one of them. Pastoral counseling is spiritual conversation, i.e., conversation that takes place either implicitly or explicitly within the commonwealth of eternal life as we know it in Jesus Christ. The way of life we have known in times past, the decisive turnings in our way of life called for in the living present, and the consideration of the end of our existence, our destiny—all these come to focus in the spiritual conversation known as pastoral counseling.

CONTEMPORARY DETERIORATION OF SPIRITUAL CONVERSATION

Thus pastoral counseling is spiritual communication about the durably meaningful things of life as they are separated from the transient things of life. But spiritual conversation has tended to go the way of many fine arts. The oil painting has given way to the photograph. The piano in the living room has been replaced by the hi-fi set. We rely upon mass media of communication for our knowledge of New York, Little Rock, Havana, New Orleans, and Laos. We have less and less face-to-face conversation of any kind, much less spiritual conversation of a special kind. Furthermore, the shorthand slogans of rapid-fire news production create thick insulations of stereotyped thinking. For example, *all* people who prefer liturgical forms of worship may be seen as sophisticated, authoritarian, and snobbish. *All* people who raise *any* question about the wisdom of the 1954 Supreme Court integration decision will be seen as reactionary, fundamentalist, and haters of the Negro. *All* people who feel that integration should take place are seen as "Northerners," "communist-inspired," etc. *All* Southerners are seen as "Bible-worshipers" and *all* Yankees are seen as not being evangelistic enough. These stereotypes are veritable idols of the market place. They are packaged ideas that prevent people from really coming to know each other's way of life.

Another evidence of decay in spiritual conversation today appears in the distinctly *religious shyness* of even the most actively religious people. David C. McClelland, Professor of Clinical Psychology at Harvard, speaks of "the taboo on religion" as a subject of conversation, both privately and publicly. He says that a colleague of his has found the "same condition exists among undergraduates" concerning "religious commitment of any kind." He says that "they talk readily enough about their sex lives, but unwillingly and with great hesitation about their religious convictions. He has concluded that it is "not sex which is a delicate subject in our generation, but religion." (David C. McClelland, "Religious Overtones in Psychoanalysis," *The Ministry and Mental Health,* ed. by H. Hofmann, p. 49; Association Press, 1961.) The forces of repression operate more effectively upon a candid confrontation of basic religious feeling, history, and commitment than upon sexual problems. This suggests that the easy equations and exchanges of the redemptive witness of the New Testament for the mythology of psychoanalysis by pastoral counselors takes the line of least resistance with counselees. Their heaviest resistances are at the point of the ultimate and permanent commitments of their lives, not in the verbalization of sexual conflicts.

But an even more serious deterioration of religious conversation today rests in the exteriorizing of social occasions today. The *objective* of social occasions is to *keep* them superficial, a studied effort at shallowness, quick changes of subject, and the use of various types of social and professional gamesmanship. For example, one knows that he *should* have read a certain "O.K." book. He should be able to pronounce the title, anyway. That is really all he would get the chance to say, accompanied by various types of sighs, grimaces, or gestures of the hands, at the average social occasion. We as theologians are capable of the same superficiality in our use of titles of books we have not read, "headline" intelligences we have picked up on the run from one place to another, and pigeonhole quotations of the latest theologians' most used phrase. The superficiality of social occasions militates against much genuine meeting of the persons attending. Time could be used much more wisely if four people who really wanted to meet each other and to converse with each other would use the same amount of time in meeting for that purpose, i.e., spiritual conversation, the exploration of what life really means or does

not mean to them. For that matter, if husband and wife would
do this periodically, we would have less need of formal counseling. The superficialities of life are the stuff of which sheer
boredom is made. Sheer boredom is the stuff of which latent
and flagrant marital unhappiness is made.

THE FATE OF SPIRITUAL CONVERSATION IN PASTORAL CARE

Historically, at least three things have happened to spiritual
conversation between pastor and parishioner. First, the original proclamation of the Christian message was a two-way
conversation in which Christians bore witness to what God
had done in raising Christ from the dead. He had called them
out of darkness into the light of the knowledge of God in the
face of the living Christ. In return, those to whom they wit-
nessed were free to converse with them, to inquire of them,
and to discuss the meaning of the Scriptures in the light of
these things. But, when the oratorical schools of the Western
world laid hold of the Christian message, they made Christian
preaching something vastly different. Oratory tended to take
the place of conversation. The greatness of the orator took the
place of the astounding event of Jesus Christ. And the dialogue
between speaker and listener faded into a monologue. Only in
pentecostal churches, street preaching, and mental hospitals
are Christian preachers interrupted with responses and questions from the audience. One wonders what would happen if
in a Sunday morning sermon some one were to arise and say:
"Brethren, what shall we do?"

In the second place, the Great Awakening followed the path
of the opening of the Western frontiers of America. To some
extent it is still following it. Evangelism was institutionalized
in the revival and took on a distinctly professional character.
Personal evangelism became a one-way conversation in which
the evangelist did all the talking. This kind of evangelism consists too often in the proposal of general propositions with
little awareness of the meaning of these to the person whose

assent is sought. But the essential problem is that spiritual conversation has collapsed because the relationship is essentially a monologue. Evangelism soon became the emulation of salesmanship just as preaching was transmuted into oratory. In both instances, spiritual conversation deteriorated for monologue's sake.

History has something to teach pastoral counselors at this point. Pastoral counseling has developed in America partially as a criticism of the destruction of the dialogue between pastor and people in perversions of Christian preaching and evangelism. We were taught that we talk too much and do not listen enough. We were positively astounded at the way in which people would respond when we learned the rudiments of listening. But once again we are beginning to lose our perspective by turning the basic dialogue of spiritual conversation into a monologue. We may become enamored of being so completely nondirective that once again genuine conversation between us and our people collapses. The impingement of psychotherapy upon pastoral counseling has taught us much about the processes of communication, but more and more inexperienced theological students are being taught that psychotherapy and pastoral counseling are synonymous. They are no more synonymous than oratory and preaching or evangelism and salesmanship are synonymous. The uniqueness of pastoral counseling emerges, therefore, when we define it as a spiritual conversation that involves both *a meeting* of two persons in the context of the Christian faith and *a dialogue* between them concerning (1) "their way of life in times past," (2) "the decisive turnings in the living present" and (3) the "consideration of the outcome of their life."

THE MEETING

The pastor cannot counsel with someone whom he has never met. Yet his parishioners too often expect him to do so. He himself, under the pressure of their expectations, often attempts to foist his services upon people. A mutually meaningful meeting of minds, a reciprocally understood relationship is necessary for a true dialogue concerning one's total way of life. Four basic elements are prerequisite to an effective counseling relationship. They provide the conditions and the atmosphere of a real meeting of the pastor as a person with the counselee as a person. *First,* the person in need must *want* to meet with the pastor enough to take a measure of *initiative* on his own. The earlier phases of the relationship may result from his having requested a visit from the pastor. But he *did* request it or warmly welcomed a routine visit of the pastor. As the relationship develops, the person should come to see the pastor if he is physically able to do so. *Second,* the pastor should expect a reasonably private, responsibly appointed, and uncompromisingly appropriate place for his counseling. For example, beyond an initial visit or two, he should not attempt to do marriage counseling in the homes of the persons in distress. He should expect them to come to his study or to his own home at a time when other responsible people are in the same building, such as a secretary, the pastor's wife, or one of the lay leaders. *Third,* the pastor should control and determine the time factor himself and not leave this entirely in the hands of the counselee. The length of the interview, the time of the interview, the number of interviews, etc., can be gauged according to the expressed desires of the counselee, but inasmuch as the time of the pastor is at everybody's disposal, he himself has to make the final decisions. *Finally,* the pastor's own role needs to be clearly defined and mutually understood by both himself and his counselees. As has already been said, the pastor has both *formal* relationships *as pastor* to persons in the community and *informal* relationships *as friend and neighbor.* To superimpose either of these upon the other leads to *confused relationships* which are filled with misunderstanding, anxiety, and distortion. The doctor, for example, avoids "curbstone consultations" apart from his controlled settings for treating persons' difficulties. The minister needs to do likewise.

Furthermore, no good doctor attempts to turn a social occasion into a diagnostic interview. The pastor would do much to localize people's difficulties and to keep down unnecessary gossip, conflict, and embarrassment if he would do likewise. Spiritual conversation takes place under responsibly intimate and emotionally healthy conditions. Otherwise, real hindrances to a genuine "meeting of minds" arise between pastor and the person who needs his understanding concerning his "conversation" of life.

Naturally, the pastor's neglect of the basic conditions for effective communication with the counselee poses the major hindrance to a true meeting of minds with his counselees. In addition to this, several other hindrances need to be mentioned. *Insensitivity to social distance* (sometimes known as shyness or timidity) breaks many counseling relationships at the outset. The pastor attempts to overcome the natural distance between him and the counselee by being exceptionally warm, charming, or outgoing. But if he is sensitive to how painful too much "togetherness" and closeness can be to some persons, he will respect the psychic space between himself and them until they stretch forth beyond it to meet him.

In the second place, the counselor needs to examine constantly his need to "help" people, lest it be of such a quality as to render the "helpless" subservient to him, placing them *under* him and him *over* them. This is what H. A. Overstreet has aptly called an "over-under" relationship. His desire to *help* may be in itself a massive assault on the integrity of the person, when the very admission of the need for counseling itself has already made severe inroads on the person's self-confidence. More subtly, the desire to "help" people may be our own taste for the luxury of other people's appreciation. We cannot forever be, as Albert Camus calls it, "eternal pacers of the top deck," enjoying the free breathing of the summits "well above the human ants." (Albert Camus, *The Fall*, pp. 23 f.; Alfred A. Knopf, Inc., 1957.) We must face ourselves and admit that our own need for the feeling of being above people and for having their ingratiating appreciation does more than just hinder our meeting them; it denigrates them as persons.

This is closely related to the third hindrance to meeting a person at the truest level. It springs from the marketing orientation of our whole culture in which we *use* people as things rather than meet them as persons. Long before Martin Buber made the I-Thou relationship lucidly and qualitatively different in our minds from the I-It relationship, Augustine distinguished between two sorts of love. *Frui* to him was a love that "enjoys"; *uti* was a love that "uses" its object. (Augustine, *Concerning Christian Doctrine,* I. iv. 4.) We *use* a plane or a train or a car to go to our home; but we *enjoy* our home for its own sake alone! This is particularly applicable to the Westminster Catechism's statement concerning the chief end of man. We glorify God and *enjoy* him forever! He is the absolute end of our striving, and we seek nothing else beyond him. In counseling, we really meet people and proclaim the unconditional love of God when we show them the appearing of the Lord Jesus Christ in the starkness of their suffering and minister to them, not for appreciation or as a means to our own self-elevation, but "in his name."

THE DIALOGUE

Such a meeting is the beginning of dialogue. Once the initial shock of unbelief and astonishment has worn off, the work of the Holy Spirit has genuinely begun to take place when the counselee accepts the pastor as someone who seeks nothing at all. Spiritual conversation can now begin. A reciprocal relationship exists between the goals and the techniques of pastoral counseling. The goal of the conversation determines the means used, and the means used reflect that character of the goals of the conversation in God.

It is no digression to say that the goals of pastoral counseling are related to but different from the goals of medical therapy.

Medical therapy takes responsibility for the removal of crippling symptoms. Whereas physicians like Tournier and Frankl do not consider the removal of symptoms as unrelated to the patient's way of life, nevertheless they cannot abrogate responsibility for the removal of symptoms. Whereas ministers in counseling do not consider the parishioner's way of life unrelated to his health, they nevertheless cannot accept medical responsibility for the removal of symptoms. This fine and moving line of differentiation between medicine and religion provides a boundary-situation in which ministers and doctors discover, on the one hand, the healing power of the Christian faith, and, on the other hand, the basic aspect of ministry in the calling of the doctor. The Protestant understanding of the ministry as being rooted in the priesthood of all believers would affirm the work of the doctor as the witness to the healing intention of God. On the other hand, the focus of the conversation about the relationship between the doctor and the minister is upon their relationship to God and not upon competitive role-distinctions in society.

The position taken here is that the minister's task is to help psychiatrists to understand better what they are doing in religious terms and at the same time to learn from the psychiatrist more about the conflict-weary and estranged condition of man. The minister may consider it his task to become a psychotherapist in the medical sense of the word, but his time can be more effectively used in development of the religious understanding of life in all of the helping professions of which psychotherapy is only one. For example, overconcentration in psychotherapy may cause the pastor to neglect the religious significance of the work of the public-school teacher, the college professor, the social case worker, and the other persons whose vocation is more deeply relevant to the relief of human distress.

THE PROCESS OF PASTORAL COUNSELING

The dialogue of pastoral counseling consists of a series of progressively more profound and complex meetings or interviews. Regardless of how many interviews take place, the dialogue tends to move through several phases. A careful analysis of these phases accentuates the inner content of the spiritual conversation known as pastoral counseling. Four phases need close scrutiny: the phase of the removal of threat, the phase of participant understanding, the phase of making covenants, and the phase of community interaction.

The Removal of Threat

The person who seeks counseling assistance is filled by and surrounded by conflict. These conflicts represent threats to his clear sense of selfhood. He is confused as to his heritage, his calling, and his destiny. The process of counseling is initiated in an atmosphere of threat that must be patiently transmuted into an atmosphere of secure trust and release of the tension of these threats. The nature of these threats can be described somewhat as follows.

The threat of domination. Both the counselor and the counselee are in a potential position of slave and master. The threat of domination and submission must be removed before an effective understanding can be initiated. The counselor can dominate the counselee with his role, his authority, and his charm. The counselee can dominate the counselor by giving him deadlines of time, by demanding authoritative answers, by complimenting or criticizing, or by simply refusing to talk except when questioned. The end result in either instance is what has already been described as an over-under relationship. By the mutual or reciprocal process of self-encounter and self-revelation, these threats can be removed. For example, a young woman, who was engaged to a divorced man, perched aggressively on the edge of her seat and told her pastor: "I want you to tell me what our church teaches about this business of divorce." In her mind she had determined, it was later discovered, that if he said the church forbade her to marry this man, she was going to get up and walk out. Instead, the pastor said: "Let us explore what this means to you. Then we can discover together what the meaning of the teachings of the church is for you. I would rather for us to learn these things together than for me to hand it down to you as a sort of edict." Thereupon the threat of domination on both sides began to relax considerably.

The threat of meaninglessness. The relationship of pastor to counselee often does not get beyond one or two interviews because neither the counselor nor the counselee find any meaning in what is happening. The counselee may perceive the counselor as a person who in one interview can "give" him the answer to his problem. The possibility of more than one interview has to be interpreted to such people in such a way as to make more than one interview meaningful. Better than this, the kind of understanding and acceptance the counselor demonstrates in the first interview may be such as to leave the person feeling that he or she has only begun to speak clearly of what is concerning them. This is the best removal of the threat of meaninglessness for which we could hope. But without such a removal of the threat of meaninglessness, the conversation tends to be dissipated. In any event, when meaninglessness takes over, the counselee usually verbalizes it by saying, "I don't see any point in continuing to come here." Or, he may say, "Where is all this getting me, and what is this all about anyway?" More often than not, he does not say any of these things. He simply does not come back, or forgets his appointments, or makes excuses for not carrying through a counseling relationship. He often has little or no awareness of *why* he did not return.

Or, on the counselor's side of the relationship, he himself may discover that he and a given counselee are "not getting anywhere," that he is bored by the counselee, or that he feels he "is doing more harm than good." The counselor has to probe his own motives as to *why* he gives much time to one person and does not give any to another. The answer will lie in the candid interpretation of the meaning of the one counselee to him and the absence of meaning of another to him. Intensive research into the motivations of counselors needs to be done. As Professor James Dittes says, the minister's own chief rewards in counseling "are not in the long-range effectiveness but in the immediately available evidence within the relationship that the minister feels he is understanding and being understood." (James Dittes, "Psychology and a Ministry of Faith," *The Ministry and Mental Health*, p. 145.) In other words, the ministry of counseling itself holds out the hope of relevance for the minister himself. Meaningfulness is reciprocally necessary for a given counseling relationship, both for the counselee and for the counselor. The absence of it in either can be sensed by the other and is usually sensed as a vague and nameless threat. This threat must be removed if the relationship is to grow.

The threat of exposure. The person who comes for counseling to his pastor usually is suffering from isolation and fear of rejection by others. He may or may not have done things about which he does not wish others to know. He may or may not want the fact that he has sought assistance from the pastor to be known to others. On the other hand, the pastor accepts a measure of responsibility for the counselee's "story." Just knowing some things is a heavy load to carry, especially when a pastor is responsible to the church as well as to the individual. On both sides, the pastor and the counselee live under the threat of exposure. How can this threat be removed? It can best be removed by the establishment of a *covenant of communication.*

A covenant of communication is much more than a promise not to tell anything the person has said, which may or may not be a wise thing to promise. A covenant of communication consists of a *mutual* understanding that both the counselor and the counselee will consult with each other *before* either of them discusses their conversation with anyone else. Thus, no one is told what has been discussed without the permission of the other to do so. Thus information will fall into at least three different categories depending upon the degree of threat of exposure inherent within the information. First, there is *community knowledge*. The pastor receives information from the counselee that is commonly known in the community. Such information may be a matter of public record if it has appeared in the local newspapers. Or, it may be known by a considerable number of other people and is therefore common information. Much that the unsuspecting pastor receives as "confidential" information is of just this order of knowledge. The person himself may have told this to many other people, each one having been told "in confidence." He probably has forgotten about these persons, and when one of them reminds him of it he is likely to think that the pastor has betrayed him. Consequently, it is standard clinical procedure for the pastor to find out to whom the counselee has talked about his problem.

Second, there is *privileged communication*. This is information which the pastor or the counselee may pass on if the other gives him the privilege of doing so. Usually, this is the kind of privilege which is granted for the communication of necessary information to other professional people who may be called upon as referral sources. Case conferences among professional people fall into this category of relationships in the use of information. The main feature of this is that privilege is granted only when necessity prevails. The question arises as to whether a pastor's wife should know about his counseling relationships. Quite often it is necessary that she know in order that she may accept her share of responsibility or in order that she may react appropriately in behalf of the counselee at times. But it is not always necessary, and when necessity does arise, the counselee should be consulted beforehand. Third, there is strictly *confidential information*. Here the counselor receives information in the most precise manner. In fact, even privileged communication is strictly confidential beyond the circle of those with whom the counselee has given the pastor privilege to confer. But ordinarily confidential information refers to that which the counselor confides to *no* one else. Usually this information is of a confessional nature, i.e., the minister received it as unto God and not unto himself. He was privileged to listen as the person told this to God, not to him. This kind of information, even within professional relationships, calls for a certain depth and quality of understanding between two people. No other person should be allowed to have the knowledge until he has this kind of relationship, and the person chooses to tell it.

However, the pastor needs to be extremely careful how he accepts such confidences. If the counselee confides it in another person, the pastor has the right to know who that person is if the necessity arises. He should at some time or other in the relationship make this clear to the counselee. This is a part of the reciprocal nature of the covenant of communication. If effectively established and clearly accepted, such a covenant tends to remove the threat of exposure. However, as we shall see in the next chapter, a suspiciously oriented person will bring confusion to this covenant in a variety of ways.

The threat of irresponsibility. Such a covenant as has just been described mutually allocates responsibility to the counselor and counselee. But this uncovers another threat: the threat of irresponsibility. Talking with other people outside the counseling relationship can be done either in a responsible or an irresponsible way. This is true of other aspects of the relationship also. For example, the pastor may have made it very clear that an effective counseling situation must be carried on in his office under discreetly private conditions. A given counselee, however, may insist upon turning every given social occasion into a rehearsal of personal problems. All the while he avoids making an appointment to deal more formally with them. Furthermore, the person who comes for the interview may distort what was actually said in the interview and leave on the community impressions severely threatening to the pastor. The pastor, in turn, may be panicky at hearing the nature of the problems the person has to tell and make a referral before his own relationship has deepened enough for his word about the referral to be understood. He may throw up his hands in helplessness and say, "There is nothing I can do to help you." On both sides of the encounter, irresponsibility can threaten the whole relationship. The solid ground of mutually shared responsibility for dealing reciprocally with the problem must be established. The threat of irresponsibility must be faced and removed before any effective counseling actually takes place. In the event this cannot be removed, the pastor should limit his relationship to that degree of responsibility which he can effectively discharge. For example, the person who refuses to discuss his problem with him except as an informal friend in social situations can be treated as a supportive friend treats his friends, but not as a person who is seriously attempting to deal responsibly with problems. Or the person, when he asks a blunt question, "What can I do about this?" can be told tactfully that there are persons in the community who can help him. He can be referred to other counselors. The pastor who is panicked by the story of a counselee can tell the person what he *can* do before he tells him what he cannot do. This gives support and removes threat.

The threat of dishonesty.   The hidden agenda in most counseling relationships is the threat of dishonesty, the possibility that one or the other person is being "phony." The danger, for example, in ministers being psychologically oriented rests in the fear people have of being "tricked" or "manipulated" by individuals who "use a little psychology" on them. This is a hideous distortion of the picture of the well-trained and competent psychologist, but it represents the threat of dishonesty nevertheless. As one counselee said, "Are you saying that because it is really true or because you think it will be psychologically helpful to me to say it?" The evidence for authenticity of utterance, of genuineness, cannot be manufactured. Basic honesty calls for self-examination as a way of life on the part of the pastoral counselor. He must renounce hiddenness and practice openness and candor. On the other hand, he must examine his own suspiciousness. He must look relentlessly at his sensitivity to being imposed upon, at his fear of being used and managed by the counselee, and at his need to be cleverer than the counselee.

The Phase of Participant Understanding

The removal of threat from a relationship develops an atmosphere of trust and security. Mutual responsibility provides a basis for both counselor and counselee treating each other as persons and not as means to some ulterior ends. Now they can participate with each other with understanding and purpose as they seek to resolve whatever difficulties the counselee is facing. They focus upon these difficulties. The counselor participates in the world-view of the counselee to the limit of his vision. As Heidegger says, he allows the self of the counselee "to see from itself that which it shows itself, as it shows itself from itself." He empties himself of his own perspective and participates with understanding in the perspective of the counselee. He does not, for that matter, *just* sit and listen when what is being said is not really understood. He seeks to clarify what the person is saying in such a way that it means as nearly as is possible the same thing to the counselor that it means to the counselee.

Understanding past and present. This self-revelation of the counselee has a specific time reference. His conversations consist largely of an alternating penetration into present difficulties punctuated by intermittent flash backs into the past. He discusses how things have always been in times past. All the while the present difficulties are being understood somewhat differently than before. The judgment of the present upon the past brings new interpretations to the times past and vice versa. For example, the person is likely to say: "I used to think, . . . but now it looks different." During this phase of the dialogue, the pastor actively listens by letting the person talk, by providing undivided attention, and by insisting upon really understanding what the counselee means by what he says. A good measure of attention will be devoted in a later chapter to the nature and importance of the religious history. Suffice it to say here that the process of pastoral counseling consists in a measure of bringing the past and the present to focus realistically upon each other. This is not the abstract process of "getting facts" from the counselee; rather, it is the living process of participating in the interpretation and reinterpretation that present and past bring to each other.

Conflicts of values. The pulling power of a participant kind of listening brings to the counselee's clear level of attention the excruciating conflicts in his value systems and in his feelings toward the people who represent these values in his life. He peers through an astringent, eye-smarting spiritual smog filled with the fumes of a technological culture. He tries to discern "between the things that differ," to sense what is vital and to disentangle himself from the dead weight of what is not vital. He has to make decisions as to the validity of the way of life that led him to the plight in which he finds himself. He ponders the meaning of those acts which he committed which seemed at the time to be done by someone else and not he himself, a sort of "not-me." Then he finds a kinship with his own acts that enables him to confess that in deed and in truth it was he who did them. For them *he* was responsible.

One little girl's mother scolded her, saying: "Mary! Only the devil could have made you push your little brother down the stairs and kick him in the face!" She replied: "The devil made me push him down the stairs, Mother. But kicking him in the face was my own idea!" If she had been a contemporary adult, she would probably have said some psychological truism like: "An uncontrollable impulse got hold of me when my little brother came around, and Mother's rejection of me made it worse." She would have learned how to interpret her own experience as a means of avoiding responsible decisions. In other words, she could say: "It was 'not me' but my parents who did this thing." But in the process of patient and participant listening, a decisive struggle is going on as to one's own responsibilities, the things he has done which are his own ideas. The conflict of values comes to the surface in the pastoral counseling relationship. The counselee runs a hard course between a darkened, compulsive, overscrupulous conscience on the one hand, and, on the other, the temptation to use the popular distortions of psychology and religion as a means of avoiding self-encounter, personal responsibility, and mature decisions.

Self-encounter. The acceptance of responsibility for oneself as he is involves making decisions as to the kind of person one really is. One meets himself in the dialogue of pastoral counseling. This is true of both the counselee and the counselor. One learns of his typical mode of life, his characteristic ways of handling his existence, his own particular ways of reacting to life. We shall discuss this at length in the next chapter, also, and the detailed patterns of self-encounter provide avenues of understanding between counselor and counselee. The point that needs to be made here is that this self-encounter is *reciprocal* at every step of the way. The counselor and the counselee both bring a distinct pattern of life to the relationship. The counselor is a trained person, but his training has made him an unauthentic being if he simply "plays a role," "acts a part," or "poses" a certain way for effect. This is the fallacy of stereotyping one particular method of counseling as normative for all relationships. Men avoid real encounter with their counselee when in behalf of a given method they react in unnatural, unauthentic, or devised ways even in the counseling situation itself. This in itself is a form of masking or avoidance of encounter.

Yet, another aspect of this needs to be emphasized. To be one's genuine self without retreat behind an assumed "pose" makes one vulnerable indeed. The vulnerability of the self involves risk in the encounter. Yet without this vulnerability, the counselee does not learn to meet himself as in deed and in fact he really is. Consequently, the process of self-encounter is more often short-circuited by focusing upon "problems," by shadow-boxing with ideological positions, and by retreating behind one stereotype after another. This kind of self-avoidance can also be reciprocal in such a way that no genuine conversation ever really takes place. This kind of studied avoidance of self-encounter particularly abounds in premarital pastoral counseling. The minister may see himself as a "friend of the family," as a "functionary of the church or state," as a counselor whose task it is to participate in the processes of understanding of the meaning of marriage. The couple may see him only as incidental to the whole procedure, as spiritual guide and interpreter of the meaning of their marriage, or as a person who asks too many embarrassing questions. Probably no particular kind of counseling which a pastor does is as fraught with as much avoidance of real self-encounter as pre-marital counseling.

But the decision to "face up to oneself" is in itself a turning point in the counseling relationship. This marks a "wheeling about" of direction in the processes of understanding. One has really taken hold of the resolving, deciding, and determining powers with which he is endowed. A definite converting of direction in his life has set in. At the very core of our need to *solve* problems is the prior necessity that the counselee *re*solve to meet himself. The counselor can provide the atmosphere in which this can take place. He can create safe and threatless conditions under which it can happen. He can wait patiently while it takes place. But he cannot make this resolution *for* the counselee. Only the counselee himself can do this. A large part of the inner wisdom of counseling rests in the patience of the counselor to wait this out and the skill with which he maintains the confidence of the counselee while waiting. Once the counselee has resolved to encounter himself as he really is, however, the relationship moves into a new phase called *the covenant-making* phase of counseling.

The Covenant-making Phase

Binswanger and others emphasize the nature of man as a "person who is responsible for his existence choosing" sort of being. (*Existence*, ed. by Rollo May and others, p. 41; Basic Books, Inc., Publishers, 1958.) In other words, man is capable of awareness of his own existence, feels responsible for his existence, and makes choices as to what he is going to do with his life. On the other hand, Martin Buber and Richard Niebuhr speak of man as a "promise-making, promise-keeping, promise-breaking being, as a man of faith." (H. Richard Niebuhr, *Radical Monotheism and Western Culture*, p. 41; Harper & Brothers, 1960.) One can go farther and say in these two respects that the image of God in man becomes vividly clear: God himself is a responsible God and has in history made the decision to be in Christ. He makes promises and keeps them. He makes covenants, in other words. He relates himself to man within these covenants. The supreme covenant is the New Covenant in Jesus Christ.

The distinct characteristic of Protestant pastoral counseling is that the covenant-making responsibility of man and the covenant of faith in Jesus Christ provide the focal center of the meaning of Protestant pastoral counseling. The Holy Spirit works within man both to will and to do God's own pleasure. A covenant within an individual or a group begins forming deep in the recesses of the unconscious. This covenant is consciously focused upon the frustration the person is suffering. It focuses and refocuses several times before the consummatory covenant is formed. These events of concentration may be called covenants in themselves in a progression of spiritual maturity. They are the covenant of confrontation, the covenant of confession, the covenant of forgiveness and restitution, and the covenant of concern. All of them require decision as to the existence of the individual or group.

The covenant of confrontation. The choice between fantasy and reality is made at the inmost recesses of a person's being. This is a painfully difficult decision because there is always just enough of reality in any fantasy to make it seem "really" real. But the dreamlike quality of this reality is such that psychological mechanisms of isolation, projection, displacement, rationalization, and, most of all, repression, must be used to make up the difference between the world in which the person as a self exists and the world that exists around him in fact. The person at some point takes a stand, makes a decision, resolves to face life as it is and not as he would like to have it be. He chooses not to try to recast "the sorry scheme of things" after his own inner design but to face up to life the way it is, with all its ambiguity, injustice, and frustration. This is really a covenant with oneself and with life itself. This covenant calls for courage, but the courage itself is an unmustered courage. This courage comes from the patience and understanding the person has already received as he has "been understood" by God and by his pastor.

But simply understanding and being understood are not ends within themselves. They lay the groundwork and provide the courage whereby the individual is *en*couraged to make a covenant to confront life itself as it is. The forces of resolve are counteracted by other forces of resistance. A conflict rages. But the individual covenants, as Perls, Hefferline, and Goodman put it, "to stand out of the way, to give the threat all (his) powers, and . . . to relax useless deliberateness, to let the conflict rage and destroy what must be destroyed." (Frederick Perls, Ralph Hefferline, Paul Goodman, *Gestalt Therapy: Excitement and Growth in Human Personality*, p. 359; The Julian Press, Inc., Publishers, 1951.) This, put in Biblical terms, is like the prodigal son "coming to himself" and choosing, whatever the cost, to face life rather than to run from it, to encounter life as it is rather than to live in a dream world of imagination, however important and treasured the imagination may be.

The covenant of confession. In the phase of participant understanding, the counselee may have told the pastor many details about himself. But pastoral counseling is not just a matter of "getting the facts," of extracting a history, from the individual. These facts must be confronted on a deeper level of reality, and this takes time. The covenant of confrontation sets this process of "working through" into motion. Then the individual resolves to confess his own resolution to change to

God. Until now his anxiety and guilt have been directed toward first one person and then another in his field of interpersonal relationships. The covenant of confrontation is followed by a resolve to relate these to God. The human idols whom the individual has both worshiped and desecrated are the source and targets of anxiety and guilt. The covenant of confession transmutes anxiety and guilt into a clearly focused sense of sin in relation to God and God alone. This refocuses the whole perspective of the counselee. The things he considered as heinous wrongs before appear to be trivial now. The things he did not consider at all become great in his mind. The vast difference between anxiety and guilt on the one hand and a clear sense of sin on the other hand resides in the fact that one is related to one's fellow human beings and the other is related to God. That which our mothers, fathers, brothers, sisters, husband or wife would consider a very grievous wrong would be easily overlooked by God. That which they would never think of would be foremost in our relationship to God, namely, our prideful unteachableness, our unwillingness to forgive, and our idolatry. The covenant of confession is in relation to God as he is known in Jesus Christ. Here is One who tells us all that we have ever done and yet accepts us, receives us, forgives us. Entry into this covenant of confession activates a deeper resolve in the counselee: a covenant of forgiveness and restitution.

The covenant of forgiveness and restitution. The person who feels that he has been accepted and forgiven moves to reconsider all the other relationships of his life. The counselee who has faced his own humanity and been accepted by God is more permissive with those about him. He ceases to expect perfection of others and can make more room for their personal shortcomings. Even though they have committed grievous errors, he can reassess his relationship to them and be more forgiving toward them. The commitment to do this is a covenant of forgiveness for the wounds one has received. This in turn reminds one of the wounds he has inflicted in the conflict with others. He is likely to discuss with the pastoral counselor at this stage the various things he can do to make restitution and to repair damages he had inflicted. This is a covenant of moral responsibility which reflects the distinctly ethical task of the pastoral counselor. One clinical note from the annals of Alcoholics Anonymous becomes relevant in most counseling relationships that reach this stage of maturity. The Alcoholic Anonymous agrees to make amends to those whom he has harmed, "except where to do so would cause more harm." Thus the covenant of forgiveness and restitution is such as to redeem and not to perpetuate the sufferings arising between people.

The covenant of concern. The genuinely profound changes that can and do take place in pastoral counseling can and do issue in a new covenant of concern on the part of the person who has changed and been changed. This is a much more crucial stage of pastoral counseling than is true of other forms of counseling. The professional counselor, for instance, has a fee-taking structure through which the counselee regularly expresses his concern and gratitude through the fees that he pays. But the pastoral counselor has the resources of the church itself to which to relate the person's concerns for other people, and especially for him as a person. However, the pastor may be so impressed by the superficial changes that have taken place in the reordering of his counselee's life that he will ignore the significance of the counselee's need to express his or her gratitude. The subtle adoration of the counselor himself may be the way the counselee covenants to make this concern known. For example, Jesus was acutely aware of the Gadarene demoniac's gratitude when the man wanted to go with him wherever he went. Rather, he sent him back to his own home village as a witness to his recovery. This was probably the most difficult thing the man could have been assigned. But Jesus chose to deflect the man's adoration from himself as an individual to the community that needed him desperately, i.e., the citizens of Gadara who were busy with the swine!

The Phase of Community Involvement

The person who has profited from pastoral counseling still lives in the same community with the pastor. His witness to the rest of the community by whatever changes have been affected in his life intimately bespeaks the quality and motivation of the pastor's work. On the other hand, his relationship to the living community of the church becomes crucial. A person who carried a burden of shame and who felt that he was "not fit" to be in a church can now attend with a new sense of joy and participation. The person who vowed that he would never attend church again because of wrongs done him by some other member of the church can now, after having received the concentrated encouragement of the intensive relationships of pastoral counseling, return to church of his own accord. The person who used the church as an atonement procedure by attending every meeting and wanting to run everything can now participate in the life of the church without as much compulsiveness.

Furthermore, the average counseling relationship refocuses in the latter phases of the interview situation. The decisions that have been made and the covenants that have been resolved must be "carried out" in daily living. The couple who were having severe marital difficulties will now begin to be concerned about their children in a way they were not previously. The young couple who underwent more intensive counseling in their engagement period will need the resources of the church in establishing their home. The older person who is bereaved by the loss of a spouse will need the continuing sustenance of the people his own age in the church. The church provides both an avenue for expressing new concerns and for receiving the concern of others.

In those instances where the process of counseling "bogged down" or the person refused to make decisions of any kind, the pastor still has the resources of the church to draw upon in ministering to the individual. The person may well be so sick emotionally that medical and psychiatric ministries are indicated. His very illness may be represented in his inability to make decisions and covenants. The pastor may well call upon professional medical resources, but he always does so in the name of the church. A clear distinction has been made here between pastoral counseling and psychotherapy. The assumption concerning pastoral counseling is that it is done by the pastor of a church, a chaplain in a hospital, or a minister who teaches in a school. In this sense pastoral counseling is one function of his total role. Only occasionally do these persons do work that approximates the psychotherapeutic relationship, technically defined. Rather, they are involved in a larger community—a church, a school, or a hospital. These institutions are integral and not incidental to the whole relationship of pastoral counseling. As has been said before, the uniqueness of pastoral counseling emerges at this very point.

The pastor and his counselee are a part of an ongoing community, and the covenant of concern that springs up within the life of the individual is tested and affirmed in his relationships in this community. The most satisfying aspect of pastoral counseling rests in the establishment of the counselee and those about him in the fellowship of faith, concern, and suffering known as the church. Furthermore, the most exacting judgments of the efficacy of pastoral counseling lie in the outcome *within the community* of many so-called successes in individual conferences. Yet, if these judgments seem harsh, the pastor's mistakes are also overruled in the larger wisdom of time and community. What he considered to be failures are later seen to be successes. But the decisive covenants made in pastoral counseling in either instance are carried out in the continuing multifaceted work of the pastor.

IX

Pastoral Counseling as Self-encounter

WE ARE INDEBTED to Lewis Sherrill for synthesizing into a meaningful theological understanding the data of contemporary psychological research on what he called the "emerging dynamic self." (Lewis Joseph Sherrill, *The Struggle of the Soul;* The Macmillan Company, 1952.) He demonstrated the pilgrimage of the self from birth to death as a venture of faith, as a struggle between the call to "cut one's way forward" in response to the redemptive love of God in Christ or to "shrink back" and thereby to lose life in an attempt to save it. Since 1951, there has been a tumultuous awakening of interest in the psychology of the self. (See Calvin S. Hall and Gardner Lindzey, *Theories of Personality,* pp. 467 ff.; John Wiley & Sons, Inc., 1957.) The term was used by William James to displace the term "soul" (William James, *Principles of Psychology,* Ch. X) and to make of the self an object of empirical study by the psychologist. Paul Tillich sought to remove the moralistic connotations from the use of the concept "self," and spoke of the self in terms of having "the courage to be," the intention to receive through faith the acceptance that God proffers to us even though we are not acceptable to ourselves. He spoke of the self as having come into conscious identity through justification by faith, the threat of meaninglessness, destruction, and condemnation having been transcended by the grace of God.

The brilliant research of Harry Stack Sullivan gave us empirical descriptions of what he called "the self-dynamism" as a person develops distinctly habitual identities as a self under threat. (Harry Stack Sullivan, *Conceptions of Modern Psychiatry*, The William Alanson White Memorial Lectures, W. W. Norton & Company, Inc., 1947.) Not until some time after their original formulation did they become influential in theological thought. Even so, the more precise formulations of Sullivan's earlier works have been unnoticed by many. Sullivan insisted that as one learns language, establishes an encounter with others, and incorporates the appraisals of others and of himself, the self-system emerges. The self consists of a composite of these evaluations and the ways in which the individual has said "yes" or "no" to them. The self encounters threat, becomes anxious, and evades, collides with, or assimilates that which threatens him.

The self can be seen developmentally, as does Earl Alfred Loomis in his book *The Self in Pilgrimage* (Harper & Brothers, 1960). Or the self may be seen cross-sectionally, i.e., in its present struggle to maintain balance, integrity, consistency, and hope. We shall see something of the meaning of pastoral counseling from a developmental point of view in our succeeding discussion of pastoral counseling as religious history. But the present task is to see the self the way the pastor has most often to deal with the individual, i.e., in the living encounters of a given moment. The processes of pastoral counseling may be said to be processes of self-encounter: of the pastor with himself, of the counselee with himself, of the two with each other, and of both of them with God in Christ. A basic premise about pastoral technique of counseling, then, is this: *Our approach in a given moment is gauged by the kind of self-confrontation going on in the relationship.* We become slaves of method when we use any given approach in every situation. Yet we become victims of our own pride, caprice, and hunches when we do not have any basic principles upon which to decide the kind of approach to use in different situations.

Therefore, the principle suggested here is that the kind of

self-confrontation which persistently takes place in a given relationship provides the basis for decision as to the technique a pastor should implement. No one can make that decision for the pastor, nor can he long avoid it himself without either breaking, confusing, or himself becoming the victim of a given relationship. In either event, pastor and counselee both inflict and receive real hurt and damage. It takes more than just common sense, more than just a set technique, such as non-directiveness or directiveness, to make such a decision. It takes disciplined understanding and knowledge of the identifiable self-systems that typically occur in human life as a whole and especially in the close-range relationships of pastoral counseling. These can be learned only under clinical conditions and careful supervision.

Several self-systems are encountered in pastoral work generally and pastoral counseling more specifically. These are, as Sullivan says, "reference frames for predicting what will and will not work" with a given person.

THE DETACHED SELF

Some persons refuse to take root anywhere or in relation to anyone. They studiously keep detached. They are "chiefly characterized by a lack of duration" in every interpersonal situation. (Sullivan, *op. cit.*, p. 37.) They expect the pastor to meet them and to serve them. Yet they avoid seemingly without effort a continuing, durable, linear, and unbroken relationship to him or to the church. They touch the pastor and the church occasionally but only in such a way as not to get involved. They refuse to make covenants, except as a means of breaking a relationship. They live through countless, fleeting, passing, and temporary relationships but never "stay put" with any one or more. The painful experiences they have with others hurt only while they are happening. They do not get bitter; they simply remain apathetic and detached.

Therefore, the pastor's efforts as a counselor are doomed

from the outset if he takes no initiative in setting a second, third, or fourth appointment. This person often does not show up for the second interview even when he himself makes the appointment. But the pastor must try to establish a continuing, durable relationship with him. Many of these persons develop relationship-breaking habits, such as borrowing money, cashing bad checks, making sexual passes of one kind or another, or, in some instances, becoming problem drinkers. They do not seem to learn anything from the mistakes they make. Though these mistakes are usually petty nuisances and not large enough to get them into real trouble with the law, they nevertheless continue to make the same mistakes over and over again. They do not learn much from their own mistakes.

The detached person is intuitively skilled in manipulating and using people. He considers himself to be exceptionally clever. He usually is a quite verbal, smooth-talking, and charming person. He makes a brilliant first impression. He is usually an aesthetic person in the Kierkegaardian sense, i.e., he is oblivious to the time factor in human existence. He lets his obligations move past due and simply follows the desire of the present moment without much memory or foresight.

From this we can see that the pastoral counselor must be unusually realistic if any self-confrontation is to take place *within* the detached person's selfhood. Many pastors are quite easily "taken in" by such a person on the first impression. They are exploited by him for the immediate ends the person has in mind. Then the pastors tend to lose patience with him and bawl him out for his "cussedness." A wiser procedure would be to concentrate on initiating, developing, and maintaining a kind of relationship which the person cannot by doing this, that, and the other thing break off or cause us to reject him. This means further that we shall not let our sympathy for him or those near him get the best of us to the point that we deprive him of the consequences of his behavior. He can do as he pleases for as long as he pleases, but he has to pay for it himself. Along with this goes the refusal to do anything for

him which would in either our mind or his require gratitude
or appreciation of him. Otherwise, he will use his seeming in-
gratitude as a basis for breaking his relationship to us.

Underlying the detached self's plight is his inability to trust
anyone except himself. He is the victim of inconsistent treatment from those who have sought to guide him. For example,
his mother may have been extremely harsh and his father
extremely sentimental and overprotective, or vice versa. They
probably quarreled much over him. He in turn learned to
think of himself as cleverer than they were. Therefore, he
played each against the other and dominated the situation. His
great need is for the good news of a consistent, firm, and yet
kindly relationship that he cannot manipulate and that he
need not fear. Rarely does he find this in the Christian community, because some sentimental person is always available
and ready to be used as a "sucker" by this kind of person.

The Handicapped Self

Jean Piaget has given us unusual insight into the effects of
the body image upon the selfhood of the individual. Alfred
Adler pointed out the way in which organic inferiority—real
or symbolically induced by culture—has upon the self-concept
of a person. The pastor meets the physically handicapped—
the person with an obvious birthmark or injury, the polio
victim, the cerebral palsied, the epileptic, the muscularly
dystrophic. He meets the mentally retarded and their
families under the impact of this difficult adjustment problem.

A great part of the pastor's task of counseling and guidance
here rests in the difficult process of acceptance of reality and
achievement of something more than a fatalistic understanding
of the suffering. Likewise, as in the instance of the pastor who
during the first month of his work in a community discovered
three families with mentally retarded children, he is called
upon to create groups whereby families with similar troubles

can sustain each other. This pastor started a special Sunday school class for the three children and a group-counseling relationship with the parents. Here everyone involved confronted reality and set about coping with it in the fellowship of the Christian community.

More subtle, however, are those symbolic handicaps thrust upon individuals by an unregenerate community. For example, a fourteen-year-old boy is sent to his pastor's study for a conference "because he can't behave like his sister does." Or, a father and mother wonder why their seventeen-year-old daughter does not have any interest in dating. Yet they have demanded that she fill the role of the boy that they wanted when she was born. They have taught her to hunt, fish, skeet-shoot, and do many other masculine things. Now they wonder why she cannot face the responsible role of a woman. She will only gradually be able to confront the feminine selfhood for which her body has been created. Even then she will fear rejection by her parents, who by implication have taught her that being a girl is a handicap.

Or, the person whose skin is black may be half persuaded by his culture that this is an inferiority. The term "half persuaded" is used advisedly. He may consciously know that this is not true. But when the pressure is on "hard and heavy" he may call for concession and special advantage because he is a Negro. He may assume that all the things that have befallen him are due to his having been a Negro and *not* to any degree due to his personal refusal to see himself as he really is, and change. In this sense, the real damage of racial discrimination lies at the point of the way it relieves the Negro of responsibility as well as deprives him of his freedom. Both he and the white man share in common their "use" of each other to avoid self-confrontation. This always happens when any segment of society is culturally rejected because of supposed or real handicaps. The ghettos of the inner self will persist long past the disappearance of the "nigger towns" of our Southern and Northern cities.

The handicapped person is likely to have companion and contradictory feelings of isolation and destiny. At one time his feelings of "differentness" will make him feel dreadfully alone, separated, estranged, and unworthy. At other times, they will make him feel unique, unusual, and appointed to a destiny that he must fulfill. In other words, the handicapped person lives eschatologically, either as a fated being or as a child of destiny. The pastor who knows this has the inner secret of pastoral care of the handicapped. He moves existentially in relation to the person and works directly with him in the clarification of his sense of calling and meaningful vocation. This speaks to him candidly at the point of his becoming a self-supporting and responsible citizen of the community. More than that, it communicates the assurances of the pastor that this person is treasured in God's design for human life and not merely an accident of birth awaiting the consummation of time to correct itself. Rather, in the midst of the handicap itself a calling and a vocation can be found that will give lasting meaning to life, not only for them but for others as well.

THE HOSTILE SELF

Another word for the "hostile" self is the "rejected" self. Rejections have been heaped upon each other until he creates situations almost automatically in which he *will* be rejected. He expects to be rejected. He comes into most situations hostile. He is rejected, just as he expected.

Therefore, the pastor's capacity to accept him, to be affectionately permissive without condescension, determines whether or not the relationship lasts. If this "son of thunder" can be accepted without having the injustice he feels blurred out, then the more positive and conjunctive emotions appear. Self-correction takes place rapidly, and reappraisal of the situation that triggered the hostility can take place. This person expresses his hostility "face to face" as Paul did with Peter at Antioch. He can be angry without letting the sun go down on his wrath. He has capacity for loyalty and deep devotion, and often becomes one of our Lord's most trusted disciples, once he has felt the warmth, tenderness, and acceptance of the love of Christ.

The pastor is often in a dire strait to give this kind of acceptance to a directly hostile person. He has not only to minister to the individual but also to cope with the effects that the person's hostility creates within the community as a whole. The pastor himself may be able to absorb much direct aggression, but many of his parishioners cannot do so. Moreover, the major emotional problem of ministers themselves, according to the detailed psychological research of Dodson, Massey, and others, is the unconsidered burden of hostility they carry. Ministers have more difficulty than other professional persons in recognizing, accepting, and expressing responsibly hostility. In fact, these hostilities many times short-circuit into sexual behavior or into depressions, or both. This makes it difficult indeed for the minister to accept hostility and aggression in others. (See *The Mental Health of the Minister*, ed. by Wayne E. Oates; Channel Press, 1961.) Consequently, the minister's own training should include considerable attention to the sources of his own hostilities in the rejections that he has had to absorb into his selfhood. Furthermore, the minister's training should include some deeper-level counseling for himself in order that he might lay hold of, rather than be the slave of, his own aggressive impulses.

With some such training and assistance, the minister has a fresh source of wisdom for accepting and channeling the blasts of hostility and aggression that he meets day after day in his work as a pastor. Good humor and large reserves of patience will find in these encounters "teachable moments" which will make lasting disciples in the Kingdom of God. The hostile person, once genuinely and openly accepted, becomes an intensely loyal and productive person. This is a subtle wisdom which Jesus repeatedly implemented in relating himself to James, John, Nathanael, and others.

THE SUSPICIOUS SELF

Contrary to the hostile self, the suspicious self does not feel as rejected as he feels *deceived*. He sees himself as being totally right at all times, and seeks at all times to determine the total course of life about him. When things go wrong, his first impulse is to suspect foul play of those about him. Treachery is in the offing. Contrary to the hostile person, also, he does not go, vis-à-vis, to the person who has supposedly offended him. He talks in an exceptionally confidential tone to everyone *around* that person. He seeks to hurt him by isolating him, undermining his success, and detracting from any good that might reside in him.

The pastor will be drawn into this kind of ambiguous situation more often than many other persons. This kind of self-structure is common among middle-class persons, who constitute most of our churches and institutions. The pastor can effectively clarify the distrust in such a person by recommending that the individual talk face to face with the person against whom he is grieved. If the person has attempted this to no avail, the pastor can offer to be a third person present while the two of them talk about these matters. If both these suggestions fail to bring the inflamed relationship under control, the pastor would do well to confer with another professional person before he moves much farther.

Such consultation would bring more technical skill to bear upon the evaluation of the situation. At the same time, the pastor would thus be sharing clinical responsibility and objectifying some of his own anxieties at the same time. The indications for referral could be assessed, and the wisdom of a limited kind of pastoral counseling could be discussed. By a "limited kind of pastoral counseling," I mean a clearly defined, supportive, and ventilative kind of listening ministry. Here it is clearly understood that both the pastor and the counselee will keep the conversations confidential and not be expected to "represent" or "misrepresent" each other to the other people involved. Many times such a tightly defined relationship will create enough security that the person may after a few interviews begin to say: "Well, I really thought last fall that Mr. X was trying to get me off the deacons' board, but I suppose it had grown too big in my mind." Or, a housewife will say, "I know that he has been unfaithful to me in the past, and I guess I've gotten to where I expect it of him when he hasn't really done anything wrong." This is self-confrontation. It takes place only when one *knows* he or she is not going to lose face for having admitted a few things to be true about his own misperception of reality. Such self-confrontation involves risk; it is painful; it takes place in an atmosphere of social safety even though personal risk is being taken. The pastor's job is to create a safe situation in which real confession and confrontation of self can take place.

Once again, however, the situation of the larger community in which the minister works as a public figure as well as a private counselor complicates considerably the pastoral care of the suspicious person. Usually the multiplex and diffuse indirection of the suspicious person comes to the attention of the pastor in what is commonly called gossip. The suspicious person may inadvertently or with deliberate design say things about the pastor himself to a closer confidant of the pastor. The unerring course of events brings this "message" to the pastor. The conscious aim of the person is to hurt both the pastor and the person who is "closer" to him. The unconscious apprehension about getting too close to anyone seems to be operative in such persons, also. Therefore, the pastor needs to be extremely careful about "moving in upon" such a person and trying to work out a hasty reconciliation. This only panics him further. Rather, he would do well to ponder the matter at least overnight and probably over many nights. Sometimes the person who "brought the message" can be of assistance in working through to a clearer understanding. At others, merely an invitation sent to the person through the "bearer of evil tidings" will encourage the person to come of his own accord and announce his distress to the pastor personally. But suffice it to say that the objective in dealing with a suspiciously oriented person is to transform the indirection and suspicion into a face-to-face hostility that is in turn accepted with humility and humor and dealt with honestly and responsibly.

Yet a pathological note needs to be entered here. The suspicious person at his worst may be acutely sick, and this possibility should never be underestimated nor neglected. Consequently, professional consultation on the part of the pastor with another pastor, a fellow staff member, and a psychiatrist, if possible, is a very wise procedure to follow in serious encounters with a chronically suspicious person.

THE AMBITION-RIDDEN SELF

The society in which we live is a competitive one. American culture, therefore, is particularly adept at producing what Harry Stack Sullivan has called *the ambition-ridden self*. They are slanted toward life with what Erich Fromm calls a "marketing orientation." As Sullivan says, these people "have to use everyone. . . . If you are no good for advancing his interest, the ambition-ridden person can find someone who is." (Sullivan, *op. cit.*, p. 40.) This kind of personality thrives on the open leadership competition of the average Protestant church. The church itself may be to him a means of advancing his particular designs in life. In fact, the Christian ministry itself abounds with the temptations of the ambition-ridden. The upward social mobility of ministers *seems* to be more rapid than that of most professions, although no specific study of this particular dimension of the ministry has yet been made. The minister himself has to ask why it is he counsels with certain individuals and not with others. Do certain counselees aid and abet his own particular ambitions whereas others do not? He is more likely to exploit people through counseling for competitive and ambitious reasons than for erotic motives.

On the other hand, he finds his counseling relationships to

certain individuals within his own congregation to be almost nonexistent, although he knows that these persons desperately need such assistance. He asks himself why it is that he cannot gain access to their confidence. One reason among many is that they are ambition-ridden personalities whose very goals in life would be threatened by admitting to such a need. The minister is valued as a person if he contributes to their status, plans, or objectives. The inner pathologies of marriage difficulties, alcoholism, or obvious neurotic or psychotic behavior are hidden or revealed, faced or avoided, in relation to the ambition-ridden self in terms of the way such behavior affects the particular social, business, or professional ambitions of the individual or family.

The main characteristic of the "ambition-ridden self" is manipulativeness. He *uses* those around him but never communicates the feeling that he really needs them as a person. He considers persons as means but not as human beings. At the inner core of his being this person is anxious and hungry but never filled. He experiences strange and persistent feelings of emptiness, loneliness, and anxiety for approval. He is hyperactive, restless, and plagued by new ideas. He is a creative, empire-building tycoon who in his own indirect way contributes much to the lives of many people. But this contribution is always a side effect, not an intention. He may, for instance, build a business that employs many people and provides work wherewith they may support their families. But this does not occur to him as a *reason* for building a corporation.

The tragedy of the ambition-ridden is that the minister rarely gets the opportunity to counsel with them. As public figure, as preacher, and as man of influence, the pastor may be "useful" to such a person. As a counselor to whom he would impart his inner selfhood and question his own patterns of living, however, the minister is not felt by him to be useful. Yet the points at which the minister does encounter this person are crucial. He meets him amid serious illness, such as a heart attack. He confronts him when children rebel and challenge or threaten the validity of their parents' ambitions. The spouse of such an ambition-ridden person pays the emotional cost of the unattended relationships to friends and relatives, particularly the children. Sooner or later the spouse, therefore, may turn to the pastor for counseling assistance. Psychoanalysis in the large metropolitan centers has done much intensive therapy with the ambition-ridden, because they are often able to pay for long-term therapy. However, the specifically sociological aspects of distinctly pastoral counseling with the "successful" and the ambition-ridden need detailed research. However, the very nature of this kind of person's place in the community makes it very difficult for the pastor to be objective in his research or to report his findings. The confidential aspects of this kind of counseling are extremely delicate to handle.

Beyond these situational problems, the main thing to be remembered in counseling with the ambition-ridden is to avoid being used by such a person. Frank resistance at this point is indicated. However, one should not be too optimistic that this will create changes, because if someone by resisting him is "no good for advancing his interest, the ambition-ridden person can find someone who is, with whom to enjoy whatever other satisfaction he had been having in your company." (Harry Stack Sullivan, op. cit., p. 40.) In other words, he will break his relationship, if indeed such was ever genuinely established.

THE DEPENDENT SELF

Dependent persons are persistently inadequate in all sorts of situations. They borrow their selfhood from others. They are constantly in debt for their existence. They are in debt to other people who tend to be ambition-ridden selves and who, as we have seen, can relate durably only to those whom they consider inferior to themselves. These persons tend to pair off each other's "ways of life." They counterbalance each other. The dependent person may have been a very obedient child for an extremely dominating parent. However, some dependency may be culturally induced. Particularly is this true of those women who have been taught by precept and example that they should let someone else make the decisions. They will function as parents, for example, by depending absolutely and not relatively upon "expert" advice about child-rearing Dependent men, on the one hand, will tend to seek positions in which major decisions are left entirely to other people. After World War II, we observed the need of this kind of person to re-enlist in a peacetime (?) army.

An understanding of dependent selfhood gives the key to several kinds of pastoral problems. For example, a passive kind of hostility characterizes *laziness*. Sometimes the only way a person can safely express his hostility is by just not getting around to doing what others expect of him. A student can express his aggression by *not doing* what has been decided for him he must do. The profound dependency into which white Americans have thrust a whole race of people by taking their freedom of decision from them is most often expressed in their not doing or not doing well what we ordered them to do. The passive resistance of Gandhi has taken hold of the Negro race in this country and has become one of the most devastating forms of aggression.

As to techniques of counseling, we must remember that the nondirective or client-centered forms of counseling were first devised in work with college students. These students are at a remarkably dependent stage of their existence, yet are filled with the *élan vital* of life and want very much to be independent in the social and courtship spheres of life at the same time that they are dependent economically and vocationally. They are often indecisive about "what is right and wrong" and are equally indecisive about "what they want to do with their lives," "what they believe about religion," and the like. Occasionally the pastor meets college students who demand that he give them final answers about the imponderables of life. They feel that a religion that has any uncertainties in it is not defensible. They require an absolute authoritarian answer, but when it is given, they reject it as inadequate.

Yet the personal history of the dependent person reflects a poignant lack of trust in him on the part of the adults in his life. They have overseen his every move and made his major decisions for him. The pastor can take a lead from this and do otherwise. He can invest trust and confidence in the dependent personality by gradual doses of responsibility. He can wait patiently and believingly while the young person learns to use the powers that were given him before he learned to be supinely dependent upon others. This takes the nondirective approach as far as basic decisions are concerned. At the same time the evenly warm climate of acceptance and trust of which Carl Rogers speaks so definitively in his works on counseling is required.

THE DESPAIRING SELF

Desperation characterizes to a certain degree everyone who seriously seeks counseling help. A large measure of their personal resources for living have been depleted. They are emotionally jaded and have undergone the attrition of self-esteem even before they reach the counselor. Yet some counselees' particular mode of existence is predominantly characterized by despair. The despairing person does not feel worthy of taking up the pastor's time. He laughs little if at all, breathes heavily with periodic sighs, complains of the pointlessness of his existence, has much trouble sleeping, and is likely to be contemplating making some rather drastic decisions. He may be thinking of selling out his business, of quitting his job, of giving up all his offices in the church (of which he may have too many), or of leaving his family because "they will be better off without me," or even of committing suicide. He may or may not have suffered some great loss already, such as the loss of someone by death or the loss of his business or fortune. Ordinarily, he has lived an exemplary life of conscientious community and church service. He is often from the "official family" of the church, a deacon, an elder, a steward, or a vestryman.

The religion of a despairing person is usually one of hard work and strenuous effort to get approval from both God and man. He is very scrupulous about even the smallest matters of conscience. He worries much about things that cause his friends to wish he were not quite so conscientious. Penitential literature through the ages has been filled with the descriptions of the despairing person's scrupulosity. (See John T. MacNeill, *The History of the Cure of Souls;* Harper & Brothers, 1952.) Luther went again and again to Staupitz, his confessor, to confess the same sins over and over. The Protestant minister of today meets this kind of repeated confession in the person who tells him that he has committed the unpardonable sin.

From the point of view of clinical care, the pastor does well to encourage the despairing person to consult his family physician. Ordinarily, sleep, which, as Shakespeare says, "knits up the ravell'd sleave of care," has been seriously curtailed for this person. The physician can prescribe medicine that will enable the person to sleep. He can explore other basic physiological functions that need attention. At the same time, he can assess the nature and extent of the depressed mood and the need for psychiatric help. Both he and the pastor can collaborate, with the person's permission, in deciding what steps can best be taken. Also, the family physician can share responsibility with the pastor for the outcome of the treatment.

The pastor himself has a ventilative, supportive, and sustaining ministry to perform, regardless of what kinds of other professional help may be required. The despairing person should be seen more often for shorter lengths of time. Thus he draws upon the sustenance of the minister's encouragement more often. The minister can effectively take the initiative toward a genuinely despairing person by visitation, a telephone call, or a personally written note. The despairing self will never exploit this. From the outset he will feel that the minister is using his time on an unworthy person. A dependent person would very early begin to demand it of the pastor, but not the despairing person.

Again, the despairing person has real difficulty in making decisions. He may ignore and procrastinate about smaller decisions of the day and act hastily and unwisely about major decisions of his life. The pastor can afford to be directive, in a way some psychotherapists would be reluctant to do, about minor decisions, and even give straight advice. For example, the person may be worrying unduly about taking a certain social engagement, such as attending a party with friends. He may really feel that he does not want to go but fears the disapproval of his friends if he does not. The pastor can "coach" the person on what he would say to his friends and gently agree with the basic desire of the despairing person. On the other hand, the pastor can with firmness and directness advise the person *not* to make major decisions about his work, his marriage, his property, and his attitudes toward God while he is this depressed. A very few rules of thumb can be set forth in Protestant pastoral counseling, but this one can: a person should never make a major decision while he is in the depths of despair. He should wait until his perspective of life is clear and accurate to do this, and steps toward a therapeutic program can be firmly advised.

But the main task of the pastor with the despairing person is that of collaborating with him concerning his way of life in relation to God. This person is often a very religious person, as we have already seen, and yet his religion is a burden rather than a joy and a resource to him. He, more than most people, needs to make the transition from a religion of ethical law to one of trusting grace. He is wretched from the bondage of an inner legalism. He is a deprived person, because life has always made demands of him but has offered little in the way of nourishing support and affectionate sustenance. God is his judge, director, employer, and law, but not his Redeemer, Friend, and Comforter. The major task of the pastor is to demonstrate this "other side" of religion to the despairing person, in his very relationship, and to challenge the legalism of the despairing person with the "free grace of the Lord Jesus Christ," which accepts in love and asks only that the acceptance be received without cost.

THE APATHETIC SELF

One of the main defenses against pain is anesthetization. This may be chemical anesthesia, as in the case of the surgical patient. Addiction to drugs, such as narcotics and alcohol, desensitizes their users to the reality around them. But these are obvious, chemical forms of desensitization and anesthesia. The human organism has its own psychological means of raising the threshold of stimulus to pain and anxiety to the point that the person does not respond, even when heavily stimulated. These psychological means of producing apathy may be temporary defenses against massive assaults on the very existence of a person. They may be adopted as a way of life, and an "apathetic self" is the kind of person whom the pastor meets.

Apathy or numbness appears in several transitory states of life. For example, the pastor meets this numbness regularly in the recently bereaved person. The person may complain of physical sensations of coldness, or he may say that he "does not know how to feel" any more, or he may complain that he "can't get interested" in anything any more. Although this is exceptionally apparent in the person who is bereaved because of the loss of someone by death, it is also much in evidence in the person who has suffered a broken courtship or a divorce. Yet these states are as a rule transitory, although the person may become fixated at this point and adopt this stance toward life as a permanent way of handling threats to the self.

Another example of the apathetic existence as a transitory state is in times of great social catastrophe, such as famine, economic depression, and war. For example, the morning's paper says that an unemployed West Virginia coal miner, upon picking up his government-given food supplies, said:

"Well, I don't have to worry about the gas and electric bill this week. They turned them off last week." His reaction was "not to worry." He was really concerned but could only become apathetic to that over which he had no control. Hachiya, the Japanese physician, wrote a diary of the first three months of his medical practice in Hiroshima after the atomic bomb struck his city. He tells of his desperate struggle to keep apathy from desensitizing him to the needs of his patients. Apathy seems to be an almost divine protection of the total organism against massive and overwhelming assaults upon the integrity of the self.

Apathy can become a way of life, a distinct patterning of the self in its habitual mode of existence. The pastor, as will be seen in the next chapter, needs to explore very carefully the religious history of the person whose indifference seems to be a way of life. He can look for an accumulation of events that have caused the individual to conclude that it is not safe to recognize his emotions, much less to respond with them. He has been hurt, and hurt, and hurt again. He has lost out, lost out, and lost out again. He has, therefore, found it much safer just not to let himself think, feel, or respond with feeling. The pastor learns much more about the areas of hurt and loss by making note of the things and persons about whom he does not talk than to probe for this, that, or the other "fact" in his history.

Formal counseling itself is very threatening to the apathetic person. The occasional kind of informal conversation, carefully used by the pastor, provides a more relaxed environment for the apathetic person. Also, the pastor depends very carefully upon his own relationship as the conduit of resensitizing this person's deprived emotional life. He takes great care, for instance, to be a faithful person in his appointments, promises, and follow-through of plans. If, for example, he talks with the person on occasion about some interest of his, the pastor takes care to develop that interest in later conversations. He may hand the person a book that he has found on the subject. He may recount an incident that is related to it, or refer another person to him, who is interested in the same subject. This may or may not be related to religious interests. The pastor is in much the same position in relating himself to the apathetic person that the physiotherapist is to the person who has lost use of a certain limb of his body. It takes time, carefully planned "exercise of interest," and a consistently faithful and nonabrasive relationship to restore the lost feeling.

Particularly is this true of apathetic persons who have lost interest in or failed to develop an interest in the Christian faith. Much that is called irreligion is apathy to that which has been presented as religion. The person is simply "left cold" by the whole interest. His religious history in itself may reveal that this is a reaction to disappointment, disillusionment, hurt, and exploitation in relation to "religious" persons, personages, and institutions. The pastor in his own way cannot restore these feelings by rational argument, by pushing group relationships too hard, or by appeals to the purely social and utilitarian advantages of the religious life. He must open himself as a person with complete vulnerability to the apathetic person as a person. Through the consistent honesty and warmth of his own interest and willingness to listen he demonstrates that the meaning of love is measured by the risks it takes in making oneself vulnerable to hurt. Strangely enough the apathetic person is quite often acutely aware of these issues and can talk about them frankly.

THE WITHDRAWN SELF

The final pattern of selfhood to be considered here is the "withdrawn self." The hostile self, as Horney says, "moves against" people. The dependent person "moves upon" other persons. The suspicious person "moves around" or circumvents persons. The ambitious self exalts himself "above" people. The apathetic person "plays dead" in the presence of other persons. The withdrawn self moves "away from" people, and his "distance machinery" works automatically and full time. Kurt Lewin calls this man's "most primitive attempt" to avoid at one and the same time both task and punishment in inter-personal relationships. He calls it "going-out-of-the-field," either bodily or psychologically. (Kurt Lewin, *A Dynamic Theory of Personaity*, p. 174; McGraw-Hill Book Co., Inc., 1935.)

In ordinary human conversation, withdrawnness is interpreted as shyness. C. G. Jung's term "introversion" has eased its way into popular speech as a description of withdrawnness, although Jung's own meaning is much richer and more diversified. The withdrawn person is a very different person from the detached self, who maintains an equal distance out of contempt for the human race. The withdrawn person both desperately wants and fears real contact with persons. He wants closeness and tenderness, understanding and love, but fears being possessed and controlled by those from whom it comes. The withdrawn person may have previously been "smothered" by someone's sentimentality, which is a counterfeit form of love. Hence, the suspicious self and the apathetic self both have dimensions of withdrawnness in them. The withdrawn person has been both deceived and hurt, misled and exploited. As a result, the power to connect with other people has been blunted. In acute forms, this person is usually thought of as a schizoid person, and highly professional care is indicated. However, this does not mean that at the same time the pastor himself does not also have a remarkably significant ministry to perform.

From a clinical point of view, the pastor must develop a special sensitivity to emotional distance and nearness to appreciate the inner pain that a normally shy person feels. This becomes especially necessary when he is tempted to be excessively "hail fellow well met" with a withdrawn person. Another basic principle of pastoral care is that people vary widely as individuals in the tempo with which they become close to and involved with others. The pastor must, therefore, sense the tempo of their existence and modulate his own pace of encounter to theirs. Becoming too "pushy," demanding, or familiar with a withdrawn person is very threatening. A more matter-of-fact, less verbal, and slowly paced kind of response makes the withdrawn person feel much more secure. Frieda Fromm-Reichmann recommends a studied nonchalance with the more acutely disturbed, schizophrenic person, underscoring the painfulness of too much solicitude and warmth, especially in the earlier phases of the relationship.

The rich values within the life of the withdrawn person have much to contribute to the life of the pastor himself. The withdrawn person is usually a contemplative, nonactivistic kind of self. The activism of the life of the average church leaves little room for appreciation of this person. He often prefers to write his thoughts rather than speak them, and the pastor does well to encourage this. Next to this, the withdrawn self prefers a more leisurely telephone conversation to a face-to-face encounter. Then he does not feel "looked at" or "observed" in conversation. In the formal situation of the counseling interview, the withdrawn person is much more comfortable if the counselor looks out a window or at a portrait on the wall away from him.

The withdrawn self moves slowly in dealing with his personal difficulties in living. The pastor does well to space his interviews with him over a longer period of time with longer amounts of time between interviews. In this respect, the withdrawn person is the opposite of the despairing self, who needs shorter interviews more frequently. Much patience and unhurriedness is required. Patient work with withdrawn persons returns long-term friendships and devotions in the pastoral ministry which more than justify the use of the time.

GENERALIZATIONS CONCERNING PATTERNS OF SELF-ENCOUNTER

Several basic generalizations need to be made concerning these patterns of self-encounter. First, the pastor needs to recognize these as varieties of *religious* experience and not merely as psychological phenomena. The person relates to God in these characteristic ways also. These are modes of religious existence. The hostile person is likely to be angry at God, as is true of the rebelling "atheist." The dependent person's prayers are mostly petition and demand, rarely adoration and fellowship. The ambition-ridden person thinks of God as being "on his side" and "pulling for him" in the competitive struggle for success. The apathetic may complain about not being able to feel that his prayers are meaningful or being answered. The suspicious person may suspect that God is persecuting him in various ways. The detached person remains uncommitted in any kind of covenant with God too.

Again, this discussion of various patterns of selfhood is not a *pure* typology of personalities. All these forms of existence are participant in the life of the typical person at different times in this life. The healthy person consciously decides to deal with first one problem and then the other in one or the other of these modes of reaction. But he *does* decide and choose; he is not driven and compelled. He is flexible and can react appropriately to a given situation with the kind of response that is most meaningful to him and those persons to whom he is responsible. He is not bound and compelled to react in *one* way to all people. For example, our Lord Jesus Christ was hostile, knew how to depend upon persons like Martha, Mary, and Lazarus. He withdrew from persons like Herod. He felt the great heaviness of soul in prayer. The ethically negative kinds of response, such as ambition-riddenness and detachedness, are almost nonexistent in him but ever-present in his temptations.

These patterns of relatedness in selfhood indicate a flexibility of technique on the part of the pastor. Tender solicitude meets the despairing person's needs, whereas it may be interpreted as a sign of guilt and appeasement on the part of the suspicious person and as a sign of stupidity and weakness on the part of the detached person. The passive, nondirective approach to the dependent person draws his inner resources into focus. The same approach will be interpreted as full-scale approval of his many plans by the ambition-ridden person, who seeks simply to use the counselor for his own ends. To suggest that the pastor should use more than one method, however, is not to suggest a willy-nilly eclecticism. Basic principles of interpersonal relationships are necessary for making a clinical decision as to the approach that should be followed in any given situation. The first of these principles has been set forth here in a description of the various modes of selfhood. Yet, these cannot be learned merely by reading them here. Intensive clinical supervision and staff collaboration provides a fund of experiential validation and clarification of these modes of reaction. Genuine sensitivity can best be developed in such clinical training.

But the pastor does not really sense the emotional tones of reference in these patterns of reaction unless he has seen them clearly in himself. He must encounter himself as a person before, during, and after his confrontation of his counselees. He must explore his own spiritual autobiography and draw some basic conclusions as to his own patterns of reaction. Then he begins to appreciate with greater clarity and deeper patience the problems of self-encounter in his counselees' lives.

X

Pastoral Counseling as Religious History

THE PREVIOUS CHAPTER dealt with the patterns of selfhood that appear in the immediate present of the encounter of a pastor with his counselee. These patterns were woven together in the process of time and of the spiritual autobiography of the person. In the presentation of the self in encounter with the pastor, the immediate relationship gives the pastor what has been called a *cross-sectional* perspective of his history. The living past is observable in the responses of the present. However, the pastor cannot be certain of his relationship without a more *longitudinal*, developmental understanding of how and under what circumstances this person came to be what he is. Similarly, the pastor cannot appreciate in depth the responses he himself gives to those with whom he works and to whom he ministers unless he has some emotional grasp and interpretation of his own developmental history.

The purpose of this chapter is to provide a framework for such reciprocal understanding between counselor and counselee, from both a psychological and a religious perspective, but especially accenting the religious history of the person. The pastor is predominantly related to the counselee, both symbolically and actually, in terms of the specifically religious history of the person. For this knowledge, he is responsible. He cannot "refer" this to others. However, in making the religious dimensions of the history most articulate, no artificial dichot-

213

omy is made with the other aspects of the person's history, particularly his medical history. To do this would be to distort the meaning of both religion and personal history, both of which embrace all of life.

THE PASTOR'S DEVELOPMENTAL PERSPECTIVE

A developmental perspective is an achievement of discipline and clinical experience, not a charismatic gift. Without it, the pastor may continue to have a static and fixed view of his task as a counselor, depending upon word magic, rabbinical rules, and his own intuitive "hunches." With a developmental perspective, the pastor takes a dynamic view of his task as a counselor. He depends upon the wisdom that the numbering of our days brings, a process relationship of trusting love, and the guidance of the Holy Spirit in the developmental life of his counselee. There are several ways a minister can achieve a developmental perspective through discipline and clinical experience.

Supervised clinical education. One of the most creative sources of developmental understanding is in supervised clinical pastoral education. Here the clinical histories of hundreds of suffering persons have been, with varying measures of efficiency and wisdom, garnered through interviews and examinations. Also, the student minister has an opportunity to participate meaningfully in staff conferences where an interdisciplinary team confers about different patients' histories. The student writes his own records, and, through the long process of pastoral visiting and interviewing the same person many times, develops his own understanding of the life cycle of the persons with whom he works. He does this under supervision of experienced chaplains whose task is to assist him in clarifying his distinctive role as a minister and in understanding the religious dimensions of the patient's life pilgrimage.

Interprofessional collaboration. Another way of achieving a developmental perspective is through on-the-job collaboration with persons of other professions in the actual care of persons within the pastor's own parish responsibilities. The family physician, the local family service agency, the guidance counselors in the local schools, social workers in welfare agencies, professors of psychology, marriage and family living, and pastoral care in nearby colleges, universities, and seminaries, gynecologists, psychiatrists, and psychoanalysts all provide potential allies in the ministry to specific individuals and families. The "feedback" of understanding in telephone conversations, letters of referral and evaluation, and personal discussions provides a source for accumulating a vastly enriched developmental perspective of human selfhood. This is not a one-way kind of learning, either. The minister has something of his own to offer in interpreting the religious history of the persons involved. He often communicates more to the person of another profession about the nature of "pure religion and undefiled before God" in his ministry to the clients of these professional persons than he would in a formal discussion of religion.

Such a learning relationship of reciprocal understanding thrives in the soil of personal friendship and mutual respect, not abstractly between persons who do not really meet each other as persons but only are self-conscious about their social roles. As such friendships continue, a further way of achieving a developmental perspective is to form study groups composed of ministers and other professional persons. This has been exceptionally productive in several communities.

Reading of developmental theory. However, the pastor does not engage in clinical pastoral education and interprofessional collaboration to any great extent without coming upon the major prevailing theoreticians of personality development. Therefore, he can further achieve a clear developmental perspective by studying the works of these men. He should bring careful theological scrutiny to bear upon their presuppositions about time and the developmental process. He should not accept gullibly everything he reads. He should be

216   PROTESTANT PASTORAL COUNSELING

informed in detail on the major theories of personality development that have been built by these authors on the basis of their clinical experience. The influential theories of psychoanalysis can be reviewed in their contemporary and classical statements in the works by O. Spurgeon English and G. H. J. Pearson, *Emotional Problems of Living: Avoiding the Neurotic Pattern* (W. W. Norton & Company, Inc., 1955), and William Healy, Augusta F. Bronner, and Anna Mae Bowers, *The Structure and Meaning of Psychoanalysis as Related to Personality and Behavior* (Alfred A. Knopf, Inc., 1938). The work of Arnold Gesell, Frances Ilg, and Louise Ames in their successive volumes, *The First Five Years of Life; The Child from Five to Ten; Youth: The Years from Ten to Sixteen;* and the composite one-volume work by Ilg and Ames entitled *Child Behavior* (all published by Harper & Brothers) give a detailed study of the characteristic patterns of attitude and behavior of children in American culture. The interpersonal theory of development devised by Harry Stack Sullivan is succinctly described in his book *The Psychiatric Interview* (W. W. Norton & Company, Inc., 1954) and in more detail in his book *The Interpersonal Theory of Psychiatry* (W. W. Norton & Company, Inc., 1954). A less technical but equally valuable book written for teachers is the one by Robert J. Havighurst, *Human Development and Education* (Longmans, Green & Co., Inc., 1953). Prescott Lecky gives a creative understanding of conflict in personality development in his small volume, *Self-consistency* (Island Press Coop, Inc., 1945).

The pastor who spends some time in serious reading of these volumes will receive a permanent contribution to his understanding of his task as a counselor. He will find specific religious value in his interpretation of these works from the point of view of his own Christian doctrine of man. For example, he will have moralistic religion roundly challenged in behalf of faith working through love. He will come to appreciate both the creative and destructive aspects of conflict in human development. His appreciation of how people learn and assimilate the new life of the Christian will be both challenged and modified. But he will not come to this kind of larger perspective without a backdrop of clinical experience under supervision by which to measure his learning. He will also find the work of Lewis J. Sherrill in his book *The Struggle of the Soul* (The Macmillan Company, 1951) and Earl A. Loomis, *The Self in Pilgrimage* (Harper & Brothers, 1960), as well as my earlier volume, *The Religious Dimensions of Personality* (Association Press, 1957), especially Ch. VII, to be helpful guides in the theological interpretation of developmental theory.

Such an educational and experiential background as has been described here is assumed in the further discussion of the more detailed aspects of the nature and function of the religious history in the process of pastoral counseling. One does not, in pastoral counseling, set out to "get a history." He dares not ignore the relational reality of the intimately personal encounter of selves that the process of pastoral counseling essentially is. Pastoral counseling (or any other legitimate form of personal assistance to suffering persons for that matter) is not a form of detectivelike "sleuthing" in order to fix blame or to hand down a decision as to what *the* problem of a person is. Therefore, the religious history of the person comes somewhat of its own accord and forms into a meaningful pattern in the "betweenness" situation of the counselor-counselee encounter. The formal detailing of a "history," as it were, comes *after the fact* of the total relationship, and should be sufficiently a part of the pastor's previous training and experiences that it is second nature to him and not a matter of self-conscious method.

The minister who lives close to his people is in much the same position as the family physician: he moves from crisis to crisis, developmental era to developmental era, with his people. He actually participates in the making of the history of an individual in a way that other counselors do not. His is a linear, durable relationship, not a punctiliar, temporary relationship. He does not "accept" and "discharge" his counselees in the way other counselors do. Therefore, he stands in a unique relationship to the history of the individual. It is not merely a factual history or a history of pathology. Rather, it is the "faith history" of the person as a child of God. Yet, in this faith history several distinct considerations require careful analysis and interpretation in the counseling relationship.

THE CULTURAL HERITAGE AS RELIGIOUS HISTORY

Religion is not only an individual expression. Religion is a structural part of the sum total of "ways of living" built up over the centuries by a group or society of human beings and transmitted from one generation to another. As a result the cultural heritage of a given individual is a part of his collective identity, his present selfhood and ongoing destiny. The pastor, therefore, should be cross-culturally educated. His own travels will have put him in touch with people of differing heritages from his own. Knowing more than one language is another way of insight into other cultures. Having studied in more than one type of school adds to his cultural breadth and depth. The specific study of anthropology in its several branches will give the pastor technical information about other cultures. A course or two taken at a nearby college or university will stimulate the minister's understanding of persons.

These are matters of background and option. The pastor really has no choice, however, in his responsibility to know the varieties of religious culture in American Christianity. His theological education is deficient if he does not have this, and his daily reading program should include the study of such books as William Warren Sweet's *The American Churches* (Abingdon Press, 1948), and Willard L. Sperry, *Religion in America* (Cambridge University Press, 1945). The study of the nuances of belief and practice among the various cults and sects also contributes to this understanding. (See Van Ogden Vogt, *Cult and Culture;* The Macmillan Company,

1951.) For example, one does not serve as a pastor long before
he encounters representatives of the Mormons, Jehovah's Witnesses, Christian Science, Unity, Theosophy, and other such
groups. In the process of pastoral care and counseling, the
Protestant pastor also encounters people who have emerged
from the cultural heritage of the great living religions other
than Christianity. Especially should he be disciplined in an
understanding of Judaism. To such an extent as his time
permits and local conditions require, he should understand
Buddhism, Hinduism, Mohammedanism, Shinto, and other
religious cultures. (See Joachim Wach, *The Comparative
Study of Religion*, ed. J. M. Kitagawa; Columbia University
Press, 1958.)

But one of his main sources of instruction is from his counselees. They provide him with "living epistles" of the strengths
and weaknesses of religious cultures, both his own and that of
others. Within Christianity he will find the varieties of religious experience that move from one extreme of legalism to
the riches of a redemption by grace through faith and to the
other extreme of a bare rationalism that considers everything
but is committed to nothing. If he opens himself to learn from
his counselee and *not to argue with him*, he will come to understand both his counselee and himself better. Here again is an
example of how the minister does not "take a history" but as
a living representative of his own cultural heritage *encounters*
the counselee as a living representative of his heritage.

However, several specific factors should be anticipated in
the encounter. First, *the age* at which the counselee made
living contact with his religious heritage is important. For
example, a family may have been inactive, nominal Presby-
terians, Baptists, Episcopalians, or the like, until the counselee
was in high school. Then the father became converted to the
Jehovah's Witnesses, and the whole family was reorganized
around this commitment of the father. The family may have
been wholly unrelated to any kind of religious heritage in another instance until the counselee himself began attending the

local Methodist Sunday school. He, being an aggressive teen-ager, had success in "enlisting" one member of his family, a younger sister, but the rest of the family jeered at their interests. Or, as is more often true, the person may have received his religious heritage as culture from birth, in "his mother's milk," and in the water of the community in which he grew up. Second, the *educational* and *vocational* aspects of the religious heritage as it takes effect in a family are important. These in turn affect *the economy* of the family. All three of these factors combine to produce a high degree of social mobility, both horizontal and vertical. Horizontal mobility refers to the geographical "moving about" of the family and its members. Vertical mobility refers to "moving up and down" the social ladder in terms of the social class of the family. Third, these movements produce deep personality changes in the counselee and his family. The counselee may well be what the anthropologists have aptly described as a "marginal man." A marginal man has, through education, vocation, increased income, and marriage, moved completely out of the original group of his religious heritage. At the same time he has not found himself at home in any other group. He is an outcast of one group—either by his own choice or the rejection of his home community or both—and has not yet found acceptance and "at homeness" in another.

Finally, the pastoral counselor should anticipate the kinds of loneliness, hostility, guilt, and defensiveness the individual may feel about his religious heritage. The "marginal man" is lonely. Sometimes he is cynical and hostile about his heritage. Yet when drawn close to his parental home, he is filled with guilt and anxiety. On the other hand, if he has held to his religious heritage, he may be defensive and fearful of rejection by others who are not "like him" in faith and order. He may be reluctant to admit his heritage without a measure of shame. He may be belligerent toward "aliens" from his particular commonwealth. Strangely enough, the pastoral counselor himself usually has these problems also. These feelings in him tend to block and impede his relationship to his counselee. He cannot "sit still," much less listen with appreciation and tender understanding to what the person is trying to communicate. The closer the person gets to his own heritage, the more difficult it may be for him to be an adequate counselor. A part of effective training in pastoral counseling is to gain understanding of and control over one's relationship to his own heritage. He should be adequately related to it without being bound by it.

THE FAMILY AS MEDIATOR OF RELIGIOUS CULTURE

Both the adequate and the inadequate communication of religious culture come through the medium of the family. The family is a molding influence, shaping the individual according to its own inner designs. It is also a sieve, screening out those influences from the larger community which it can and letting through those which it chooses. The pastor who has worked long in a community finds the powerful determination of the family structure upon the religious history of the individual and group life of his church. Several dimensions of the religious life of the family are specifically significant for the religious history of a given counselee.

"The family name" and religion. The family as a family has an identity of its own. Often this is associated with "the family name," and religious attitudes toward life are suggested by this name. "The Edwardses are all Baptists." "Our family has always gone to the Presbyterian church." The heavy contributors to a given religious institution often have buildings named after them, and this identifies the family name with the religious culture. A child growing up under the aegis of "family name" religion has an identity problem of his own as an individual. The minister's child and the children of prominent professors of religion cope with the way in which their own names have become institutionalized as formal expressions of religion. To be able to talk about this is a great

relief to many counselees. Even a batted eyelash of under-standing of their need to be a person in their own right comes as good news to them. Similarly, the child who bears a "family name" of irreligion and disrepute has the same problem, only obversely defined.

Family patterns of conflict and co-operation in religion. The minister's very role draws out the underlying affinities and antipathies in the family relationships. These are usually ex-pressed to him in terms of the interest or lack of interest, the appreciation or hostility, the family members may feel toward religion as such. Also, the members of a family, quite apart from the relationships between them and the minister, will tend to group as individuals according to religious preferences, antagonisms, and indifferences. A counselee will say: "My sisters went with Mother, but Dad and I belong to a different church." Or another will say: "Mother and I believe you ought to be at the church every time the doors open, but the rest of the family sleep late on Sunday mornings and go to church only when there is a funeral or a wedding." These references say much about the inner constellation of personal relation-ships in the family in addition to the problems of religious connections.

Patterns of conformity and rebellion in family religion. Family religion becomes intermixed with the patterns of family rearing. These patterns in and of themselves, apart from their religious content, are fraught with submission and domi-nance, conformity and rebellion, on the part of the child in relation to the parent. When religion becomes the motif of the relationship, these patterns are wrought out along the lines of attitudes toward religion. The pastor should be neutrally sen-sitive to these emotional frames of reference toward religion and enter them into his understanding of the religious history of the individual. Naturally, religion as law or grace becomes the crucial theological issue in these relationships. The pastor steers a hard course between the legalism of formal family religion and the antinomianism of the rebelling child, between the total absence of religious concern on the part of the family and a rigid religion of defense on the part of the growing child and adult. The grace of the Lord Jesus Christ is always his point of departure, and a religion of grace and faith challenges the distortions of both the legalist and the antinomian.

Family rituals and individual memory. Every family develops its own private rituals of eating, sleeping, working, playing, worshiping, etc. The counselee will say: "Our family used always to . . ."; or "In our family we always did . . . this way . . ."; or "I can remember how, every Sunday morning, we used to get up and all of us shine our shoes at the same time . . ."; or, "When we would get ready to go on a trip, my dad would get us all together and pray for a wise and safe journey." These rituals flower into more elaborate ones, depending upon the religious tradition out of which the individual comes. For example, the Jewish child will recall events around the Passover, Yom Kippur, or other religious occasions in which family ritual is used to transmit the faith to the child. The Protestant child, reared in a rural community, will remember the way his mother prepared meals for the visit of the minister over the weekend. He may remember how his father and mother insisted on giving the proceeds of a certain acre of ground to the church. The pastoral counselor listens particularly to the "feeling tone" attached to these memories in the religious history of the counselee, whether they be conjunctive or disjunctive emotions.

Family mobility and the religious history. The movement of the family from one place to another or from one social class to another becomes the focus of real upheavals in the religious life of the family and its individual members, as has already been said. However, these movements also affect the relationship of the individual to his group of friends. Sullivan's developmental understandings suggest that these moves would interfere with the development of the child of six to ten in relationship to his playmates. The preadolescent would be bereaved of his chums. The adolescent would be concerned about the peer-group "place" he occupied and the kind of effect his moving would have on his relationship to the opposite sex. The interaction of these very human factors with the religious outlook of the growing individual should be of especial note to the pastor in the perspective of the religious history.

THE INDIVIDUAL'S HISTORY OF RELIGIOUS RESPONSES

The individual's responses to the meaningful events of his spiritual pilgrimage are the central concern of the counselor in developing a picture of the counselee's religious history. A detailed listing of several specific events to which the individual's response is highly important in Protestant pastoral counseling is as follows:

1. *Specific interpretations the counselee may have of the meaning of his own birth.* Each individual carries deep within himself a subliminal interpretation of the meaning of the "day of his birth." One Southern boy had a painful memory of his mother's recounting of what was said by his father at his birth: "She said that my father took one look at me and said, 'The damn little nigger!' and left home and never returned." Or, an adopted child may be filled with a sense of mystery as to who his parents *really* were and what it meant to them to have him. The prophets of the Old Testament and the apostle Paul talked about their vocation in terms of having been set apart from their mothers' wombs. These retroactive interpretations of the meanings of one's birth are candid portraits of the selfhood of the individual. The pastor should pay close attention also to christenings, dedications, and other rituals performed by the church at the time of birth.

2. *Specific moral or religious evaluations the child has received from his parents and siblings.* The child may have been told by his parents that "he has a destiny to perform." They may have prayed for him that he would be a minister. During an illness they may have rededicated themselves and

him to the Lord with their prayers for his recovery. These are evaluations of him as a person *before God*. To negative evaluations, also, the individual responds as if they were before God. The parents and siblings, particularly the "religious ones," may say: "You are no good and never will be." "God hates the likes of you." "You and your kind can never be counted on except for meanness." Such evaluations are lasting residues in the memory of the individual's selfhood. They should be carefully noted by the pastor. These are large-scale judgments of the value of the individual as a person. The pastor should be sensitive to the "heavy-ladenness" of the individual with either an intolerable sense of expectation and demand on the part of the parent or an equally crushing weight of rejection, as the case may be.

3. *Specific bereavements and other losses that the individual has suffered.* The pastor is a "natural" person to whom the individual communicates his sense of grief and loss. These should be carefully noted by the pastor as a vital part of the religious history. The loss of a mother or father, brother or sister, by death and the circumstances under which the deaths took place reveal much about the interior design of the self-hood of the individual. His interpretation of these events in relation to his religious faith gives deep evidence as to his stand before God. Furthermore, the loss of members of one's immediate family may not be as significant as other losses, such as the death of a grandparent who reared the person while the parents worked, or the roommate in college who became that co-operative being with whom the individual felt genuinely understood and accepted for the first time. The death of a favorite teacher, pastor, or camp counselor may make a deeper impression upon the inner life of an individual than even that of a relative.

Bereavement, as has been indicated in one of my earlier volumes, *Anxiety in Christian Experience* (The Westminster Press, 1955), is often much deeper in the face of the loss within life itself than by death. Death cuts with a clean knife. Certain

situations in life are severing forces, but with a very jagged
and dull knife. For example, anyone who would understand
the spiritual history of the apostle Paul must appreciate what
a pain it was for him to be separated from his brethren whom
he left behind in Judaism. Also, one cannot appreciate the
meaning of Sören Kierkegaard's theological thought apart
from an understanding of his grief over the loss of his beloved,
Regina Olsen. The shift from one religion to another is an
occasion of separation. Such a change should be carefully assessed when counseling with individuals who have been converted to the Christian faith from other religions and cultures.
Experienced missionaries remind us that these changes are
radical and deep. Broken courtships should be attentively considered in the religious history.

Major conflicts in the personal biography take on a bereavement quality. When a man is fired from his job, this is an
intolerable assault on his personal identity, for example. When
he has lost all that he has in a financial fiasco, he becomes a
different person. When he is ejected from the family business,
his whole life undergoes a metamorphosis. When he is convicted of a felony and his status as a citizen removed, he
undergoes a loss that easily infects his whole existence with
destructive emotions. Or one considers the conflicts an unwed
mother feels about releasing her baby for adoption by stran-
gers. The pastor needs to bear in mind that the individual
tends to place a *theological interpretation* on the experiences.
Others in the "helping professions" may be related to these
crises in many different ways, but the pastor is concerned both
with their empirical effects on the individual and with the
ultimate meanings "before God" with which he endows his
experiences. A case can be made for interpreting the whole
pastoral ministry in the light of the unique functions of the
pastor in response to loss and limitation. However, to do so is
to overemphasize these to the neglect of the more positive
experiences that people must assimilate into their interpretation of their relationship to God.

4. *Specific "great events" of self-transforming power.*   Grief and adversity are often more courageously absorbed than are remarkable successes. For example, in one counselee's biography, her high school musical recital resulted in a nation-wide television audition and contract. This will become a "focalizing" event in her life, one that will come more nearly to being a determinative date than any other. Remarkably enough, many people who have such experiences become so heavy-laden by the changes worked in their lives that they prefer not to discuss them. This is particularly true of persons who later suffer severe reversals. For example, the author of a best seller who tries in vain to write a *second* best seller suffers "has-been cramps" and may be reluctant to mention his previous success. The pastor is a counselor to people who live in a competitive world. He may well look upon himself as a hospital-corpsman for the casualty list of the failures and the successes in such a world.

5. *The religious significance of the medical history of the individual.*   Both as clinician and as pastoral theologian the pastor has a responsibility for becoming acquainted with the significant illnesses the counselee has suffered. The nature and the extent of the illnesses can often be estimated without any questioning, for the person tends to confide these matters in the pastor as a matter of course if the relationship is secure. When references to illnesses are made, the pastor can "follow the lead" given and encourage the counselee to "tell me more about this." Or, if no reference to illnesses is made, the pastor may ask a general question as to whether or not the counselee has always been in good health. Particularly significant are the counselees' interpretations of these illnesses, for the *meaning* of the illness may completely outweigh the clinical symptoms. Many times the person associates specific religious experiences of mystical encounter with God, of vocational decision, and of marital choice to illnesses. The advent of or recovery from an illness has always had, and probably always will have, "sign" value in the religious history of people. (A

thorough discussion of the symbolism of illness can be found in Carroll A. Wise's book, *Religion in Illness and Health;* Harper & Brothers, 1942. This is an older book; nevertheless, it was far ahead of its time when it was published and deserves careful attention.)

6. *Specific religious events in the life of the individual.* The issues mentioned thus far tend to provide a "feeling context" in which the religious "specifics" of the person's history can be discussed. The kinds of *religious education* the counselee has received are important to note. Also, the *conversion* experience or experiences should be explored with considerateness and appreciation of the detail and personal meaning. For example, a person may come complaining that he has come to the conclusion that God cannot save him, that he has committed the "unpardonable sin," etc. It is helpful to ask him to discuss his conversion or commitment of self to Christ previously, how he felt about it at the time, and how he feels about it now. Also, subsequent times of *recommitment* and spiritual deepening should be explored with sensitivity and appropriateness. These are "easy" for the person to talk about and provide a basis for appreciating the person as a whole. Specific times of *turning away* from God are important, many times much more real from a religious point of view than some of the conventional formalities in which the counselee may have participated.

Closely associated with the turnings toward and away from God are the counselee's *educational* and *vocational* motivations. The total educational and work history of the individual is, in a sense, the religious expression of the person's life as a whole. His reasons for going to college, or not going to college, his reasons for choosing the work he is in, or his feeling that he had no choice in the work he does—all these provide much of the content of the individual's ultimate meanings or meaninglessness in life. They are what he is doing with his life as far as his conscious choices will take him. Therefore, even when the pastor cannot establish rapport with a counselee about specifically religious content, he can find his way into the religious direction of the counselee's life by exploring the educational and vocational history of the individual with him in a considerate, appropriate, and interested manner. Much pastoral counseling revolves around the problems associated with work and vocation, and the pastor does well to take this seriously.

7. *The religious dimensions of the marital intentions or experience of the individual.* The large majority of pastoral counseling problems are, on the surface at least, connected with marriage and the family. A comparative study of pastoral counseling in San Francisco and Boston reflects that these problems were first in frequency. (E. F. Namache and Tilden H. Edwards, "The Minister and His Counselee," *The Ministry and Mental Health,* ed. by H. Hofmann, p. 225; Association Press, 1960.) More attention will be given this particular kind of counseling in the next chapter for this very reason. However, the marital history as it is related to the explicitly religious concerns of the counselee is a necessary part of the religious history. The pastor can initiate a train of historical references to the marriage itself by simply asking: "How did you and your wife meet each other and come to know each other?" If the pastor becomes somewhat passive and noninterfering at this point, the counselee will provide the relevant historical details from the time the two met each other. The kind of pastoral attention the couple received, the kind of wedding they chose to have, the attitude they have had toward the coming of their children into the world, and the relationships they have to their children are all important data for a complete religious history.

The parental experience of the couple deserves special exploration. Their sense of identity is wrapped up in their perception of themselves as parents. The wholeness and normality of children is a deeply appreciated blessing from God to even the most conventionally irreligious. The birth of a handicapped child awakens religious dialogue with God in an almost primitively unique way. These feelings cluster around the references to children which the pastor may tend to pass by with little sensitivity as to their importance for the total religious outlook of the counselee.

8. *The prayer life of the individual counselee.* The final and most important relationship in the religious history of the individual is his pattern and experience in communication with God himself in prayer. The pastor often discovers this dimension of the counselee's existence in the early phases of the counseling relationship. In his initial exploration, he may ask the counselee: "What have you tried in your efforts to solve these problems you are facing?" The counselee reviews a pattern of repeated frustration in the endless cycle of his distress. He may tell then of his efforts at prayer in the desperation of his situation. Or the pastor may deliberately introduce this into the relationship as he suggests that the two of them engage in prayer. Or he may simply ask: "Would you like to tell me how you think God feels about these matters and how your prayers and conversations with him have gone?"

Involved in the prayers of the counselee are his feelings of "fate" or of hope, his sense of doom and destiny. The degree of hope is to the pastoral counselor what the body temperature is to the physician. It gives him an index to the whole organism in action and failure of action. The pastor is the apostle of "steadfast hope" in Christ. He is concerned that the person not be carried away in the unrealism of groundless and fantastic hope or trapped in the necessities of a distorted pessimism. The prayer life of the individual, granted that he is not too shy religiously to converse about it at all, provides an entree for the pastor into the source of renewal within the life of the counselee.

THE PASTORAL INTERPRETATION OF THE RELIGIOUS HISTORY

The pastor concerns himself and the counselee with the total design or meaning of life. The Gestalt psychologists' interpre-

tation of the whole pattern of a person's life provides a symbolism for the interpretation of the meaning of life. Different
part-processes contribute to the present "figure" or configura-
tion of the individual's whole life under God. At the same
time these part processes provide the "ground" and context for
the Holy Spirit to continue to reveal the will and intention of
God to the person. We have not discussed the religious history
of the individual apart from his relationship to organized
Christianity. Nor have we confined ourselves to this "con-
nectional" meaning of religious history. Rather, we have
moved to the more diffuse sources of religious concern and
sought to focus them at various points within the total field of
the person's life as a whole. The role of the pastor is to participate *with* the counselee as he searches the "starry heavens
above" and the "moral law within," as Immanuel Kant put it,
for the discernible and durable design of his life under God.
The pastor functions as Bunyan's "Mr. Interpreter," providing
resources and relationships for the counselee in his spiritual
pilgrimage. He even gives awe-infused evaluations. The counselee is given the right to accept or reject, try on, take off, and
consider these evaluations in terms of the larger counsel of the
Holy Spirit as to what is imperative *for him.* The pastor's task
is not that *his* will and *his* interpretations be taken as definitive "gospel." The pastor's task is to be a faithful steward, both
of the confidence the counselee is willing and able to invest in
him and of the miracle of redemption and calling that God in
Christ has wrought in his own life as a fellow sinner beside
the counselee.

The religious history *means* something in its detail and its
total design to the counselee. The assignment of meaning to
his experience is, in varying degrees of ability and freedom,
the province of every person. When a counselee comes to a
pastor, this assignment of meaning is in large measure the
epitome of his struggle. From the outset to the conclusion of
the counseling process of the revision of selfhood the pastor
participates in this assignment and reassignment of meaning

and significance to the events of the individual's life. Yet, the religious history cannot be accurately interpreted unless the factual basis of interpretation itself is also a shared knowledge between pastor and counselee. The pastor as counselor cannot function effectively as a religious interpreter of the meaning of life unless he is willing and disciplined enough to take the life history of the person seriously. The unwilling and undisciplined nature of the "quickie" and "advice-giving" kinds of pastoral exhortation and coercion are the most stringent condemnations that can be brought against them. In the intention of the Lord Jesus Christ, the good pastor concerns himself with "all that men ever did," and focuses this history in Christ, who gives freely of the renewing waters of the eternal meaning of life.

However, the pastor cannot expect a simple, one-two-three outline of things he must say and do in the interpretation of the religious history. This interpretation is not a monologue from the pastor to the counselee; it is a dialogue that is worked out between the counselee and the pastor under the tutelage of the Holy Spirit. The pastor can grasp this most easily when he has really faced his own religious history in the light of the preceding suggestions of this chapter. Any pastor who has given his own personal religious history careful attention would consider as sacrilegious the easy, one-two-three answers as to the meaning of his own life under God. Rather, he would say that the minister who extended pastoral care *to him* must counsel with his "whole being." He would need all the theological breadth and depth and personal preparation of a genuinely educated and devout person. Therefore, even as the minister would that others do unto him, he himself should be unto his own counselee. Out of the fullness of his treasure he should bring things both new and old for the interpretation and encouragement of the life of his counselee.

XI

The Protestant Pastor
as a Marriage Counselor

THE FIELD OF MARRIAGE COUNSELING is both an emerging
new profession and a correlative or cognate function of
the older professions of medicine, the law, social work, and the
ministry. The position taken in this chapter is that the minister,
priest, and rabbi do much counseling on family problems as a
normal outgrowth of their ministry. However, only in a few
instances is marriage counseling being practiced as a subspecialty of the ministry. The main concern of the churches
seems to be in the direction of expecting the minister to be a
sympathetic marriage counselor in relation to his total task as
a pastor rather than as a specialist in this area.

The Protestant pastor functions distinctively as a marriage
counselor in relation to his total ministry in more than one
respect. For example, the Protestant pastor is usually a married
person, and his task differs qualitatively and quantitatively
from that of the Roman Catholic priest because of his status
as a married person and as a parent. In addition to this, the
Protestant pastor as a marriage counselor tends to have a
quite different ethical perspective of matters such as birth
control, artificial insemination, and the intermarriage of people
of different faiths. These dimensions of Protestant pastoral
counseling in marriage and family relationships are thoroughly
discussed in Joseph Fletcher's book *Morals and Medicine*
(Princeton University Press, 1954) and in James A. Pike's book
If You Marry Outside Your Faith (Harper & Brothers, 1954).

233

Again, the Protestant pastor's work as a marriage counselor is done within the shaping environment of the group life of the church. Therefore, family life education groups are a necessary part of the work of the pastor as a marriage counselor. He cannot, however, with safety to the families involved conduct such groups unless he is also ready and able to provide individual counseling to persons who have problems that cannot be dealt with in the group context. Genuine safeguards must be set up to protect the interests and needs of persons in the church who are single, widowed, or divorced. Many times pronounced emphases upon the "family-centered church" tacitly exclude these persons. The church becomes idolatrously centered in the importance of the family when this happens. The sovereignty of Christ challenges the subtle presuppositions upon which much "family-centered" thinking rests. (For more detailed attention to these problems, the following resources should be consulted: Clark E. Vincent, *Readings in Marriage Counseling;* The Thomas Y. Crowell Co., 1957. Roy W. Fairchild and John Charles Wynn, *Families in the Church: A Protestant Survey;* Association Press, 1961. Charles William Stewart, *The Minister as Marriage Counselor;* Abingdon Press, 1961. Wayne E. Oates, *Premarital Care and Counseling;* The Broadman Press, 1958. Nathan W. Ackerman, *The Psychodynamics of Family Life: Diagnosis and Treatment of Family Relationships;* Basic Books, Inc., 1958.)

However, the focus of this chapter is not upon the educational and preventative aspects of the work of the pastor as a marriage counselor. Rather, the point of concentration will be upon the process of conflict within marriage that leads ultimately to divorce and the specific steps a pastor can take to anticipate, stop, reverse, or set aright the process of marriage conflict. The pastor will not have dealt with many marriage counseling situations before he discovers that the persons who come to him for pastoral care and counseling on marriage difficulties usually do so only after their difficulties are in the advanced stages of deterioration. This suggests two basic principles of pastoral care which are still calling for careful research. First, marriage conflict goes through a process that needs to be observed, charted, identified, and described. Second, the process itself happens within the interacting field of many persons in the family, church, and community. The couple themselves are only two among many people. The pastor is one among many people who are "giving advice," "counseling," and "exerting influence." The process of conflict tends, therefore, to be conditioned by the kind and quality of communication between and among these persons.

With these two principles in mind, the author spent two days a week for eighteen months working with a group of about seventy-three couples in a counseling service that he initiated in Louisville. His purpose was to see what needed to be done pastorally for persons at the *different stages* of marital conflict and disintegration. But before this he had to identify what these stages were, what characterized them, and with what understanding a pastor should be endowed as he encountered people at the varying stages of stress.

THE PROCESS OF MARRIAGE CONFLICT

Marriage conflict moves from the typical "growing pains" of marital adjustment through serious assaults upon the covenantal nature of the marriage to chronic conflict as a way of life or to acute conflict as a problem-solving experience. This latter problem-solving experience can be of a destructive or creative character. It can result in either divorce in the one instance or in personality change, based on insight and understanding in the instance of creative conflict. Marital conflict was charted as moving through at least seven definable stages:

The Stage of Typical Adjustmental Conflicts

This stage is filled with the conflicts that "are common to all marriages." If a couple does *not* have conflict over these things, one might guess that they are leaving some of their "homework" undone. One might ask if the conflicts are actually going on and they are not aware of them. This happens very easily when the couple are enjoying the first glow of sexual freedom in marriage after years of continence. But these conflicts are both tangible and intangible.

The more tangible conflicts arise over such problems as *when* to have the first experience of intercourse, who will accept full responsibility for birth control, the husband or the wife, and how much money will be spent on the honeymoon. The husband, for instance, can be extremely anxious about spending money staying in a hotel that has "atmosphere" and *decor* when a good commercial hotel is cheaper. In other words he will be penny-wise and feeling-foolish. The non-recurring aspect of his expenses here will not occur to him. Usually people are married only once. They are married the *first* time only once in every instance!

Upon return home, the tangible problems take a new form. Whether or not the wife works, what will happen if she becomes pregnant, where they are going to live, and the adequacy or inadequacy of the arrangements for living quarters made prior to marriage—these are just a few of them. Whereas the fears and anxieties of courtship and engagement were relatively abstract, they become more concrete and tangible in marriage. Fatigue and preoccupation can as a result become the atmosphere of the first few weeks of marriage.

But the obvious tangibility of these problems should not obscure four necessary adjustments which are not so apparent. These persist from the beginning to the end of any marriage and are the hinges upon which the whole thing swings:

1. *The development of an agreed-upon schedule of work, rest, play, love-making, and worship.* A steady course has to be driven between being overscheduled and simply leaving the whole matter of time and schedule-planning to chance. The earliest quarrels in a marriage tend to center on failures to synchronize masculine and feminine uses of time. For example, he may sleep late in the morning and go to bed late;

she may get up early and go to bed early. A couple like this can, conceivably, go a whole week and never talk with each other.

2. *The development of a deeper-level and mutually satisfying plan of communication.* The couple should "pause for station identification" daily, weekly, monthly, and yearly to sketch out the schedules of these blocks of time, gear them in with their over-all goals and aspirations, and simply "get to know each other" as persons. They actually learn to talk with each other in a dramatically verbal way. Up to now they have depended upon kisses, motions of the body and hand, and the rituals of making dates and going places. But now the question is, Can they stay in the same room with each other for an evening of conversation? Do they lay plans for their lives together or do they just throw their minds out of gear and let their lives go where circumstances push them?

3. *The development of a comradely understanding as to their masculine and feminine roles, i.e., what a man is "supposed to do" and what a woman is "supposed to do."* More than this, under God they should develop an understanding of why it is he made them in his image and yet created them as male and female. They thus find out what they are to *be,* and the everyday tasks of life are shaped according to this identity, their *being* man and woman. This calls for real conflict. The new confrontation in the intimacy of marriage calls for personal ability to learn from each other. The things they have "always thought" are necessarily reshaped by the greater truths about what *this* man and *this* woman conceive their role *as* man and *as* woman to be. This confrontation brings to the surface their parents' ideas about the roles of men and women. For example, the wife who works will have very different feelings about the management of money as compared with those of the mother of her husband, who never had to work outside the home. Likewise, the husband, having been raised by that mother, will have different expectations of the wife from those her father had of her mother, especially if her mother worked full-time and the father was an invalid.

These things must be talked and worked through. Much conflict attends the process.

4. *The development of a spiritual welcome and joyous acceptance of the first child in the family.* The early, typical adjustments of the couple are consummated in the incorporation of the first child into the life of the family. The word "incorporate" is used advisedly. It literally means to "embody the child" into the life of the family as a whole. All other conflicts of schedule, communication, and masculine and feminine identity are either faced before the coming of the child, or they become *forced issues* when the first child comes. The element of option in adjustment is now removed. A baby with a high temperature does not ask if the husband is accustomed to going to bed early. A baby yet two months to be born does not ask whether the family can get along without mother's pay check. A baby who is hungry at two A.M. does not ask whether Daddy would prefer that Mother be out at a party or giving him her full attention! In other words, the adjustment of parenthood removes fantasies of freedom from the minds of a couple. Parenthood demands that they accept responsibility of the freedom they have already exercised in creating a child.

These basic changes should and must take place in the life of a married couple during the years prior to the birth of the first child. Left unattended or unmet, these conflicts will form the basis for the symptoms that emerge in the later stages of conflict. Now let us discuss these phases.

The Stage of a Disrupted Covenant

Marriage is a covenant of trust. Legal complications occur only later, long after the covenant of trust has been disrupted. The second phase of marital conflict is the disruption of the covenant of trust. It may even be more serious than this: the covenant may have been defective from the beginning and only now does this become apparent. For example, a husband withholds the fact that he has a criminal record, must report to a parole officer, and cannot buy real estate because he has no rights as a citizen until he is paroled. He does not tell his wife this. She discovers it several months later when they attempt to buy a house. Or the wife does not tell the husband that she has been previously divorced and that she continues a clandestine relationship with the former husband who returns to town only occasionally. These are *defective covenants,* i.e., they were not openly arrived at and they represent matters large enough to undermine confidence in the integrity of the partner.

But ordinarily, the covenant was established in something that approaches good faith if not good faith itself. Then, because of a neglect of the problems mentioned above, there is called into question the *willingness* of the partners to make the marriage work. They lose touch with each other and withdraw as selves from each other. Isolation increases and the degree of suspicion mounts in proportion to the isolation. Soon assaults are made upon each other's integrity: "I *suppose* you worked last night; I don't really *know* what you did." "It is hard for me to get through to you without yelling; I sometimes think you are just plain stupid." "Well, I would have told you what I was doing, but I knew you wouldn't believe me."

The hallmark of this stage of conflict is repeated failure of communication. The situation progressively deteriorates until the couple simply live in silence. They talk about only the most superficial things and tend to go their separate ways. Each feels that the other does not understand and does not want to understand, does not care and does not want to care. The only vestige of a covenant that remains is a mutual feeling of hopelessness: "What are we going to do?" Contact of selves, not communication, takes place through tears, profanity, and brutality. Occasionally violent efforts at overcoming the chasm are made by hyperactive sexual behavior between the estranged persons of the marriage. But this is not a communion of tenderness and respect. It is a hostile encounter in itself with the violent hope that passion itself will overcome the barrier of isolation.

The Stage of Private Misunderstanding

One thing characterizes the couple up to this point most significantly: they have not told anyone else of their distress. Up to this point they have "kept up appearances." They have carefully covered for each other. They have even lied for themselves and each other. But the individual isolation, loneliness, and feeling of not being understood creates a vacuum that must be filled. Sometimes the distress is communicated through illness on the part of one or the other. Various organs of the body, depending upon the individual constitution, fall prey to disorders in one way or another. Stress may reactivate an old disease, such at latent tuberculosis; it may introduce a new one in a previously healthy person; it may cause an already present one to mean more to the individual and to become the organizing center of his or her reactions.

At other times the marital distress is communicated and the vacuum of anxiety filled by behavioral reactions. Excessive spending is one form of allaying anxiety and at the same time expressing hostility. Alcohol or drugs become more useful in calming jittery nerves, and giving depressed spirits a momentary lift. Contemporary advertising probes heavily into these weak spots in order to make sales and to create the illusion of security in desperately anxious persons. (Some attention to the ethical issues at stake in modern advertising needs to be given at this point as well as many other. Here is one vital point of connection between pastoral counseling and social ethics.)

Disease, behavior difficulties, such as alcoholism, drug addiction, excessive spending, absorption in cheap literature, and excessive soap-opera viewing, are accompanied by other symptoms of isolation. The husband may frequent prostitutes, he may become a "masher" in trying to "pick up" strange women without revealing his identity. He may temporarily revert to earlier homosexual pick-up behavior. Similar behavior can and does happen in neglected, lonely, isolated married women. This behavior is symptomatic of the private misunderstanding that has happened in the marriage itself. When, however, this loneliness and isolation become unbearable, one or both of the marital partners break away to someone in their environment *with whom they feel they can talk.* This inaugurates a new stage of marital conflict.

The Stage of Social Involvement

One or the other member or both members of the partnership may break away to other people. This may be done wisely or unwisely, in a responsible or irresponsible way. They may go to their parents for guidance as they did in former years. Sometimes this is not possible. Instead, they may involve a brother or sister who has been particularly close to them. The wisdom of doing this depends entirely upon the kind of persons these people are. Are they wise? Often they are. More often they are not. On the other hand, they may choose to go to a physician, a minister, or a former teacher. Marriage counseling is a cognate function of many different kinds of professions, and all these persons should be alert to the family overtones of the kinds of problems presented to them. The happiest thing that could happen at the time of the first breakout of the isolation is that the person would go to a responsible, wisely devout, and skilled person for understanding. The prayer and commitment of a faithful pastor should be for a more and more sensitive and durable relationship of trust that will enable people to come to him at a time like this. For this is *the* most propitious moment, when a married couple can best be helped, i.e., *to be the first person to whom they break away from the isolation of the stage of private misunderstanding.*

But often this is not the way the movement out of isolation occurs. Too often one or the other person talks indiscriminately to everybody whom he or she meets. A random stranger on the telephone inquiring of the husband's whereabouts in order to buy a piece of merchandise from him is met with this: "I don't know where he is. He never tells me anything. Here I sit all day with these kids too!" Or instead of this, the husband or wife, and sometimes both of them, find another member of the opposite sex "who understands." The other person may or may not have unalloyed motives of his own. He may simply be looking for a little sexual pleasure or for someone whose mate he can further alienate. Ordinarily, though, this may begin in an honest attempt to be helpful and only gradually become more and more involved. The new person in every instance, however, becomes a part of the problem, and not the solution. The thing we should do with our more intimate personal friends when they present marital problems is to call for the help of a more detached person, who can deal with them more professionally and less informally. For community gossip and extramarital involvements tend to be formed just this way. Often pastors say that we should beware of counseling with people about marriage difficulties, especially women, because we can become involved too easily. One observes, however, that ministers do not get involved with counselees nearly as often as they do with their secretaries, educational directors, deacons' wives, and other persons who are associated with them in the distinctly administrative and personal aspects of their social lives. These persons come to the pastor in an uncontrolled informal relationship. The pastor thus becomes the "third person" in a marriage "triangle."

The Stage of Threats or Attempts at Separation

The marital conflict is further inflamed when separation is threatened or seen as the only way out. Separation may take place on a socially acceptable plane, on a planned and legal basis, or on a chaotic and compulsive basis. Socially acceptable separations occur under the guise of changes of the husband's work. For example, the wife goes away for a long summer vacation, or the husband "stays in town" while she lives in the suburbs, or he may reactivate a military tour of duty. Many other stratagems may be available at the moment and become socially acceptable foils for marital conflict.

Under professional guidance, or by reason of wisdom on each other's part, the couple may be led to plan a manifest, open, candid separation. They may do this while each of them is getting some counseling assistance. This is often done in order to prevent further infections from arising. It especially protects the children from scenes between the parents. But the objective of such separation is creative and usually aims at improving rather than dissolving the relationship. Sometimes the separation is set up on a legal basis for a "cooling off" period to see if a divorce is really what is wanted. Many dramatic changes have been observed in formal, legal separations as a trial period for a divorce. In fact, some state laws recognize two years' separation as the only valid ground for divorce. From a legal point of view, and from a therapeutic point of view, this is one of the wisest conditions for divorce.

But the more common kind of separation is the chaotic one, done in anger, vindictiveness, or as a means of manipulation and coercion. One person walks out and goes home to his or her parents. Another kicks the partner out the first time he comes home with alcohol on his breath. Another becomes violently outraged by a skirmish at infidelity on the part of his wife. These become lighted torches that set the whole marriage on fire. In many of these instances, processes of vindictiveness are set in motion which are irreversible. Many times the separation is neither done nor taken seriously, but becomes a repeated form of transient petulance between immature people. But often the separation is only a prelude to the next phase of conflict.

The Legal Phase of Marriage Conflict

Several signals indicate that this phase has set in, regardless of whether separation has taken place. They are sometimes subtle and sometimes obvious signals. The subtle signal appears in the kind of demand that is laid on a pastor, for example. He is expected to "decide who is to blame." The couple present their evidence and expect him, without the help of a judge, jury, or fee to function as a lawyer—to be a judge and a divider over them. The pastor does well to refuse this role as did Jesus in another connection when he said: "Who made me a judge or divider over you?" (see Luke 12:13 ff.). The pastor not only should be alert to this, but he should resist being pushed into this legal role. Such problems of affixing blame, for example, cut the pastor off from the person blamed. Lawyers do not mind this, but the pastor must be related durably to both partners, not legally and punitively to one at the expense of the other. More and more, however, lawyers are looking upon themselves as "counselors at law" and charging for services of counsel apart from specific "piece-work" on legal papers drawn up. In these phases of conflict such problems emerge as feelings of hopelessness and self-depreciation on both sides. Economic anxiety and insecurity flood out much rational insight. The conflict of devotions between spouse and children rages. Social pressure from both sides forces "joiners" in sympathy for this spouse or that one. Few remain objective enough to be a part of the solution rather than the problem. The end result is that many divorcees change their whole set of friends by moving to a new environment. (See William J. Goode, *After Divorce;* The Free Press of Glencoe, 1956.)

The Stage of Divorce

Competent studies of divorced persons indicate that the real shock and numbness of the grief situation occurs long before the actual granting of the divorce. We should not be deceived by the seeming lack of feeling that many demonstrate in the court room. Nor should we be enchanted by those few miracles that do occur where people are reconciled on the eve of the divorce decree and live happily ever after. Much that has happened has taken the marriage beyond the point of no return. Many things can yet be done, as we shall see, but not all of a sudden. People that belong together do not need to be glued together, but much has been done to separate them that is modifiable by wise pastoral care. This is not a hopeless situation, but it is a hard one.

The thing the pastor must concentrate upon at the point of the decree of divorce is the next phase into which the couple goes almost immediately.

The Postdivorce Bereavement Situation

More and more we are seeing pastoral care during critical incidents as a unique ministry to people in their losses. Divorce is a loss in much the same sense that death is. As has been said in connection with religious history, death in a sense is more easily assimilated than divorce: it is clean, final, and definitive. Death cuts with a sharp knife. Divorce cuts with a dull, dirty, and rusty knife. And it accentuates the poignancy of the grief. A flood of grief, characterized by much hostility and vindictiveness as well as the tears of frustrated love and devotion, follows with a heavy depression of emotions. Loneliness and social awkwardness due to the new role and status as a "divorcee" complicate the process of readjustment. As one divorcee, a man, put it to me: "I feel more of a second-class citizen than any Negro in the South."

All this is compounded by the recharting of affections and the discovery of a new meaning in life apart from the previous marriage. Many find this meaning in their work, and this is easier for professional people than for nonprofessional persons. Others find the new meaning in their children, and this is much easier for mothers than for fathers. Some find new meaning in the life of their church, but this depends upon the conditions under which the divorce took place and conditions within the church itself. Others find new meaning in completely relocating and starting over where they are not known. Pioneer areas of the country are filled with divorced persons who have "amputated the past" to the best of their ability. Even so they are like men without a country or lost sheep of the house of

Israel as far as their relationship to the churches is concerned. The majority of divorcees find new meaning in remarriage. This has become the prevailing pattern in our society. But it puts them in opposition to the church whose teachings hitherto allowed them no room.

PRINCIPLES OF PASTORAL COUNSELING IN THE PROCESS OF MARRIAGE CONFLICT

The foregoing discussion of the process of marriage conflict provides the groundwork for evolving some principles of pastoral counseling at the different stages of conflict. Obviously, the pastor must carefully reflect on the meaning of these different stages. Again, he must have a dynamic, developmental view of human life and the marriage relationship before this whole approach makes much rhyme or reason to him. He cannot approach a marriage conflict situation as a static, legal contract but as a personal covenant that is characterized by life, growth, deterioration, etc. This attitudinal orientation is best gained in a clinical setting where a staff of ministers discuss these problems. Reading this brief description of the stages can point one in this direction. However, the minister can compare his previous experience with what has been said here and learn much from his own experience. As he does this, he will see several principles emerging for devising specific techniques in a given situation.

The Principle of a Controlled Counseling Relationship

In everyday speech we talk of some situations as being "well in hand" and others of being "out of control." This is especially true of the pastor's relationship to a marriage conflict situation. As has been previously said, the initiative of the person *wanting* help in the marriage situation is required. This must be gained honestly and aboveboard and not covertly and surreptitiously. For example, if one member of a marriage comes to the pastor, he or she may suggest that the pastor come by the home for a visit when the other partner is there "without their knowing that he knows about the trouble." This is a form of deceptiveness which should be avoided. It puts the pastor in the position of being manipulated by one partner against the other. Rather, the pastor would do much better to write, call, or visit on an above-the-board basis. Many counselors write a brief note to the other spouse. They do this with the permission of the person who did come to them. In the note they invite the other person to come by to see them. This leaves a large measure of freedom with the other spouse and at the same time "clears the atmosphere" of any covertness.

In addition to initiative, the pastor needs a place of discreet privacy, either in his home or his study at the church, for conferences with people about marriage difficulties. Furthermore, he needs enough time in which to do the work of counseling. For example, if the couple are demanding that he visit in the home and "settle things for them" at some late evening hour, the pastor does well to interpret that conflict as a process of accumulated distress that will take time. Then he can reschedule an appointment after his visit in the home for later times in his office. Thus the pastor brings the whole situation under the control of his own professional relationship as to initiative, time, and place.

But these factors are external controls as compared with the distinctly spiritual awareness of the kind of relationship the pastor has to the individual or couple. The role of the pastor should be clearly and mutually understood. The person should understand clearly that the pastor is not just another *neighbor* peering into the situation, not just another *friend* trying to be nice and friendly, not just another *relative* with a vested interest and a "side" in the matter, and not just a *preacher* looking for illustrations with which to dramatize his sermons. Rather, he is a *pastor* appointed by men and called by God to minister with confidence and commitment to all concerned. This role of his should be clear, lest his motives be interpreted wrongly. Otherwise, he could be seen as a competitor for the wife's affections. The wife, on the other hand, might see him as another man that the husband has "ganged up" with against a poor defenseless woman. Both partners may see him as a father who is supposed to spank them and send them back to play peacefully. Or, as in the case of the persons at *the legal phase* of the conflict, the pastor may be pushed into the role of a judge and a divider over them, to decide who is to blame and how the property should be divided. Clarity of role will facilitate communication, and the pastor must be explicit and forceful enough to make these things clear to the couple. In acute marital conflict passivity can be nondirectiveness, but more often it is irresponsibility.

Developing an Interprofessional Team

The minister learns very early that no matter how skilled he is, he cannot work effectively as a marriage counselor in isolation from other professional people. Such isolation goes hand in hand with failure. At the points of detection, diagnosis, treatment, and convalescence, the pastor is deeply in need of colleagues such as the physician, the schoolteacher, the social worker, the lawyer, the judge, the juvenile probation officers, and the hospital officials. For example, it is almost routine to expect each couple to have a thorough medical examination. Often specific medical problems have been discovered which either contributed to or caused the trouble. Early signs of mental illness can be checked by a physician as routine in such an examination. Specific medical therapies can be recommended to stabilize the situation while the counseling continues. Likewise, employers have been of vital assistance in work difficulties that aggravate the marital situation, and in turn pastoral assistance to the counselee has often made a better worker of the person. Public-school teachers have often called stress situations to pastors' attention and in turn been coached by them on the needs of the children without the children ever being aware that their pastor was ministering indirectly to them through their teacher.

Identifying the Stage of Conflict

The pastor must carefully develop ways of identifying the stage at which he has found the conflict. *The kind of communication going on in the total situation is the basis of determining the stage* at which the pastor has found the conflict. For example, the couple in the typical, adjustmental stage of conflict are likely to come to the pastor together. They will talk even with humor and a few tears about quarrels they have had about their routine, their differing interpretations of the roles of men and women, their inability to talk with each other, and the like. But, at the stage of serious conflict where the covenant has been threatened, they may never say anything to the pastor, although he may sense that something has gone wrong. He will see them come to different services at church for no obvious reason. They look unhappy. They may seek to depreciate each other with humor in a crowd or avoid the pastor, whereas they have hitherto been very open. He may hear about unusual things they have done that are not typical of their routine.

In the stage of private misunderstanding, he may notice that the husband has bought a car that is just too expensive. The wife may have started dressing in a style that is out of keeping with her budget. They may go in over their head for a house. Or, the counselor may detect the stress between the lines of a story about an illness. He may note that the couple has begun to drink or to drink more heavily.

When they do come to the pastor or open up to him when he goes to them, he can be assured that he has met them in the stage of social involvement. They probably have talked with other people before coming to him. Therefore, it is routine practice to ask: "To whom else have you felt free to talk?" From this point he can consult with them about whom else they *plan* to talk to. Thus he can bring some influence to bear upon regulating the communication processes. Localizing the spreading conflict is a major job. On the other hand, some people really should be conferred with by the counselee, and this is ordinarily what we mean when we speak of referral. This does not mean sending the person away from us as if they were "beyond us." It means calling in the assistance of others. As representatives of the love of God in Christ, neither they nor the people whose assistance for them we seek are ever "beyond his loving care."

Furthermore, when a couple have reached this stage they usually are not able to talk with each other meaningfully. Whereas in the earlier stages of conflict, a pastor would see the couple together, he probably will want to schedule separate interviews with husband and wife until the communication is clarified.

Stabilizing and Reversing the Process of Conflict

The next strategic objective of the pastor in dealing with marital conflict is to stabilize and reverse, if possible, the destructive process. For example, when an individual or a couple comes to the pastor in the stage of imminent divorce, they usually are coming out of desperation. He can free the situation a bit if he tells them that if they go ahead and get a divorce, he still wants to be a pastor to them. If they expect him to accept responsibility for conferring with them toward a reconciliation, they will necessarily have to "freeze" the divorce procedures until a considerably later date. He disavows any role as a miracle worker. He uses delaying procedures to create a free situation in which responsible counseling can take place.

In this situation, the pastor may, if he has succeeded in stabilizing the process just short of divorce, attempt to reverse it to the next earlier stage. He may suggest that they confer with their lawyer as to the possibility of a *legal separation* as a basis for a divorce in the future if they so choose. This will give them time to try the new identity before they finally accept it. They can use the intervening time span for further counseling. This will assure them that they have done everything possible to work things out. It will give them a greater measure of freedom from later regrets. Sentimental appeals to the good of the children, to the "poor mother's breaking heart," and to "how it will look for Christians to be divorced" simply galvanize the rebellious into action. The pastor can hasten the stampede by using such appeals. Appeals to their own self-esteem for having taken time to act wisely and to their need for counseling help make much more sense.

When the couple come in the stage of separation, the objective of the pastor is to keep it from further deterioration. But more than that, he looks back at the earlier stage and sees that his task is not to "glue these people back together" with a kiss, but to assess carefully the kinds of social pressures being exerted upon them by other people. This becomes the stuff of his separate conversations with them. He knows that it only adds fuel to the fire to talk to them together. But when he talks with them separately, the hidden "deals" that have been made with the "other woman" or "the other man" emerge. The threats that have been leveled by their mothers or fathers, brothers or sisters, of "never having anything to do with them again if they do go back to that brute or that wench," appear.

When we see couples in the quiet, silent desperation of the stage of private misunderstanding, we can involve them in group discussions along with those in the earlier stages of conflict. Sometimes group work will make it easier for them to open up to the leader on a personal basis. If a particularly loaded question comes at the pastor, he can ask if he can confer with the person for a moment after the group meeting so that he can give this more personal attention. At other times, the group work itself resolves the difficulty through straight intercommunion with other more experienced couples. Reading helps some couples, but not nearly so many as we would think or like it to help. Simpler, briefer, nontechnical and poetic material is of more use than the gobbledygook of much literature written by specialists in counseling. For example, one of the best self-help books on marriage was written by

William Lyon Phelps, a professor of English literature! (William Lyon Phelps, *Marriage;* E. P. Dutton & Co., Inc., 1941.)

When we find couples in the years just prior to and following the birth of the first child, pastors should devise family life discussion groups for them. This is the place to do preventive work, even more than with teen-agers. Here the couple finds out that *no* marital choice is perfect, and that we learn to live with the one we *did* choose, not the one the books say we *should* have chosen.

The distinctly exhortative "use" of religion in this process is not as helpful as a consistent mood and atmosphere of prayer. The pastor has chosen to place his own personal faith between the lines of his conversations rather than in them. He loves God, not because he tries, but because God loved him and he can't help loving Him now that he has encountered and been encountered by the Lord Jesus Christ. If this is so, and he is not fooled in it, then the counselees have already felt it in the times together with the pastor. If it is not so, then all his special pleading about religion is in vain. Many counselees have heard this from their youth up, but an authentic person of faith in Christ is new every day to them. The first principles of the faith set forth in this book provide the basis for describing the very demonic itself at work in the shattering of marriages. The pastor's job requires that he be as wise as a serpent and as harmless as a dove in the confrontation of the distortions of sin.

This volume on the theory and practice of Protestant pastoral counseling has been designed to provide a sort of anatomy and physiology of the processes of sin. And it has been demonstrated that no such description is usable by the pastor except in the light of his knowledge of the availability of redemption in Jesus Christ.

Index

SELECTED SUBJECTS AND AUTHORS

253